The Filioque Impasse

Perspectives on Philosophy and Religious Thought

6

Perspectives on Philosophy and Religious Thought (formerly Gorgias Studies in Philosophy and Theology) provides a forum for original scholarship on theological and philosophical issues, promoting dialogue between the wide-ranging fields of religious and logical thought. This series includes studies on both the interaction between different theistic or philosophical traditions and their development in historical perspective.

The Filioque Impasse

Patristic Roots

Michelle Coetzee

gorgias press

2014

Gorgias Press LLC, 954 River Road, Piscataway, NJ, 08854, USA

www.gorgiaspress.com

Copyright © 2014 by Gorgias Press LLC

2014 ˌ

ISBN 978-1-4632-0403-7   **ISSN 1940-0020**

Reprinted from the 2012 Gorgias Press edition.

Library of Congress Cataloging-in-Publication Data

A Cataloging-in-Publication record is available from the Library of Congress.

Printed in the United States of America

TABLE OF CONTENTS

v

CONTENTS

FOREWORD

This worthy publication is an extremely thorough contemporary investigation of the roots of the *filioque* impasse in patristic thought. Michelle Coetzee is able to demonstrate that the roots of the impasse lie not in differing conceptual frameworks (as assumed by many theologians), but rather, more deeply in an apophatic/mystical/experiential exposition as opposed to speculative/ phenomenological/neo-platonic idea of revelatory truth outlined initially by Augustine.

Additionally, she shows that the concept of "person" used in relation to the Trinitarian Persons underlies not only the impasse under investigation but deeper problems that beset Eastern (Orthodox) and Western Trinitarian theology.

Augustine had tended to use the word "person" as a synonym for "individual". Thus, in his Trinitarian thought, there is only one "subject" or "self" subsisting in three subsistents. This means that one subject expresses himself in a threefold way (is this not Modalism?, Ms Coetzee asks). In Orthodox thought there are three unique, ineffable "Subjectivities" that transcend and constitute the divine nature. Each is a Person because they have "self-awareness" (to use a Western way of saying it). "Person" here means, in addition to self-awareness, something like an interpersonal centre of consciousness. The unity then is not supplied by "substance" or "being" but by "communion"; an interpersonal communion of love is then the "substance" of God.

I think Ms Coetzee has demonstrated in her research the core of the East–West impasse concerning the *filioque*; that is, the significant divergence in thought between the two traditions' understanding of the Trinity. Thus, the problem is not the *filioque* alone, but the deeper issue of Trinitarian faith. There are differing experiences and approaches and indeed different criteria of truth. Is truth experiential (mystical) or reflective (conceptual or rational) or both?

The fundamental point of departure is differing understandings of the word "person" and divergent understandings of the divine unity. The problem is compounded because in patristic texts there is often much linguistic confusion: the same language can and is used to denote different meanings. Ms Coetzee's insights are indeed valuable and essential for ongoing East-West dialogue.

Given the aim and scope of the research, Michelle Coetzee has done what she set out to achieve in this publication. It is penetrating in its analysis, extremely well structured and coherently argued. It is a substantial contribution to the advancement of theological knowledge in the area of the *filioque* debate. My unreserved congratulations are offered for a work well done.

Rev. Professor Rodney Moss
St. Augustine College of South Africa
20 March 2012

PREFACE

This work was originally written in fulfilment of the requirements for the degree of Master of Philosophy in Theology. It was submitted to St Augustine College in Victory Park, Johannesburg, South Africa. I was awarded the degree with distinction in April 2010. I chose to research the patristic roots of the *filioque* impasse both due to my dismay at the East-West schism and because this issue had direct bearing on my own personal choices. Also, attempts to discuss it with both Eastern and Western priests did not yield satisfactory answers, either due to the ignorance of those I spoke to or because the answers I received presupposed an allusionary base with which I was not sufficiently acquainted.

My aim in undertaking this research was therefore simply to come to grips with this thorny issue for myself, to identify the underlying problems and to share my findings with whoever might be interested. As such, by sharing this work with you, the reader, I am sharing a stage of my own journey and it is my hope that it will be as helpful to you as it was to me.

I believe this small contribution will be useful to two sets of readers. First, I am hoping it will be of benefit to students of theology who are attempting to get their heads around the *filioque* impasse that has contributed to the ongoing East-West schism in the Church. With this in mind I have retained the exploratory nature of the work so as to carry the reader with me on my own journey from confusion to clarity. The early chapters therefore reflect first impressions and as the work progresses the central issues become increasingly clear.

Second, I think this research will be of interest to academics concerned with this subject, both because of its fresh approach and because of the particular angle I have taken. I focused primarily on the divergent understandings of divine personhood in East and West as the fundamental issue underlying the *filioque* impasse.

While much has been written by Orthodox writers on the Eastern understanding of divine personhood in relation to Western thought, I have not encountered any work in which this theme is specifically related to the problem of the *filioque*.

Of course, as I progressed I realised that the issue of personhood goes hand-in-hand with divergent understandings of several key terms and concepts, and that underneath this difficulty we have the key problem of differing approaches to theology.

To complicate matters, the fact that polemicists from both traditions assume an allusionary base that is foreign to the other means the two traditions have been speaking at cross-purposes.

I therefore aim to make the thought of each tradition accessible to the other in the simplest way possible.

As an exploratory work and also due to space constraints, I do not posit any resolutions to the impasse. My hope at this stage is simply to offer a fresh perspective on this centuries-old problem.

Michelle Coetzee
14 March 2012

ACKNOWLEDGMENTS

I would like to thank my supervisor Dr Rodney Moss for his advice, patience and support while I was engaged in this research. I also thank Metropolitan Hierotheos Vlachos, whose book *The Person in the Orthodox Tradition* was my inspiration for the mysticism-versus-philosophy angle that came to constitute the heart of my research, as well as Metropolitan John Zizioulas, whose book *Being as Communion* was decisive in my decision to tackle this extremely difficult topic.

ABBREVIATIONS

NAOCTC	North American Orthodox-Catholic Theological Consultation
PCPCU	Pontifical Council for Promoting Christian Unity

Ad Haer.	*Adversus Haeresus* (St Irenaeus of Lyons)
Cat.	*Catechism of the Roman Catholic Church*
Conf.	*Confessions* (St Augustine)
Frs.	*The Fragments* (Heraclitus)
Magn.	*Letter to the Magnesians* (St Ignatius of Antioch)
Myst.	*Mystagogy of the Holy Spirit* (St Photius)
S.Th.	*Summa Theologica* (St Thomas Aquinas)
Trin.	*On the Trinity* (St Augustine)

Non-English words are always in italics.

INTRODUCTION

When I began this research I had no strong opinions either way regarding the issue of the *filioque*. My sincere aim was therefore to get behind the seeming ideological positions often expressed in the polemics related to the controversy and to get a sense of the real issues that underscore the impasse. I hoped to find that East and West believed the same things, but articulated this shared perspective differently due to using differing conceptual systems. I found that the reality was somewhat more complex than this.

The ordering of the material strictly follows the research process, with certain omissions, so as to carry the reader on the same journey that I took. I first researched the history of the East-West schism with a view to setting the *filioque* issue in its proper context. I had to omit this chapter due to space restrictions, but retained a few central points. I then searched through books I had at hand and on the Internet, starting with popular websites, for an overview of the arguments posited by the Eastern and Western traditions for and against the *filioque* and then followed the clues from there. My supervisor, Dr Rodney Moss, also made some valuable suggestions regarding reading material on the Roman Catholic position.

My first priority was to get a sense of the current state of the *filioque* debate before attempting to understand the patristic roots of the arguments posited by the two traditions. It soon became clear to me that East and West were talking at cross-purposes, with each tradition appropriating the arguments of the other within its own conceptual system. I consequently set about researching how post-modern writers explain the Fathers of their own traditions, so as to avoid misappropriating the words of the Fathers within the context of an unrelated conceptual system.

The result is that much of this research is concerned with post-modern interpretations of the Fathers, leaving me the time and the space to read only a few key texts from the Fathers themselves. What particularly stood out for me was that key concepts and words were imbued with entirely different meanings within the context of each tradition's Trinitarian theology.

My early research indicated that a pivotal difficulty was that the two traditions use the word "person" differently in relation to the Divine Persons. I therefore angled the discussion on the word "person" as it is used in Trinitarian theology in East and West, but later discovered that there is also an interrelated divergence in the use of the word "substance" or "essence", consequent on differing notions of the divine unity.

Moreover, I found that this disparity is underpinned by irreconcilable approaches to theology and truth, which are in turn a function of the different experiences and approaches of St Augustine and the Cappadocian Fathers – whose incompatible perspectives appear to constitute the point of departure between Eastern and Western Trinitarian theology.

Consequent on these points of departure, the "subtext" of the Trinitarian thought of the two traditions seems to be radically different, so much so that one has to consciously make a paradigm shift when switching from the thought of one tradition to the other, setting aside all one's assumptions, if one is to truly "see" what each tradition holds to be true. When one does so, each argument make perfect sense when assessed in terms of the presuppositions and truth criteria of the tradition concerned, meaning that this issue has to be resolved on the level of truth criteria.

The breadth of this subject means that I have had to impose certain restrictions on myself: I have examined only the thought of the Cappadocian Fathers in the East, Tertullian, St Ambrose and St Augustine in the West, and St Athanasius as representative of the theology of Nicaea I. Post-modern interpretations of Athanasius' thought are illustrative of significant differences in how Nicene thought has been appropriated by Eastern and Western thinkers, a development again traceable to the differing approaches of Augustine and the Cappadocians. However, due to space constraints I have had to omit the chapters on Tertullian, Ambrose and Athanasius, although I have worked some aspects of their thought in elsewhere.

References to the thought of other early Christian thinkers are taken from summaries or references to them in the writings of post-modern writers. I investigated Tertullian and St Ambrose because they are credited, along with St Hilary of Poitiers, with positing pre-Augustinian versions of the *filioque*. What is in question is whether these thinkers meant the clause in the same way that Augustine explicated it – an argument I have had to set aside for now. What is of more importance is the way in which Augustine appropriated the phrase, the definitive meaning with which he imbued it in his conception of the Trinity and whether this meaning is consistent with the apostolic faith. The deleted sections are not vital to this central question.

I have also had to leave out my own analysis on the crucial issue of the divergent criteria of truth operative in East and West, although, once again, I have retained a few key ideas. I hope to revisit these omitted sections at a future date.

In the meantime, I simply aim to demonstrate that:

(a) The East-West impasse over the *filioque* is not simply a misunderstanding, as some Roman Catholic polemicists attempt to show. The *filioque* represents a significant divergence in thought between the two traditions' conceptions of the Trinity.

(b) Moreover, there has been a great deal of talking at cross-purposes between the two traditions, because often the same language is used to denote different meanings.

(c) The fundamental point of departure is different understandings of the word "person" in Trinitarian theology and parallel divergent understandings of the divine unity.

(d) These differences are in turn consequent on differing experiences, approaches and consequently criteria of truth.

This means that this issue ultimately has to be tackled on the level of truth criteria.

1 THE *FILIOQUE*: MEANING AND ARGUMENTS

In this chapter I shall briefly sketch a few key points about the historical context in which the *filioque* impasse is rooted, and then proceed with an overview of the arguments posited by the West to explain this clause and the Orthodox objections to it.

1.I HISTORICAL BACKGROUND

It is particularly significant that the Council of Nicaea I was primarily an Eastern affair, at which the bishop of Rome was represented by only two presbyters[1] and Constantinople I an exclusively Eastern council.[2] Also, the theology that underpinned the "one *ousia*, three *hypostases*" the formula of the council and the addition to the Creed regarding the Spirit – "[…] the Lord, the Giver of life, who proceeds (*ekporeuetai*) from the Father […]", was largely the product of the thought of the Cappadocian Fathers - Ss Basil of Caesarea, his brother Gregory of Nyssa and friend Gregory of Nazianzus.[3]

The Symbol of Faith as articulated at Constantinople I was formally received by Rome only at the Council of Chalcedon in

---

[1] Kenneth *Latourette, A History of Christianity, Volume 1: Beginning to 1500* (San Francisco: HarperSanFrancisco, 1953/1975), 161–163; Khaled Anatolios, *Athanasius* (London: Routledge, 2004), 11

[2] The North American Orthodox-Catholic Theological Consultation (NAOCTC), *The Filioque: A Church Dividing, Issue?* 2003, [online]. http://www.usccb.org/seia/filioque.shtml (accessed 13/09/2008), n.pag

[3] NAOCTC, *op.cit*, n.pag; Anthony Meredith, *The Cappadocians* (London: Geoffrey Chapman, 1995), 44; Gregory of Nazianzus, *5th Theological Oration* in *Theological Orations* [online]. http://wwwnewadvent.org/fathers/ (accessed: 22-02-2008)

451. In the meantime the Latin Church had begun to develop a divergent Trinitarian theology[4] and would have received this Symbol in light of this tradition. Thus the *Catechism of the Catholic Church* (n247) notes that Pope Leo I had confessed the *filioque* as early as 441, "following an ancient Latin and Alexandrian tradition".

The findings of Constantinople I had been communicated to Pope Damasus (366–384) in a synodical letter following a post-conciliar synod in 382. However, the document contains only a brief summary of the doctrine of the council and makes no attempt to explain the underlying presuppositions. It simply states: "According to this faith [the ancient faith, the faith of our baptism] there is one Godhead, Power and Substance of the Father and of the Son and of the Holy Ghost; the dignity being equal and the majesty being equal in three perfect *hypostases*, i.e. persons".[5]

The document then briefly states the heresies this formula opposes, namely those of Sabellius, Eunomius, Arius and the Pneumatomachi, and guides the reader to the tomes of the councils of Antioch and Constantinople I, though the acts of the latter were apparently lost.[6]

Against this backdrop it seems likely that the West formally received the modified Creed (a) without being fully cognisant of the thought that underpinned it[7] and (b) that the West read the document through the lens of Western presuppositions. The misunderstanding that ensued is the primary focus of my research.

---

[4] Pontifical Council for Promoting Christian Unity (PCPCU), *The Greek and Latin Traditions about the Procession of the Holy Spirit*, 1995, [online] www.newadvent.org (accessed June 24, 2008), n.pag

[5] *Synod of Constantinople (A.D. 381): The Synodical Letter* (from *Nicene and Post-Nicene Fathers, Second Series, Vol. 14*, H Percival, trans, 1900 (Buffalo, NY: Christian Literature Publishing Co, 1900.) Revised and edited for New Advent by Kevin Knight. [online] http://www.newadvent.org.-fathers/3809.htm (accessed 12/03/2009)

[6] NAOCTC, *op.cit*, n.pag

[7] *Ibid*

1.II. MEANING AND OBJECTIONS

The *filioque*, meaning "and the Son", is the Western addition to the Niceno-Constantinopolitan Creed found in the clause referring to the Holy Spirit: "We believe in the Holy Spirit, the Lord, the Giver of Life, who proceeds from the Father *and the Son…*" The second Council of Lyons (1274) dogmatised the formula that "the Holy Spirit proceeds eternally from the Father and the Son, not as from two principles but as from one single principle (*tamquam ex uno principio*)".[8] *The Catechism of the Catholic Church* (n246) sums up the meaning of the *filioque* by quoting from the Council of Florence (1438), which constitutes the Roman Catholic Church's final dogmatic statement on the matter:

> The Holy Spirit is eternally from Father and Son; He has his nature and subsistence at once (*simul*) from the Father and the Son. He proceeds eternally from both as from one principle and through one spiration […] And, since the Father has through generation given to the only-begotten Son everything that belongs to the Father, except being Father, the Son has also eternally from the Father, from whom he is eternally born, that the Holy Spirit proceeds from the Son.

The Eastern Church argues that the Spirit proceeds from the Father alone and that the *filioque* compromises the monarchy of the Father as the source of the Trinity by positing two causes of divine *hypostases*. Furthermore, Orthodox polemicists argue that the clause is rooted in a false conception of the Trinity that (a) begins with the essence rather than the Divine Persons, consequently making the essence rather than the Father the source of unity in the Godhead, and (b) reduces the Divine Persons to mere relations.[9]

---

[8] PCPCU, *op.cit*, n.pag

[9] Anonymous, *Filioque Controversy: General Information*, St. John in the Wilderness Adult Education and Formation, [online] http/www.-stjohnadult.org (accessed 09/04/2008), n.d, n.pag; *Byzantine Theology* (New York: Fordham University Press, 1974/1979), 60–61; c.f. George Bebis,

As a symptom of this false notion of the Trinity, the *filioque* also subordinates and depersonalises the Spirit.[10] The Orthodox also have canonical objections to the *filioque*: They argue, firstly, that the Western Church had no right to unilaterally modify the Symbol of Faith without the consent of an ecumenical council that represented the whole Church.[11] Second, the addition is a violation of the anathemas of the councils of Ephesus (431) and Chalcedon (451) against making any insertions into the Symbol of Faith.[12]

However, while noting that canonical considerations mean the *filioque* debate dovetails into the questions of papal primacy and infallibility, I shall not deal with this issue here, but focus only on the theological and philosophical arguments relating to the clause.

1.III. SCRIPTURAL EVIDENCE

1.iii.a. Western arguments

The online *New Advent Catholic Encyclopedia* quotes Anthony Maas's argument that, because Scripture refers to the Holy Spirit as the Spirit of the Son/Christ/Jesus Christ (Gal 4:6; Rom 8:9; Phil 1:19) in the same way that they refer to Him as the Spirit of the Father (Matt 10:20) and the Spirit of God (1 Cor 2:11), the "inspired writers" attribute to the Spirit the same relation to the Son as to the

---

(PhD), *Orthodox Church Beliefs* [online]. http://www.mb-soft.com/-believe/txw/orthobel.htm (accessed 18/01/2008), 2007, n.pag

[10] Kallistos Ware, *The Orthodox Way* (New York: St Vladimir's Seminary Press, 1993), 121–122; Alasdair Heron, *The Holy Spirit* Philadelphia (Westminster Press, 1983), 94

[11] George Bebis, *op.cit*, n.pag, GW Bromily, "Filioque Controversy: Advanced Information" in *Elwell Evangelical Dictionary* [online]. http://mb-soft.com/believe/txn/filioque.htm (accessed 07/08/2008); c.f. St Photius, *Mystagogy* 5, c.886 [online] http://geocities.com/trvalentine/orthodox/-mystagogy/html (accessed 03/09/2008)

[12] Antony Maas, *Filioque* in *New Advent Catholic Encyclopedia*, 1909 [online]. www.newadvent.catholic.org (accessed June 24, 2008), n.pag; c.f. *Myst.* 5; Michael Pomazansky, *Orthodox Dogmatic Theology* (New York: Holy Trinity Monastery, 1994), 91

Father. Furthermore, Scripture speaks of the Son sending the Holy Spirit (Luke 24:49; John 15:26; 16:7; 20:22; Acts 2:33; Titus 3:6) just as the Father sends the Son (Romans 3:3, etc.) and the Spirit (John 14:16). On this basis, Maas argues:

> [...] The very idea of the term "mission" implies that the person sent goes forth for a certain purpose by the power of the sender, a power exerted on the person sent by way of a physical impulse, or of a command, or of prayer, or finally of production; now procession, the analogy of production, is the only manner admissible in God. It follows that the inspired writers present the Holy Ghost as proceeding from the Son, since they present Him as sent by the Son.

Maas goes on to quote John 16:13–15, where Christ says: "What things soever He [the Spirit] shall hear, He shall speak; [...] He shall receive of mine and show it to you. All things whatsoever the Father has are mine." He argues that a double consideration is in place here:

> First, the Son has all things that the Father hath, so that He must resemble the Father in being the Principle from which the Holy Ghost proceeds. Secondly, the Holy Ghost shall receive "of mine" according to the words of the Son; but Procession is the only conceivable way of receiving which does not imply dependence of inferiority. In other words, the Holy Ghost proceeds from the Son.

The PCPCU, wrapping up its 1995 document *The Greek and Latin Traditions about the Procession of the Holy Spirit* (which has no page or paragraph referencing), which is widely referred to as "The Clarification", argues from Scripture that the Spirit is the love between the Father and the Son; the Father is love at its source (2 Cor: 13:13; 1 Jn 4:8:16) and the Son is the Son that He loves (Col 1:14). Thus "a tradition dating back to St Augustine has seen in the Holy Spirit, through whom 'God's love has been poured into our hearts' (Rom 5:5), as the eternal Gift of the Father to his beloved Son" (Mk 1:11; 9:7; Lk 20:13; Eph 1:6). The Clarification states that the Father gives the Spirit to the Son in order to exist consubstantially through the Son in the person of the Spirit: "This takes into account," the document continues, "the fact that, through love, the Holy Spirit orients the whole life of Jesus towards the Father in the fulfilment of his will." This is followed by the quotation of several texts to demonstrate the involvement of the Spirit with Christ in the incarnation:

> The Father sends his Son (Gal 4:4) when Mary conceives him through the operation of the Holy Spirit (cf. Lk 1:35). The Holy Spirit makes Jesus manifest as Son of the Father by resting upon him at Baptism (cf. Lk 3:21–22; Jn 1:33). He drives Jesus into the wilderness (cf. Mk 1:12). Jesus returns "full of the Holy Spirit" (Lk 4:1). Then he begins his ministry "in the power of the Spirit" (Lk 4:14). He is filled with joy in the Spirit, blessing the Father for his gracious will (cf. Lk 10:21). He chooses his Apostles "through the Holy Spirit" (Acts 1:2). He casts out demons by the Spirit of God (Mt 12:28). He offers himself to the Father "through the eternal Spirit" (Heb 9:14). On the cross he "commits his Spirit" into the Father's hands (Lk 23:46). "In the Spirit" he descended to the dead (cf. 1 Pt 3:19) and by the Spirit he was raised from the dead (cf. Rom 8:11) and "designated Son of God in power" (Rom 1:4). This role of the Spirit in the innermost human existence of the Son of God made man derives from an eternal Trinitarian relationship through which the Spirit, in his mystery as Gift of Love, characterises the relation between the Father, as source of love, and his beloved Son.

In short the *filioque* is rooted in biblical texts that speak of the Spirit being the Spirit of the Son, of the Son sending the Spirit into the world, of the Son having all that the Father has and the Spirit's role in pouring the love of God into the hearts of believers.

1.iii.b. Orthodox argument

The Orthodox counter that the West has wrongly deduced truths about the immanent Trinity from the economic Trinity: references to the Son sending the Spirit relate to the sending of the Spirit into the world, not to the eternal procession.[13] Thus the Orthodox have no difficulty with St Ambrose (c. 339–97), for example, saying that the Spirit "proceeds from (*procedit*) the Father and the Son" without ever being separated from either,[14] as long as it is said to refer to the economic activity of the Trinity. But they object to the idea that this statement refers to the relations of origin. St Photius,[15] (c. 810–c. 893), the disputed patriarch of Constantinople who was the first Easterner to formulate a detailed polemic against the *filioque* in his *Mystagogy of the Holy Spirit*, argues that the Son Himself stated that the Spirit proceeds from the Father (alone) in John 15:26. Thus Scripture texts that refer to the Spirit as being the Spirit of the Son cannot be interpreted to mean that the Spirit proceeds eternally from the Son, but rather refer to the fact that the Son and the Spirit are of one "essence, glory, dignity and dominion".[16]

Photius focuses on the word "of" at length, pointing out that if one follows Western logic, one might argue that, since Christ is the Light of the world, the Son proceeds from the world, or since the Spirit is called the Spirit of understanding or knowledge or love, etc., one might say that the Spirit proceeds from these gifts.[17] Alternately, arguing the *filioque* from references to the "Spirit of Christ" would mean that the Spirit proceeds eternally from the Son's humanity, as "Christ is a designation that refers to the Son's incarnate life".[18]

He also cites several texts that the Clarification uses to support the *filioque* – such as those referring to the Holy Spirit descending upon the Son at His baptism and abiding upon Him (John 1:32), Christ saying: "The Spirit of the Lord is upon me, because He has anointed me" (Isaiah 61:1; Luke 4:18), "If by the

---

[13] Michael Pomazansky, *op.cit*, 90

[14] *On the Holy Spirit* 1.11.20

[15] The West does not consider him a saint

[16] *Myst.* 1; 48–51; see also Photius in MA Pugliese, "How Important is the Filioque for Reformed Orthodoxy?" in *Westminster Theological Journal* (66), 161–2; Michael Pomazansky, *op.cit*, 89

[17] *Myst.* 55–58

[18] *Ibid* 90, 93

Spirit of God I cast out demons…" (Matt 12:28) and "by the Spirit of the[19] Father" (Matt 10:20), and St Paul: "The Spirit of Him that raised Christ" (Rom 8:11)[20] – to argue that the Spirit is said to be of Christ because He anoints and is in Christ [i.e. in His humanity], not because He proceeds from the Son eternally.[21] Orthodox apologist Fr Michael Pomazansky[22] also quotes Blessed Theodoret as saying that the Spirit is "the Spirit of the Son as being One in essence with Him", not as proceeding from Him.

Photius also rejects the use of John 16:14 to support the *filioque*: "The Spirit will receive of Mine and will proclaim it to you".[23] He argues that this means the Spirit receives equally everything from the Father that the Son receives, that all that "is mine" is in the Father and therefore the Father Himself, thus the Son and Spirit share everything by virtue of their consubstantiality with the Father.[24]

The irony of all this argumentation is that both traditions understand these texts to denote the consubstantiality of the Son and the Spirit; the problem is that the Orthodox cannot see how the *filioque* is necessary to demonstrate this, for reasons that shall become clear as we proceed.

Another difficulty is the idea that the Spirit is the Gift of Love from the Father to the Son, based on biblical texts "which clearly refer to the divine economy and not to the immanent Trinity," as Metropolitan John Zizioulas (co-chair of the joint commission for

---

[19] Current Western texts read *your* Father

[20] *Myst.* 85; 90

[21] *Ibid* 94; in his polemic against Aetius, St Basil argues that it is the "students of vain philosophy" who interpret such terms in light of the rules of their own discipline. However, the Biblical writers "were not laying down a rule but carefully distinguishing the *hypostases*". He attacks these innovators as those who "pervert the simplicity and artlessness of the faith" – see *De Spiritu Sancto* 2.5; 5.7; 6.13

[22] *Op.cit* 89

[23] *Myst.* 20ff

[24] *Ibid* 29

East-West dialogue) says in paragraph 4 of his *One Single Source: An Orthodox response to the Clarification of the Filioque*.[25] He continues:

> We seem to encounter here the usual difficulty between the Western and Eastern theological tradition, namely the problem of the distinction between the eternal and the economic level of God's being. […] the *filioque* at the level of the economy presents no difficulty whatsoever to the Orthodox, but the projection of this into the immanent Trinity creates great difficulties.[26]

These examples illustrate that the issue cannot be decided by appeals to biblical texts, because different assumptions are being read into Scripture; what is needed is to uncover the frames of reference that underpin the two perspectives in order to make these presuppositions explicit.

1.IV. ECONOMIC AND IMMANENT TRINITY

1.iv.a. Western view

The Western conception is underpinned by the conviction that the immanent Trinity can be deduced from the economic Trinity.[27] For example, according to a summary by an anonymous author on the *St. John in the Wilderness Adult Education and Formation* website, in St Augustine's thought this idea is an underlying assumption in his notion that, just as the Holy Spirit is the bond of love between believers, so too within the Godhead the Spirit is the bond of love between the Father and the Son. Catholic theologian Karl Rahner (1904–1984) goes so far as to say that the economic Trinity *is* the immanent Trinity, the summary continues.

---

[25] At http://www.orthodoxresearchinstitute.org/articles/dogmatic/-john_zizioulas_single… (2007) (accessed 06/06/2008)

[26] *Ibid*

[27] *Cat.* 244

Rahner describes the Father as "God as such", and the Son/Word/*Logos* and the Spirit as "distinct modes/manners of subsisting" or "modes of God's givenness". He sees the Son or Word or *Logos* as God's self-communication as "knowledge" and the Spirit as God's self-communication as "love".[28]

Gerald O'Collins echoes Rahner. Commenting on the Creed of Constantinople I, he remarks:

> "[…] God's self-communication *ad extra* through the missions of the Son […] and the Spirit […] in the history or 'economy' of salvation presupposes and reflects the self-communication *ad intra*: the eternal generation of the Son and procession of the Spirit. Thus the 'economic' Trinity […] on which the Creed largely focuses reveals the immanent Trinity and is identical with it." [29]

1.iv.b. Eastern perspective

In Orthodox thought, the immanent Trinity cannot be equated with the economic Trinity because there is much more to God as He is in Himself than we can experience in creation; the inner essence of God is transcendent, unknowable and incomprehensible.[30] So, for example, while in Western thought humanity will one day enjoy the beatific vision – i.e. God as He is in Himself – in Eastern thought humanity will only participate in the "energies" of God; we will never fully know the essence of God, that is, God as He is in Himself.[31]

Kallistos Ware explains: "When Orthodox speak of the divine energies, they do not mean by this an emanation from God, an

---

[28] Karl Rahner, *The Content of Faith* (New York: Crossroad, 2000), 375–376

[29] Gerald O'Collins, *The Tripersonal God* (London: Geoffrey Chapman, 1999), 126

[30] Michael Pomazansky, *op.cit*, 89

[31] St. John in the Wilderness Adult Education and Formation summary, *op.cit*, n.pag

'intermediary' between God and man, or a 'thing' or gift that God bestows. On the contrary, the energies are God Himself in His activity and self-manifestation."[32] However, because God reveals Himself personally – as Father, Son and Holy Spirit – in His energies (or acts), one can arrive at true (personal) knowledge of God if three elements are present: religious awe, personal encounter and participation in the acts or energies of God.

Bebis adds that this distinction, which has its roots in the Cappadocian Fathers, was developed by St Gregory Palamas and given official sanction at councils of 1341 and 1351 in Constantinople, which confirmed a real distinction in God between the unknowable essence and the acts or "energies".[33]

While the Trinity is revealed in the incarnation, all we can know of the origin of the Son and Spirit from the economy is what Scripture tells us: that the Father is the source of divinity, the Son is begotten by the Father and the Spirit proceeds from the Father.[34] This was sufficient for the Cappadocians to distinguish the origin of the Son from the Spirit and show that there are not two Sons.[35]

Thus St Gregory Nazianzus says in *Oration 31:8* that as the Spirit is neither Father nor Son, so He is neither unbegotten (like the Father) nor begotten (like the Son), but proceeds (John 15:7). St Basil likewise says the Spirit is from God (the Father), not by way of generation, like the Son, but as "the breath of His mouth".[36] Pomazansky quotes St John Damascene's (676–749) *On the Orthodox Faith* 1.8:

> Although we have been taught that there is a distinction between begetting and procession, what this distinction consists

---

[32] Kallistos Ware, *op.cit*, 27–28

[33] *Op.cit*, n.pag; c.f. Hierotheos (Vlachos), *The Person in the Orthodox Tradition*, (Levadia-Hellis: Birth of the Theotokos Monastery, 2002), 200–203

[34] George Bebis, *op.cit*, n.pag; Hierotheos (Vlachos), *The Person in the Orthodox Tradition*, 200–203

[35] Gerald O'Collins, *op.cit*, 131

[36] St Basil, *De Spiritu Sancto* 38, 46; c.f. Alasdair Heron, *op.cit*, 81; St Athanasius, *Letter to Serapion* 1.31

of, and what is the begetting of the Son and the procession of
the Spirit from the Father – this we do not know.[37]

1.v. PROOF TEXTS FROM THE FATHERS

In its attempt to demonstrate the harmony between Roman Catholic and Orthodox thought, in its 1995 Clarification the PCPCU
cites several texts from the Greek Fathers that seem to support the
filioque. Ss Basil, Maximus and John Damascene are quoted as stating that the Spirit proceeds (*ekporeuomenon*) from the Father *through*
the Son, which is taken to have the same approximate meaning as
from or *by* the Son.

The council adds that this should be the basis for future discussion. Zizioulas agrees, provided it is understood to mean the
Father is the only personal cause of the Spirit.[38] Also, most Orthodox thinkers insist that while many Eastern Fathers used the expression "through the Son" they were usually referring to the prov-
idential action of the Trinity in the world, not to the relations of
origin.[39]

In a footnote to its explanation of the Spirit as the love between the Father and the Son, the Clarification also quotes Aquinas
(following Augustine), writing that "if we say of the Holy Spirit that
he dwells in the Son, it is in the way that the love of the one who
loves reposes in the loved one".[40] The Clarification goes on to assert that "this doctrine of the Holy Spirit as love has been harmo-
niously assumed by St Gregory Palamas into the Greek theology of
the *ekporeusis* from the Father alone". It quotes Gregory as saying:
"The Spirit of the most high Word is like an ineffable love of the
Father for this Word ineffably generated. A love which this same

---

[37] Michael Pomazansky, *op.cit*, 82; see also Kallistos Ware, *op.cit*, 43;
Hierotheos (Vlachos), *The Person in the Orthodox Tradition,* 179–180; 183–
184; Irenaeus in Gerald O'Collins, *op.cit*, 98

[38] John Zizioulas, *One Single Source: An Orthodox response to the Clarification of the Filioque*, 2.c

[39] Michael Pomazansky, *op.cit*, 90

[40] *S.Th.*, la, q. 36, a. 2, 4um

Word and beloved Son of the Father entertains (*chretai*) towards the Father: but insofar as he has the Spirit coming with him (*sunproelthonta*) from the Father and reposing connaturally in him".[41] The Clarification later links the notion of the Spirit as love to the "Trinitarian order", in terms of which the Spirit cannot precede the Son because it is the Son who characterises the Father as Father:

> But the spiration of the Spirit from the Father takes place by and through (the two senses of δια [*dia*] in Greek) the generation of the Son, to which it gives its Trinitarian character. It is in this sense that St John Damascene says: "The Holy Spirit is a substantial power contemplated in his own distinct *hypostasis*, who proceeds from the Father and reposes in the Word".[42]

Zizioulas strongly objects:

> Neither of these two theologians bases the above references to the Spirit's relation to the Son on the relation of these two Persons in the economy, as St. Augustine seems to do and as the Vatican document also does. The *filioque* in no way can be projected from the economy into the immanent Trinity, and the same is true also of any form of *spirituque* that might be detected – this is in fact possible – from the relation of Christ to the Spirit in the history of salvation.[43]

These examples again illustrate that Western thinkers read the sayings of the Eastern Fathers through the lens of a conceptual system that differs from that of the East. As we shall see, the converse is also true. This underscores the need to grapple with the broad contours of thought that underpin the positions that were ultimately received by the two traditions, rather than fixing on iso-

---

[41] *Capita Physica* XXXVI, PG 150, 1144 D–1145 A

[42] *De Fide Orthodoxa* I.7

[43] John Zizioulas, *One Single Source: An Orthodox response to the Clarification of the Filioque*, 4

lated statements, and to allow Eastern and Western apologists alike to interpret their own traditions.

1.VI. THEOLOGICAL ARGUMENTATION

It is not easy to set out a clear line of argumentation because East and West argue from diametrically opposed paradigms, which has resulted in the two traditions arguing at cross-purposes, making it is no easy task to untangle it all. But I shall do my best to present the theological rationale of each tradition, with some cross-referencing between the two sets of argumentation. At the centre of the difficulty, it seems, are contrasting notions of divine personhood. The NAOCTC seems to agree:

> The Greek and Latin theological traditions clearly remain in some tension with each other on the fundamental issue of the Spirit's eternal origin as a distinct divine person. By the Middle Ages, as a result of the influence of Anselm and Thomas Aquinas, Western theology almost universally conceives of the identity of each divine person as defined by its "relations of opposition" – in other words, its mutually defining relations of origin – to the other two, and concludes that the Holy Spirit would not be *hypostatically* distinguishable from the Son if the Spirit "proceeded" from the Father alone.[44]

I shall therefore angle my discussion on this pivotal issue.

1.vi.a. West: The Divine Persons are relations of origin

In Western thought, the Divine Persons can be distinguished only by their relations of origin. This idea is traceable to St Augustine, who converted to Christianity in 386 A.D., five years after Constantinople I, and who worked out his thought independently of the Greek Fathers. In V.3.15 of his *On the Trinity*, he posits the

---

[44] NAOCTC, *op.cit*, n.pag

double procession in order to explain why the Spirit is not also a Son. He concludes his argument by saying: "[…] the Father and the Son are a Beginning in the Holy Spirit, not two Beginnings; but as the Father and Son are one God, and one Creator, and one Lord relatively to the creature, so are they one Beginning relatively to the Holy Spirit." I do not wish to deal with Augustine's thought in detail at this stage. For now I would like to note the footnote to the online translation from which I took this quotation:

> […] when the term ["beginning" (principium)] refers to the relations of the persons of the Trinity to each other, it denotes only a modifying energy, whereby an existing uncreated substance is communicated by generation and spiration. […] When it is said that the Father is the "beginning" of the Son, and the Father and Son are the "beginning" of the Spirit, it [means] that the Son by eternal generation receives from the Father the one uncreated and undivided substance of the Godhead, and the Spirit by eternal spiration receives the same numerical substance from the Father and Son. The term "beginning" relates not to the essence, but to the personal peculiarity. Sonship originates in fatherhood; but deity is unoriginated. The Son as the second person "begins" from the Father, because the Father communicates the essence to him. His sonship, not his deity or godhood, "begins" from the Father. And the same holds true of the term "beginning" as applied to the Holy Spirit. The "procession" of the Holy Spirit "begins" by spiration from the Father and Son, but not his deity or godhood (italics in original).[45]

Arguments such as these evoke the Eastern objection that in the Latin-Augustinian approach God is seen as simple essence, "within which a Trinity of Persons can be understood only in terms of internal relations", as opposed to the personalistic approach of the Greeks, in terms of which the "starting point" of Trinitarian

---

[45] http://www.ccel.org/print/schaff/npnf103/iv.i.vii.xiv, (accessed 26/01/2008)

thought is the Divine Persons.[46] Meyendorff argues that the *filioque* therefore presupposes that essence precedes the personal existence of the three *hypostases*, as against the Eastern insistence that the Father is the origin of the Son and the Spirit, not by nature but in virtue of his *hypostatic* existence.[47] As Zizioulas says: "The Greek Patristic tradition, at least since the Cappadocian Fathers, identified the one God with the person of the Father, whereas, St Augustine seems to identify Him with the one divine substance (the *deitas* or *divinitas*)."[48]

Patristic historian Michel Rene Barnes questions this essence *versus* person schema, traceable to Théodore de Régnon (1898), and laments the fact that it has been unquestionably adopted by a host of modern and post-modern systematic theologians, although it in fact conceals as much as it reveals and leads to an idealistic reading of particularly Augustine's work.[49] What is true is that the Orthodox have traditionally understood the Western conception to "begin with the essence". Thus Photius objected: "For it is not [...] the nature [...] which is worshipped, but the specific *hypostatic* properties through which theology discerns the *hypostases* of the Trinity."[50] The NAOCTC[51] insists that this is a misconception of the Catholic position, but does not explain further. The problem appears to be that while in Western (as in Eastern) thought person and essence are seen as identical in God,[52] this notion is worked out differently by the two traditions.

---

[46] John Meyendorff, *Byzantine Theology*, (New York: Fordham University Press, 1979) 60–61; John Zizioulas, *Being as Communion*, 40–43, 88

[47] *Ibid*

[48] John Zizioulas, *One Single Source: An Orthodox response to the Clarification of the Filioque*, 2; for a fuller explanation see John Zizioulas, *Being as Communion*, 40ff

[49] "Augustine in Contemporary Trinitarian Theology" in *Theological Studies* (*Vol. 56 Issue*, 1995), 237–239; Gerald O'Collins (*op.cit.* 135) also refutes it

[50] *Myst.* 47; c.f. Richard Cross, "On generic and derivation views of God's Trinitarian substance" in *Scottish Journal of Theology* (UK: SJT, 56(4), 2003), 471

[51] *Op.cit, n.pag*

[52] Thomas Aquinas, *S.Th.* 1.a. q. 39. art 1. ans.

It seems that in Western thought the essence is identified with the One God, who is also identified with the person of the Father. Thus Aquinas argues that the Father *is* the essence; so when one says that the Son is begotten of the essence of the Father, it is the same as saying that the Son is "of the Father, Who is essence".[53] Richard Cross[54] argues that in the Western tradition this does not imply that the substance is prior to the Persons or a cause of the Persons. Rather, the Father is seen as the source of the Son and the Spirit and the substance is seen as an "item" common to the three Persons. The substance is a constituent element of the Father's being. This implies that the Father communicates His own substance to the Son and the Spirit in the begetting and spirating; thus the divine attributes belong equally to all three and the end result is that the essence is common to all three. However, Cross continues, citing Aquinas, speaking of the substance independently of the Persons is merely an abstraction; in fact God is nothing other than a trinity of Persons.[55] Thus, it seems, contrary to the Orthodox perception, (a) the West does not see the essence as prior to or constitutive of the Persons and (b), as in the East, the West identifies the One God with the Father and sees the Father as the source of the Trinitarian life, which means the monarchy of the Father is not technically at issue.

However, the idea that Father is the essence is equally problematic, because in Eastern thought all three Persons are the essence, as we shall see. Western thinkers will argue, as we shall also see, that this is also true of the Western conception. However, there is a fundamental difference, which relates to the different way in which the two traditions use the words Person and essence, resulting in divergent emphases. While in the East the three Persons are essentially three "Subjectivities" who tri-mutually constitute the essence, in Western thought the way in which the Persons and essence are identified gives the impression that in the Trinity there is only one real Person in the sense that the Orthodox understand the word. Rahner, for one, makes it abundantly clear that in Western

---

[53] *S.Th.* 1.a, q. 41. art. 3 r.obj.2
[54] *Op.cit*, 464ff – see especially pp. 466–467, 472 and 476
[55] Richard Cross, *op.cit*, 474–476

thought the Divine Persons are not persons as we understand the word today. He describes the Son and Spirit as "two modes of factuality" of God the Father's "self-communication as *Logos* and love".[56] He continues:

> When *today* we speak of person in the plural, we think almost necessarily, because of the modern meaning of the word, of several spiritual centres of activity, of several subjectivities and liberties. But there are not three of these in God – not only because in God there is only *one* essence, hence *one* absolute self-presence, but also because there is only *one* self-utterance of the Father, the *Logos*. The *Logos* is not the one who utters, but the one who is uttered. And there is properly no *mutual* love between the Father and the Son, for this would presuppose two acts. But there is self-acceptance by the Father and this self-acceptance gives rise to distinction.[57] (Italics in original)

He continues that there is consciousness in each "person" about Himself and about the other two, but it is not three consciousnesses; "one consciousness subsists in a threefold way":[58]

> The subsistence itself is as such not "personal", if we understand this word in the modern sense. The distinctness of the persons is not constituted by a distinctness of conscious identities nor does it include the latter. This distinctness is conscious. However, it is not conscious for three subjectivities, but it is the distinctness of this awareness in only one consciousness.[59]

O'Collins, summarising the thought of Aquinas, states similarly that "there is only one mental state in God, a mental state that

---

[56] Karl Rahner, *op.cit*, 375–376

[57] *Ibid* 378–379

[58] *Ibid* 379

[59] *Ibid*

has a plural subject (the Father, the Son and the Holy Spirit) [...]
Apart from the two events in God's life (the generation and spiration) that cause the opposition of relationship, every perfection is
simply one in God."[60] Rahner goes on to justify the continued use
of the word "persons" in relation to the Trinity, using expressions
such as "the One God subsists in three manners of subsisting" or
"manners of being"; "the Father, Son and Spirit are one God each
in a different manner of subsisting"; "God as subsisting in a determined manner of subsisting (such as Father) is 'somebody else'
than God subsisting in another manner of subsisting, but he is not
'something else'"; "the one and same divine essence subsists in
each of the three distinct manners of subsisting".[61]

What we have, effectively, is a God who is an individual and
who knows and loves Himself through two *persona* that are subjective only in the sense that the One God subsists in them – or *as*
them: the One God eternally constitutes Himself as Father by begetting Himself as Son; and in His subsistence as Father and Son
He spirates Himself as Spirit. As the One God in His subsistence
as Father is the originator of the other two "Persons", He is identified with the One God and the One essence. While not every
Western thinker agrees with Rahner, his perspective represents an
underlying presupposition in Western philosophical thought regarding the Trinity, namely that the One God is an individual in
whom there are three relations – a notion that is also traceable to
Augustine, as we shall see below. Thus Leonard Geddes explains
that the Divine Persons are subsistent relations:

> For the constitution of a person it is required that a reality be
> subsistent and absolutely distinct; i.e. incommunicable. The
> three Divine realities are relations, each identified with the Di-
> vine. A finite relation has reality only in so far as it is an acci-
> dent; it has the reality of inherence. The divine relations, how-
> ever, are in the nature not by inherence but by identity. The re-
> ality they have, therefore, is not that of an accident, but that of

---

[60] Gerald O'Collins, *op.cit*, 146; see also p. 74ff
[61] Karl Rahner, *op.cit*, 380–381

a subsistence. They are therefore one with *ipsum esse subsistens*. Again every relation, by its very nature, implies opposition and so distinction. It the finite relation this distinction is between subject and term. In the infinite relations there is no subject as distinct from the relation itself; the Paternity is the Father […]; the Filiation is the Son. The Divine realities are therefore distinct and mutually incommunicable through this relative opposition; they are subsistent as being identified with the subsistence of the Godhead; i.e. they are persons.[62]

McCarthy brings us full circle by outlining Aquinas's explanation of Augustine's argument as to why the Son and Spirit cannot both originate from the Father alone:

> Now, St. Thomas argues that, if such an idea were true, the Person of the Holy Spirit would not be distinct from the Person of the Son, and there would, therefore, not be a Blessed Trinity […]. St. Thomas says: "It is necessary to believe that the Holy Spirit is from the Son. For, if He were not from Him, in no way could He be personally distinguished from Him." His reason is that "only by relations are the divine Persons distinguished from one another" and "relations cannot distinguish Persons except according to the fact that they are opposite". Hence, if the Father had two relations of origin which were not opposite to each other, the Son and the Holy Spirit would be one Person having two relations opposite to the two relations originating from the Father. "Therefore, it is necessary that the Son and the Holy Spirit be related to one another by opposite relations. But there cannot be in the Godhead any other relations than relations of origin".[63]

---

[62] Leonard Geddes, "Person" in *New Advent Catholic Encyclopedia*, Vol 11, New York: Robert Appleton Company, 1911 [online] http//www.newadvent.org/cathen/11726a.htm (accessed 24/07/2008)

[63] John F McCarthy, "On the Procession of the Holy Spirit" in *Living Tradition*, no 66 (September, 1996), 7–8

This brings us back to the Eastern objection that the *filioque* implies the reduction of the *hypostatic* (personal) existence of the Divine Persons to mere relations.[64] But this protest would be unintelligible to the Western mind unless one understands what the Orthodox mean by "person-*hypostasis*" in relation to the Divine Persons and how they therefore understand the constitution of the Trinity.

1.vi.b. The person in Orthodox thought

Metropolitan Hierotheos of Nafpaktos[65] describes how Basil of Caesarea (329–379), speaking of the Divine Persons in his argument against Sabellian Modalism,[66] first separated the term *ousia* (essence) from *hypostasis*, which until then was identified with essence – as in the First Ecumenical Council.[67] Basil's argument was that the essence or nature is held in common in the Trinity and that the *hypostases* are the particular ways of being of the Father, the Son and the Holy Spirit. He arrived at this distinction by arguing that no nature exists "in the nude" but always has its mode of existence.[68] Or, as Hierotheos puts it: "Essence cannot subsist by itself, since formless essence does not subsist, while in the *hypostases*, or individuals, are found both the essence and the intrinsic differ-

---

[64] John Meyendorff, *Byzantine Theology*, op.cit, 60; George Bebis, op.cit, n.pag

[65] *The Person in the Orthodox Tradition*, 70–72; 193–194

[66] A form of Monarchianism named after Sabellius, its most famous exponent (early 3rd century), who, wanting to preserve both the monarchy of the Father and the unity of the Godhead, taught that the only differentiation in the Godhead was a succession of modes or operations; i.e. Father, Son and Spirit were one God in three modes – see E. A Livingstone (Ed), *A Concise Dictionary of the Christian Church* (London: Omega Books Ltd, 1988), 341; 342; 451

[67] Athanasius also used "*hypostasis*" in this way. See John Zizioulas, *Being as Communion*, 36

[68] John Zizioulas, *Being as Communion*, 88; see e.g. Basil, Ep 38:2; Gregory of Nyssa, *Letter to Ablabius*

ences."[69] Second, he identified the *hypostasis*, in the Stoic sense of the distinct substance of the individual, with the word "person" and applied the term to each Divine Person, arguing: "For it is not sufficient to enumerate the difference in the persons, but it is necessary to confess that each Person subsists in a true *hypostasis*."[70] Thus Hierotheos remarks:

> Until that time "person" [*prosopon*] had meant something 'unreal', the mask. From the time of Basil the Great [...] the person has acquired ontology and substance. [...] Thus the *prosopon* – when identified with the *hypostasis* – which is the essence with the particular peculiarities – takes on great value, losing its impersonal and abstract character and acquiring ontology.[71]

To explain his meaning, St Basil argued illustratively in his *Letter 214 to Terentios*, drawing an analogy from human existence: "Essence is to *hypostasis* as common is to particular. Each one of us partakes of being by the common notion of essence, but we are this man or that man by our own individuality."[72] And elsewhere that "substance and person (*hypostasis*) have the distinction that the general has with reference to the particular"; for example, just as "a 'living creature' has with reference to 'a particular man'. For this reason we confess one essence for the Godhead [...], but we confess a person that is particular".[73] The particular peculiarities indicate distinct individuality.

---

[69] Hierotheos (Vlachos), *The Person in the Orthodox Tradition*, 74

[70] *Letter 210*, LCL, vol.3, p. 211 in ibid; c.f. Vladimir Lossky, *Orthodox Theology: An Introduction* (New York: St Vladimir's Seminary Press, 1978), 41

[71] Hierotheos (Vlachos), *The Person in the Orthodox Tradition*, 71–72; c.f. John Zizioulas, *Being as Communion*, 87–89

[72] In Georges Barrois (trans/ed), *The Fathers Speak: St Basil the Great, St Gregory of Nazianzus & St Gregory of Nyssa,* (New York: St Vladimir's Seminary Press, 1986), 128

[73] *Ibid* 71; here he quotes St Basil's *Letter 36 to Amphilochios* (LCL, vol. 3, pp. 401–403)

In n39–43 of his *Dialectics*,[74] St John of Damascus similarly describes the person as "one who by reason of his own operations and properties exhibits to us an appearance which is distinct and set off from those of the same nature as he". That is, a person is one who appears as somebody in particular among the many of his kind. For example, he continues, the Archangel Gabriel who "was one of the angels and belonged to a particular species, was at the same time a particular individual "distinct from the angels consubstantial with him". Similarly, while the Apostle Paul "was one among the number of men, by his characteristics and operations he was distinct from the rest of men". In short, the Eastern Fathers made the simple point that the Divine Persons were real Persons – but not individuals in the Aristotelian sense. Vladimir Lossky links Basil's notion of personhood to *perichoresis (circumincessio)*:

> *Ousia* in the Trinity is not an abstract idea of divinity, a rational essence binding three divine individuals, as humanity, for example is common to three men. […] It is rather an unknowable transcendence; the Bible envelops it in the glorious radiance of the divine names. As for *hypostasis* – and it is here, under Christianity, that a true advancement of thought emerges – it no longer contains the individual. The individual is part of the species, or rather he is only a part of it: he divides the nature to which he belongs […] there is nothing of that sort in the Trinity, where every *hypostasis* in its fullness assumes in its fullness the divine nature. […] The *hypostases* […] are infinitely united and infinitely different; they are the divine nature, but none possess it […] precisely because each person opens itself to the others, because they share one nature without restriction, that the latter is not divided.[75]

This distinction between "person" and "individual" is vital, as some Westerners tend to believe the Orthodox conceive the Divine Persons as individuals, a misconception fuelled by the fact that

---

[74] In Hierotheos (Vlachos), *The Person in the Orthodox Tradition*, 74–75
[75] Vladimir Lossky, *op.cit*, 41

the Cappadocians sometimes used the word individual in their expositions, as we have seen. However, they were using the word illustratively, not to denote an Aristotelian meaning, and certainly not in the sense of the meaning it came to acquire in the West through thinkers such as Thomas Aquinas, who defined the person as a "distinct subsistent in a rational nature"[76]. One also has to view the Eastern patristic use of the word individual in context. As Lossky puts it:

> One is present then, with the Fathers, at a true transmutation of language; using either philosophical terms or words of the current language, they change their meaning until they are rendered able to encompass this prodigiously new reality which Christianity alone reveals: namely that of personhood – in God as in man, since man is the image of God; and in the Trinity as in regenerated humanity [...].[77]

Ware elaborates in light of the Western scholastic idea of the word individual:

> There is in God genuine diversity as well as true unity. The Christian God is not just a unit but a union, not just unity but community. [...] He is triunity, three equal persons, each one dwelling in the other two by virtue of an unceasing movement of mutual love. [...] Thus Christ prayed to His Father on the night before His Crucifixion: "May they all be one as thou, Father, art in me and I in thee..." (John 17:21). [...] God is *personal* and God is *love*. Now both these notions imply sharing and reciprocity. Now a "person" is not at all the same as an individual. Isolated, self-dependent, none of us is an authentic person but merely an individual, a bare unit as recorded in the census. [...] If the most precious element of our human life is the relationship of "I and thou", then we cannot but ascribe

---

[76] *S.Th.* 1a.30.3 ad 4 in Gerald O'Collins, *op.cit*, 176
[77] Vladimir Lossky, *op.cit*, 40

this relationship, in some sense, to the eternal being of God Himself. And that is precisely what the doctrine of the Holy Trinity means. At the very heart of the divine life, from all eternity, God knows himself as "I-thou" in a threefold way, and he rejoices eternally in this knowledge. […] in Him these things mean infinitely more than we can ever imagine. (Italics in original)[78]

Here Ware is teasing out the thought of the Cappadocians. For example, Gregory of Nyssa says in *Letter 38*: "The difference of the *hypostases* does not disintegrate the community of the *ousia*, nor does the community of the *ousia* confuse the particularity of the individual characteristics."[79] Notice the idea of unity as community. As Basil says: "For absolute and real existence is predicated in the case of things which are mutually inseparable."[80] Following this perspective, Ware summarises the meaning of Nicaea I and Constantinople I:

But although Father, Son and Spirit are one single God, yet each of them is from all eternity a person, a distinct centre of conscious selfhood. The Trinity is thus to be described as 'three persons in one essence'. […] There is distinction but never separation. Father, Son and Spirit have only one will and not three, only one energy and not three.[81]

Thus when Archimandrite Sophrony Sakharov (1896–1993), the disciple and biographer of St Silouan, says that "in the Divine

---

[78] Kallistos Ware, *op.cit*, 31–35

[79] In Anthony Meredith, *op.cit*, 108; some scholars attribute this letter to Basil

[80] *De Spiritu Sancto* 63 [online]. http://wwwnewadvent.org/fathers (accessed 02/05/2008)

[81] Kallistos Ware, *op.cit*, 37

Being the *Hypostasis* constitutes the innermost esoteric principle of Being",[82] he speaks of each Divine Person.

In this context, the Orthodox see the *hypostatic* origin of the Son and Spirit as Persons to be an ineffable mystery that cannot be comprehended or described in human categories of thought.[83] The meaning of begetting and proceeding is ineffable because we cannot know how a divine "Subjectivity" originates.

In terms of this understanding of divine personhood, in Eastern thought the Son and Spirit are not "modes of subsistence", but unique, "self-conscious" Persons who themselves constitute the common essence and give it its ontological content.[84] The one God eternally constitutes Himself as Father by begetting the Son and bringing forth the Spirit in love, so constituting the Trinitarian being as a communion of love.[85] Within this conception of the Trinity there is one God because there is one Father, who *has* a Son and a Spirit, who are God by virtue of their divine origin and by virtue of the fact that they are by nature an eternal communion of love that originates in the Father.

In this context, (a) the phrase "God is love" is understood to mean that the nature of God the Father is love, and the Father consequently constitutes the intra-Trinitarian communion as love, in which the three Persons eternally indwell one another in a relationship of total self-giving and receptivity (*perichoresis*). Thus Zizioulas[86] says that love, as the "supreme ontological predicate" of being and "as God's mode of existence, *hypostasizes* God, constitutes His being". Thus: "The substance of God, 'God', has no ontological content, no true being, apart from communion".[87] Thus the common nature is distinguished by the *hypostatic* attributes shared in common by all three Persons, such as love, eternity, om-

---

[82] From *His Life is Mine*, n.d: 22, in Hierotheos (Vlachos), *The Person in the Orthodox Tradition*, 80

[83] See for example Photius, *Myst.* 6 and Athanasius, *Letter to Serapion* 1.18 in Khaled Anatolios, *op.cit*, 217

[84] Vladimir Lossky, *op.cit*, 42–44

[85] *Ibid* 41; 44

[86] *Being as Communion*, 46

[87] *Ibid* 17

niscience, etc., but the three Persons *are* the threefold essence. Thus (b) Orthodox theologians argue that the Father is the source of union because He is the source of the Son and Spirit as unique, self-conscious Persons, who subsist eternally in Him in a relation of love and to whom He eternally gives Himself completely. Ware explains that this is why the origin of the Son and Spirit are defined in terms of their relationship to the Father alone.[88]

This emphasis enables Eastern thinkers to affirm the monarchy of the Father *contra* the perception that the West sees the Persons as being constituted by the essence and to emphasise that the essence is not a common entity that unites the Three, but an interpersonal communion that has its source in the Father. Hierotheos offers an important corrective to the views of both those who maintain that the unity in the Godhead is due to the Father alone and to those who say it is due to the common essence alone:

> The first view ends in overemphasis on the Persons [resulting in the perception of three individuals], the second ends in overemphasis of the essence and creates an abstract theology. I think that apart from the partial truths which are hidden within such isolated views, the truth is that the oneness of the Persons of the Holy Trinity is due both to the Father, Who begets the Son and sends out the Holy Spirit, and to their common essence. The first shows the cause of the existence of the other Persons and describes their hypostatic characteristics, and the second underlines the common energy.[89]

---

[88] Kallistos Ware, *op.cit*, 39–40; c.f. John Zizioulas, *Being as Communion*, 40–41; Gregory of Nazianzus' *Oration at Constantinople I*

[89] *The Person in the Orthodox Tradition*, 219–220; both emphases are found in the Cappadocians' writings; for example, St Basil stresses the community of nature in *De Spiritu Sancto* 45; St Gregory of Nazianzus also uses this reasoning in his *Fourth Theological Oration*, but more often stresses that the Father is the source of the unity. See also *Oration* 42.15 in Meredith, *op.cit*, 106. I should think the point is that the unity of essence is due to the fact that the Son and Spirit come forth from the Father; thus the shared essence and origination from the Father are really making the same

It seems there are two senses of the "oneness" of God; it can refer to the unity of the Trinity and also to the fact of there being One God. The second is fundamental to the Orthodox understanding of the monarchy of the Father: in the Orthodox conception the Father is the One God "as such" by virtue of His being the unoriginate cause of the other two Persons and thus the origin of the Trinitarian life.

So, as Zizioulas says: "To make the Son equally the cause of the Spirit would be to acknowledge two ontological origins in the Trinity and thus two Gods."[90] Thus, while the Western conception does not technically violate the Father's monarchy, it does empty the doctrine of its intended content.

1.VII. SUMMARY

Both traditions seem to identify the One God with the Father, who is "God as such", to use Rahner's phrase, and both agree that the Trinity is One by virtue of the shared essence and the Father's monarchy. Both agree that God is a self-aware, personal being. The fundamental difference is that the West identifies this self-awareness with the One God only, while the Orthodox ascribe it to all three Persons. Thus in Western thought there is only one conscious Self in God, who subsists in three relations, while in Eastern thought three "self-conscious centres of activity" subsist eternally in a communion of love. There are several implications:

First, the notion of the oneness and threeness of God has been worked out differently in the two traditions. In the West there is only one God because there is only one centre of consciousness or Self who subsists in three subsistences. Thus the Son and the Spirit are God – and therefore equal to and consubstantial with the Father – by virtue of *being* the one God in two incommunicable

---

point: the Son and Spirit are one with the Father because they are inseparably of His (*hypostatic*) being.

[90] John Zizioulas, *Lectures in Christian Dogmatics* (London: T&T Clark, 2008), 78

subsistences. In the East there is one God proper because there is one (unoriginate) Father/God who causes two other (self-conscious) Divine Persons who are God in a *derivative* sense, if I may use this expression, by virtue of their divine origin, but also by virtue of their eternal communion with and in the Father.[91] The Son and Spirit are equal to the Father by virtue of their consubstantiality with Him, not by *being* Him. Being the sole cause of the other two Persons is precisely what identifies the Father as "God as such". This is why the Orthodox assert that there can be only one cause of *hypostases* in the Trinity; to introduce two causes would introduce two Gods "as such".

Second, there are implications for the relationship between person and nature in God. In the Catholic model, the substance can be abstracted as a constituent element of the Father, whereas in the Orthodox model this is impossible because the Father is essentially a personal Subject, as are all three Persons. Thus within the Western schema, because *each* Person is not seen as essentially subjective and because the Father is identified with the whole essence, one has the impression that the Father constitutes Himself as Son and Spirit precisely by communicating His essence in particular subsistent ways. Thus the Son and Spirit are individuated only as a function of their origin. From an Orthodox perspective this would mean the Son and Spirit are functions of the essence. In the Orthodox view, by contrast, the nature (communion of love) is a function of the three ineffable, unique and self-conscious Persons. Add *perichoresis* to the mix and the Orthodox arrive at the view that the three Persons (unique, ineffable identities) tri-mutually constitute the essence of the Godhead by their mutual indwelling. Hence the Three *are* the essence. Thus the Persons and nature are indivisi-

---

[91] It is also true that one finds expressions such as "We have one God, because there is a single Godhead" in the writings of the Eastern Fathers, for example in Gregory of Nyssa's *Letter to Ablablius* and in the *Letter to Damasus* quoted above; however, this emphasis is found in the Fathers when the stress is on the Divine Unity – the end result of the divine processions; when the monarchy of the Father is at issue in the context of the divine processions, the emphasis seems to be on the uno-riginateness of the Father as cause of the other two Persons.

ble; the nature is delineated by that which is common to the Three, while the Persons are distinguished by those properties that are unique to each One. Third, notions of identity are worked out differently. In the Western model the identities of the "Persons" can be defined only by relationship of origin: the Father is who He is because He is the unoriginate Father to the Son (i.e. He *is* the Paternity), the Son is Son because He originates in the Father only (He *is* the filiation) and the Spirit is Spirit because He originates by spiration (He *is* the spiration); ergo, the "Persons" are subsistent relations of opposition within the one unbegotten God/essence. If the Son and Spirit both came forth from the Father alone, there would be two Sons; thus the only way to define the Son and Spirit is by their relations of opposition. Ergo the perceived need for the *filioque* – the Spirit proceeds from the Father (primary principle) and the Son (secondary principle). Thus Western thinkers are able to show that the Son and Spirit fit the description of Person as being subsistent (*hypostatic*) and distinct, without denoting separate individuals, but also without denoting three "self-aware" Subjects. In the East, the "begetting" and "proceeding" distinguish the manner of origin of the Son and Spirit from the Father and tell us something about their identities, but because the Persons are seen as distinct "Subjectivities", they are ontologically more than their relations.

Nevertheless, the idea that the West "begins with the essence" appears to be a misconception and, technically, the West upholds the monarchy of the Father; both East and West identify the Father as the One God and therefore see the Father as the source of the Trinity. However, the way in which this notion is worked out differs, with the result that, from an Eastern perspective, in the Western conception of the Trinity the Father's monarchy is upheld at the expense of the personal existence of the Son and the Spirit. Thus the Orthodox objection to the Persons being reduced to "mere relations" remains a fundamental difficulty. The primary question is whether the notion of self-conscious personhood can be properly applied to the Father (the One God) alone or to all three Persons. It is also apparent that the same words are often used by the two traditions in differing ways – most notably person, *hypostasis* and substance (*ousia*). For example, in the West *hypostasis* simply means subsistence, whereas in the East it denotes a subjective Person in the context of Trinitarian thought.

Finally, the underlying reason for the differing ideas about the relationship between the economic and immanent Trinity becomes clear: for the West the Trinitarian existence is a self-expression of the One God/Self; there is therefore no conceivable reason why God should manifest Himself differently in His immanent life than He does economically. For Easterners the Trinitarian communion is the inner life of the threefold Godhead, so the Persons' self-communication to creatures must be distinguished from their immanent communion.

2 UNTANGLING THE ARGUMENTS

The fact that Latin and Greek theologians premise their arguments on radically different understandings of divine personhood means that the two traditions have been arguing at cross-purposes and a great deal of energy has been spent addressing the symptoms of the problem while not making explicit the underlying difficulty. I shall attempt to demonstrate this by examining the Orthodox objections to the *filioque* in more detail, in juxtaposition with recent Catholic attempts to clarify their position and in light of our findings with regard to the differing conceptions of divine personhood.

2.1. ORTHODOX OBJECTIONS PREMISED ON THREE REAL PERSONS

The arguments Photius posits in his *Mystagogy of the Holy Spirit* show that he interprets the *filioque* within the paradigm of the Orthodox understanding of divine personhood. He argues:

First, one would have to also say that the Son proceeds from the Spirit to affirm the equality of the Spirit, because reason demands the equality of all three *hypostases*. Thus, following Western logic that the Son's property of procession signifies equality with the Father,[1] all three Persons would have to possess the properties of causality of *hypostases* and each would have to share in the origin

---

[1] As at the 589 Council of Toledo, where this argument was posited against the Arians – see George Bebis, *op.cit*; Kenneth Scott Latourette, *op.cit*, 303; PCPCU, *op.cit*, NAOCTC, *op.cit*; Philip Schaff, *Historical Excursus on the Introduction into the Creed of the Words 'and the Son' from Nicene and Post-Nicene Fathers: Series II/Volume XIV in Filioque Controversy*, 2007, n.pag [online]. http://www.mb-soft.com/believe/txn/filioque.htm (accessed 07/08/2008)

of the other two.[2] Photius caricatures this notion by saying that one might as well have an endless number of processions, with each *hypostasis* bringing forth another.[3] But, he asks: "Then where is the much-hymned, divine majesty of the Monarchy?"[4] Photius' underlying argument is that a property can be either common to all three Persons by virtue of the common essence, or it must be a unique property of one Person.[5] Thus, to give the Son the property of being a cause of a *hypostasis* is to either divide between the Father and the Son a property of the incommunicable identity of the Father or to suggest that the Son's property of causation (as a secondary principle) is less than that of the Father's, which renders the Son unequal anyhow.[6]

Second, the *filioque* confuses the properties unique to each *hypostasis*. The ability to beget or produce is the characteristic that makes the Father the Father, so by attributing the power of procession to the Son one either robs the Father of His identity, or implies that the Father and Son have a shared *hypostasis*, or that the Son supplements the Father, which means that the Father is not perfect in Himself.[7]

Third, granting both the Father and the Son the power of procession places the Father and the Son on the same level ontologically and the Spirit on a lesser level, compromising the dignity of the Spirit, since the Spirit is the only divine *hypostasis* who does not have the power of procession. The Trinity effectively becomes a duality with two causes.[8]

Fourth, if the Spirit has two causes, this introduces the idea that the Spirit is a composite, which contradicts the divine simplicity and begs the question: what does the Spirit receive from the Son that He did not receive from the Father in His original procession

---

[2] *Myst.* 3; 6; 18
[3] *Ibid* 37; 47
[4] *Ibid* 11; here he appeals to the *lex orandi, lex credendi* principle
[5] *Ibid* 17–19; 35–36; 46; 63–64
[6] *Ibid* 39
[7] *Ibid* 16
[8] *Ibid* 4; 9; 12; 32–34; 40–44; 52

from the Father as first cause?[9] Or it suggests that He is synthesised from cause and caused and therefore imperfect in Himself.[10]

Fifth, the *filioque* implies that the Spirit has an immediate and a remote cause, which either introduces the concept of time into the intra-Trinitarian life or implies that the cause comes into existence at the same time as the caused.[11]

Sixth, the clause separates the *hypostasis* of the Father into two *hypostases* [of Father and Son, who are "one" in relation to the Spirit]. He argues that "the essence is not the cause of the Word: the Father is the *hypostatic* cause of the *hypostasis* of the Word"[12] [...] "For the *hypostasis* comes before the distinctions in energies and operations".[13] Thus: "If the Father is cause of the *hypostases* produced from Him not by reason of nature, but by reason of the *hypostasis* [...] then there can be no way the Son is cause of any *hypostasis* in the Trinity".[14]

Finally, he posits the alternate view of the Scriptural texts that speak of the Spirit being "of the Son": the Son is the Son because He is consubstantial with the Father, not simply because He is begotten, and "when we sacredly proclaim the Spirit is of the Father and of the Son, we unambiguously indicate by these phrases the Spirit's consubstantiality with both. Now He is consubstantial with the Father because He proceeds from Him, and He is consubstantial with the Son, but not because He proceeds [from Him ...] but rather because His procession from the same one, indivisible, eternal cause brings each of them into the same rank".[15]

Photius further cites Nicaea I and Constantinople I, which, he points out, were received by the Western Church and which clearly confirmed the consubstantial essence of the Spirit by stating that the Spirit proceeds from the Father.[16]

---

[9] *Ibid* 4; 7; 31; 43; see also Photius in M.A. Pugliese, *op.cit*, 161–2
[10] *Ibid* 44
[11] *Ibid* 62–64
[12] *Ibid* 16
[13] *Ibid* 63
[14] *Ibid* 15
[15] *Ibid* 52–53
[16] *Ibid* 80

Photius' argumentation would be gobbledegook to a Western-er who does not understand the Eastern meaning of *hypostasis*. But if one understands *hypostasis* – in the context of Trinitarian theology – to mean a real, distinct personal Subject, it becomes clear that he understands the *filioque* to mean that the Son, as a distinct, real Person with His own peculiar properties, participates in the origin of the Spirit as a real Person with His own properties.

So let's take, for example, Photius' sixth point, that the *filioque* divides the *hypostasis* of the Father into two because the property of causing other *hypostases* is a distinct property of the Father. McCarthy reminds us that, in terms of the Thomist [and Augustinian] understanding, the assertion that the Father and Son are one principle in relation to the Spirit is a statement of relationality rather than ontology, "for it is only by relations that the Divine Persons can be distinguished from one another."[17]

But such an argument confuses the issue even more, because in Western thought the Persons *are* the relations (of origin), while ontology seems to refer to a substance that is abstracted from the relations themselves. In Eastern thought, on the other hand, the Persons are the essence. There are two different ontologies at play.

What is clear is that divergent views of identity in relation to the Divine Persons lead directly to opposing notions about the procession of the Spirit: to Catholics, origination of the Son and Spirit from the Father alone confuses the identities of the Son and the Spirit, while to the Orthodox double procession from the Father and Son confuses the identity of the Father with that of the Son. To an Easterner, the identity of the Father as "God as such", to use Rahner's term, is linked to His being the sole originator of *hypostases*; so, from an Eastern perspective, the *filioque* threatens the identity of the Father.

But before analysing any further, let us juxtapose the Orthodox perspective with the arguments posited in the PCPCU's 1995 Clarification and some of the commentary on the Clarification.

---

[17] John F. McCarthy, *op.cit*, 4; Aquinas *S.Th.* a, q. 36, art.2, corp

2.II. WESTERN CLARIFICATION

The PCPCU, aiming to show the harmony between the Eastern and Western conceptions, emphasises the Western Church's subscription to the dogma of the monarchy of the Father by stressing that "the Father alone is the principle without principle (*arche anarchos*) of the two other persons of the Trinity, the soul source (*peghe*) of the Son and of the Holy Spirit. The Holy Spirit therefore takes his origin from the Father alone *(ek monou tou Patros)* in a principle, proper and immediate manner".[18]

The council stresses that there is a misunderstanding regarding the monarchy of the Father due to confusion caused by the word proceed (*procedit or processio* in Latin). The Clarification differentiates between *ekporeusis*, the word used by the Greeks to convey the Spirit's eternal procession from the Father, and *processio (proienai)*, used by the Latins to express the procession of the Spirit from the Father and Son, and emphasises that inaccurate translations in the past created a "false equivalence" between the two expressions. While *ekporeusis* signifies the relationship of origin from the Father alone as the "principle without principle of the Trinity", the Latin procession "is a more common term, signifying the communication of the consubstantial divinity from the Father to the Son and from the Father, through and with the Son, to the Holy Spirit" – a precedent for which is cited in St Cyril of Alexandria (376–444), while St Maximus the Confessor (c. 580–662) is cited as supporting this teaching in his *Letter to Marin of Cyprus*.[19] The Clarification emphasises that it is not the divine essence that proceeds in the Son (i.e. the essence does not precede the Persons); rather, the Father and Son have it in common through the begetting and both communicate it to the Spirit. The Clarification quotes the Fourth Lateran Council:

> The substance does not generate, is not begotten, does not proceed; but it is the Father who generates, the Son who is be-

---

[18] See also *Cat.* 248; Gerald O'Collins, *op.cit*, 139

[19] The NAOCTC also stresses the importance of this distinction in its 2003 statement

gotten, the Holy Spirit who proceeds: so that there is distinction in persons and unity in nature. Although other (*alius*) is the Father, other the Son, other the Holy Spirit, they are not another reality (*aliud*), but what the Father is the Son is and the Holy Spirit equally; so, according to the orthodox and catholic faith, we believe that they are consubstantial. For the Father, generating eternally the Son, has given to him his substance [...] and so the Father and the Son have the same substance. So the Father, the Son and the Holy Spirit, who proceeds from them both, are one same reality.[20]

The Clarification posits that, inasmuch as the *filioque* expresses the consubstantial communion between the Father and the Son, the essential faith of the East and the West is not compromised, while differentiating between the Spirit's origin as Person and His reception of the divine substance from the Father and the Son:

> "Even if the Catholic doctrine affirms that the Holy Spirit proceeds from the Father and the Son in the communication of their consubstantial communion, it nonetheless recognises the reality of the original relationship of the Holy Spirit as person with the Father, a relationship that the Greek Fathers express by the term *ekporeusis*."[21]

In an attempt to overcome the objections that the *filioque* subordinates the Spirit to the Son, the council argues that, while it affirms that the Spirit proceeds from the Father and the Son in their consubstantial communion, "it is in the Spirit that this relationship between the Father and the Son itself attains its Trinitarian perfection":

> Just as the Father is characterised as Father by the Son he generates, so does the Spirit, by taking his origin from the Father,

---

[20] DS 804–805
[21] C.f. *Cat.* 248

characterise the Father in the manner of the Trinity in relation
to the Son and characterises the Son in the manner of the
Trinity in his relation to the Father: in the fullness of the Trinitarian mystery they are Father and Son in the Holy Spirit. The
Father only generates the Son by breathing (προβαλλειν
proballein in Greek) through him the Holy Spirit and the Son is
only begotten by the Father insofar as the spiration (προβολε
/*probole* in Greek) passes through him. The Father is Father of
the One Son only by being for him and through him the origin
of the Holy Spirit.[22]

The statement goes on to describe the "Trinitarian character
that the person of the Holy Spirit brings to the very relationship
between the Father and the Son" as the original role of the Spirit in
the economy with regard to the mission and work of the Son,
which we described earlier: The Father is love in its source (2 Cor
13:13; 1 Jn 4:8,16), the Son is "the Son that he loves" (Col 1:14)
and the Spirit is described as the eternal Gift of the Father to his
"beloved Son" (Mk 1:11; 9:7; Lk 20:13; Eph 1:6):

> The divine love which has its origin in the Father reposes in
> "the Son of his love" in order to exist consubstantially through
> the Son in the person of the Spirit, the Gift of love. This takes
> into account the fact that, through love, the Holy Spirit orients
> the whole life of Jesus towards the Father in the fulfilment of
> his will. [...] This role of the Spirit in the innermost human ex-
> istence of the Son of God made man derives from an eternal
> Trinitarian relationship through which the Spirit, in his mystery
> as Gift of Love, characterises the relation between the Father,
> as source of love, and his beloved Son.

---

[22] In its footnotes to this paragraph the council cites St Gregory of
Nazianzus, saying: "The Spirit is a middle term (*meson*) between the Unbegotten and the Begotten. (*Discourse* 31, 8) and St Cyril of Alexandria saying: "The Holy Spirit flows from the Father in the Son (*en tou Uiou*)", *The-
saurus*, XXXIV, *PG* 75, 577 A).] The Clarification adds: "[...] the spiration
of the Spirit from the Father takes place by and through (the two senses
of δια/*dia* in Greek) the generation of the Son, to which it gives its Trinitarian character."

In short, the Clarification argues that (a) the Orthodox mis-conception that the Father's monarchy is compromised is due to language difficulties, (b) that the *filioque* is in harmony with the Orthodox faith inasmuch as it demonstrates the consubstantiality of the Persons and (c) that the Spirit, as the love between the Father and the Son, is not subordinate to the Father and Son because the Father and Son subsist consubstantially in the Spirit.

2.III. ANALYSIS

The Clarification's comments regarding the words *processio* and *ekporeusis* point to a need to revisit the language used in this debate. McCarthy notes that the word "monarchy" (*monarchia*), meaning "origin" or "beginning", could also be misleading as Westerners could take it to mean that the Father is the ruler of the Trinity.[23] Likewise, the word "energies" (*energia*) used by the Orthodox to denote the manifest activities of the Divine Persons could be interpreted by Westerners to denote an impersonal power. But, the words person and *hypostasis*, which seem to be the most problematic, are not given a mention.

We have already shown that the monarchy of the Father is not technically compromised by the *filioque*, as the Clarification asserts. What is compromised by the Western conception of the monarchy, from an Orthodox perspective, is the identity of the Father and the notion that the three Divine Persons are really persons.

Further implications of the divergent views of divine person-hood become apparent when we examine, for example, ideas about the equality of the Persons, consubstantiality and divine essence. Both traditions agree that the Father, Son and Spirit are equal by virtue of their consubstantiality and that the divine essence of the Father *is* divine personhood; that is, the Father is essentially personal being. However, the West uses the *filioque* to denote consubstantiality within the paradigm of the Father (who is the essence)

---

[23] John F. McCarthy, *op.cit*, 5; this is how Tertullian understood the word – see *Against Praxeas* 3–4

originating the Spirit (another subsistence of the Father) jointly with His subsistence as Son.

Thus in the Western paradigm consubstantiality with the Father – and therefore equality with the Father – is synonymous with being the Father Himself in another subsistence. But in Orthodox thought begetting and *ekporeusis* would denote the origination of a distinct, real Person; the Three are therefore equal as distinct Persons by virtue of being equally divine and the Son and Spirit are consubstantial with the Father in the sense that divine personal Subject originates divine personal Subject, as Photius intimated (point six above) and by virtue of their mutual indwelling.

That is, in the Orthodox schema the three Persons subsist as one by virtue of their eternal communion of love, not by virtue of being bound by an indivisible "substratum". Thus, in terms of the affirmation of *perichoresis*, one could say that the Father and Son eternally "communicate" the divine essence to the Spirit by communicating themselves to Him in love. But this would be equally true of each Divine Person in relation to the other Two, so why emphasise this notion only in respect of the Spirit? In terms of this paradigm, the Western use of the *filioque* to demonstrate the consubstantiality of the Father and Son would be fallacious. Also, using the *filioque* to demonstrate consubstantiality means "Roman Catholic theologians are [...] confusing [...] the dogma of the personal existence of the *Hypostases* and the dogma of the Oneness of Essence, which is immediately bound up with it, although it is a separate dogma," as Pomazansky[24] insists. Thus the Clarification's assertion that the essential faith of East and West is not compromised inasmuch as the *filioque* expresses the consubstantial communion between the Trinitarian Persons is misleading, as is its claim that the Eastern emphasis on the monarchy and Western emphasis on consubstantiality are complementary. The subtext is radically different.

The notion that the Spirit proceeds (*ekporeusis*) from the Father as a Person but that the Father and Son communicate the consubstantial divinity to Him would also be baffling to the Orthodox mind. The Orthodox would understand it to mean (as Photius

---

[24] Michael Pomazansky, *op.cit*, 89

does) that the Spirit is a composite, receiving His personhood from the Father but His essence from the Father and the Son together. In this context Photius has to ask what this divine essence is that is communicated by the Father and the Son to the Spirit that He does not already have by virtue of His *hypostatic* origin in the Father? Catholic theologian George Tavard asks the same question in his 2001 response to the Clarification[25] and goes on to suggest that Ockham's razor might be put to good use here.

On the other hand, the idea that the Spirit comes forth from the Father as Person but receives the essence from Father and Son does not square with what was said previously; to go back to our discussion of Photius' sixth point, if the Spirit is only a relation then the implication is that He is principally from the Father in terms of substance, but as a relation ("Person") receives His *hypostatic* identity from the Father and the Son. Here the Clarification seems to be saying the opposite, without correcting the idea that the Persons are "mere relations" or noting an alternative notion of personhood.

Zizioulas is rather conciliatory. He acknowledges, on the basis of the distinction between *ekporeusis* and *processio*, that an argument can be legitimately made for the idea that there is a sort of *filioque* on the level of essence but not of *hypostasis*, because the Greek fathers used an equivalent word, *proeinai*, to denote the Spirit's dependence on the Son by virtue of their shared essence, which they both receive from the Father alone.[26] This concession should, I believe, be seen in tandem with Zizioulas' observation, noted earlier, that a sort of *spirituque* could also be gleaned from Scripture. If I understand Orthodox thought correctly, what this means is that, while Scripture refers to the Son sending the Spirit, it also testifies to the Spirit making the Son present in the Incarnation. The Clarification, ironically, provides a sample of Scripture texts to support this idea (see 1.iii.a above), regarding the annunciation, Christ's

---

[25] George H. Tavard, "A Clarification on the Filioque?" in *Anglican Theological Review* (Evanston: Summer, Vol. 83, Iss. 3, 2001), pp. 507ff

[26] John Zizioulas, *One Single Source: An Orthodox response to the Clarification of the Filioque*, *op.cit*, 3

baptism, the Spirit resting on the Son in His ministry, the Spirit raising the Son from the dead and so on. One could add that while the Spirit "is communicated to us particularly in the Eucharist by the Son upon whom He reposes in time and in eternity (John 1:32)",[27] it is also by the Spirit that the Son is made present to us as Bread and Wine. Ware[28] adds that the Spirit also makes Christ present to us inwardly as our personal Saviour. This reveals the Spirit as a real Person, because only a person can reveal another person.

While the Orthodox would not read any of this back into relations of origin, this does reveal a co-operative or reciprocal relationship between the Son and Spirit in the economy, as Ware[29] points out. Thus the *filioque* appears to lay an unbalanced emphasis on the Son's role in the activity of the Spirit without counterbalancing it with a statement about the Spirit's involvement in the Son's being. If one were to read these relations back into the eternal relations of origin and take into account the fact that, as the Clarification asserts, "The Father only generates the Son by breathing through Him the Holy Spirit and the Son is only begotten by the Father insofar as the spiration passes through Him", it might be more accurate to say that the Son is generated eternally by the Father in the Spirit and the Spirit proceeds eternally from the Father in the Son – in the same way that a word is communicated in the breath and the breath in the word.

Furthermore, in light of the Orthodox understanding of divine personhood, Zizioulas asks whether "the expression *principaliter* necessarily precludes making the Son a kind of secondary cause in the ontological emergence of the Spirit?"[30] McCarthy[31] effectively answers in the negative. He bemoans the fact that the Clarification obscures the Thomist meaning of the *filioque* and notes a difficulty with the use of the word "alone" in the Clarification's "The

---

[27] Joint Commission's 1982 report in the Clarification; see also George Tavard, *op.cit, n.pag*

[28] Kallistos Ware, *op.cit*, 124–126

[29] *Ibid* 22

[30] John Zizioulas, *One Single Source: An Orthodox response to the Clarification of the Filioque, op.cit,* 2a

[31] John F. McCarthy, *op.cit*, 4–5

Holy Spirit therefore takes his origin from the Father alone *(ek monou tou Patros)* in a principle, proper and immediate manner". He argues that the word "principally" used by Augustine and Aquinas to denote the Spirit's procession from the Father does not mean "chiefly"; the Latin word *principium* used by Augustine and Aquinas rather means "beginningly" as in "take His first origin from". Thus the Spirit proceeds immediately from the Father and mediately from the Son.[32] McCarthy nuances his response further by again quoting Aquinas:

> This answer raised for St. Thomas another question. If the Holy Spirit proceeds from the Father through the Son, does He proceed more from the Father than from the Son? St. Thomas replies: "If the Son received from the Father a numerically other power for spirating the Holy Spirit, it would follow that He would be like a secondary and instrumental cause, and He [the Holy Spirit] would thus proceed more from the Father than from the Son. But numerically one and the same spirative power is in the Father and the Son, and, therefore, He proceeds equally from both; although sometimes He is said to proceed principally or properly from the Father on account of this that the Son has this power from the Father."[33]

Coffey[34] also insists that the Clarification downplays the meaning of the *filioque* to appease the East by omitting the words "by a single spiration" from the formula of Lyons II, as well as the pronouncement of the Council of Florence, which states expressly that the Spirit is eternally of (as in caused by) the Father and the Son, from whom He receives both essence (consubstantiality) and subsistence (personhood). By omitting this, the council reduces the

---

[32] *Ibid*; see also David Coffey, "The Roman 'Clarification' of the Doctrine of the Filioque" in *International Journal of Systematic Theology* (Oxford: Blackwell Publishing, Vol 5, 2003), 15

[33] Aquinas, *S.Th*, Ia, q. 36, art. 3, ad 2um in McCarthy, 5; C.f. *Cat.* 28

[34] *Op.cit* 8–10 & 13–14

filioque to the Western understanding of *per filium* (through the Son). This clarification of the Clarification takes us back to Photius' argument that the *filioque* implies that the Spirit has an immediate and remote cause and comes into being simultaneously with the cause and the caused (point 5 above), as well as to the Eastern objection that the *filioque* confuses the *hypostases*, divides the *hypostasis* of the Father in two and/or confuses the properties of the Persons. Of course, untangling it all is complicated by the fact that there appears to be disagreement between Western thinkers about the meaning of the *filioque*. One would expect the PCPCU's "authoritative" Clarification to accurately represent the Western position, but as it contradicts Augustine and Aquinas, whose thought seems to be definitive in the West, one cannot be sure.

Nevertheless, this example does demonstrate that resolving the issue of divine personhood will take us a long way towards consensus. This becomes even clearer when we view the issue in relation to the paradigm of love.

The Augustinian notion that the Spirit is the love between the Father and the Son illustrates the fact that the Spirit is not seen as a real Person in Western thought. In terms of the Eastern perspective, while the Father originates the Trinitarian love, the three Persons together constitute the communion of love. The attribute of love is therefore common to all three and thus belongs to the nature, not to one Person. To identify one of the Trinitarian Persons as personified love without proper qualification would constitute confusing an attribute that is common to all three with one Person and imply that the Father and Son are a dyad united by an attribute of their own nature, as Photius indicates (third point above).[35]

Gregory Palamas also speaks of the Spirit as the love between the Father and the Son, as the Clarification indicates. However, in the context of Orthodox Trinitarian thought as a whole and because he sees the Spirit as a real Person, the expression takes on a very different meaning to the Western notion. We shall return to this below. But in the Western conception, on the other hand, the impression is created that the Father and Son are real Persons who love *hypostatically*, while the Spirit is the nature (common item) that

---

[35] See also Vladimir Lossky, *op.cit*, 43–44

is communicated. Apart from the fact that this idea cannot be reconciled with the notions that the Father is the essence and the Son is a mere relation, rendering the argument incoherent, Photius' objection is understandable: that the Spirit is on a lesser level than the Father and Son ontologically, even though He is equal consubstantially, because in this schema the Spirit is not a real Person. Ware says this is a primary difficulty with the *filioque*:

> [...] the Orthodox tradition firmly teaches two things about Him. First, the Spirit is a *person*. He is not just a "divine blast" (as I once heard someone describe him), not just an insentient force, but one of the three persons of the Trinity; and so, for all his seeming elusiveness, we can and do enter into a personal 'I-thou' relationship with Him. Secondly, the Spirit, as the third member of the Holy Triad, is *coequal* and *coeternal* with the other two; he is not merely a function dependent on them or an intermediary that they employ. One of the chief reasons why the Orthodox Church rejects the Latin addition of the *filioque* to the creed [...] is precisely our fear that such teaching might lead men to *depersonalise* and *subordinate* the Holy Spirit. [36] (Italics in original)

Coffey[37] states that this is not the case. He argues that the Spirit is seen in the West as a real Person but, as an analogy, the notion of the Spirit as love cannot demonstrate every aspect of the Spirit's being. He argues that the Spirit's personhood is shown elsewhere. "Firstly, as a distinct subsistence in the divine nature, he must be a Person," he says. Second, he quotes Bernd Hilberath's rather beautiful description of the Spirit as the Person who mediates the being-in-each-other of the other two Persons.

This indicates that Coffey and Hilberath might understand the divine personhood differently to Rahner, which again leads one to wonder whether Western theologians agree on what they believe.

---

[36] Kallistos Ware, *op.cit*, 121–122
[37] *Op.cit*, 17–19

Coffey goes on to suggest that the notion of the Spirit as love could be a means of demonstrating that the Western and Eastern faiths are not mutually exclusive, primarily on the grounds that it preserves the Father's monarchy: the Father's monarchy is preserved by being the first (principle) source of love, while the Son communicates the Spirit back to the Father, constituting the Spirit as mutual love personified.[38] However, even if the Spirit is understood to be a real, self-conscious Person within this schema, Hilberath's description would still be problematic to the Orthodox. First, it would be seen as wrongly reading back into the intra-Trinitarian relations the Spirit's soteriological activity of effecting communion between human persons and the Father and Son, while still ascribing to one Person an attribute that is common to all three. Second, by making the Spirit the source of unity in the Trinity, the Orthodox would argue that the West is now ascribing to the Spirit a property that belongs to the Father. Third, if the Spirit, as mutual love personified, is a real *hypostasis*, then we are back to the difficulty of the Son being a co-originator of a Divine Person, with all the accompanying objections.

Rahner denies that the Spirit is mutual love, as we saw earlier, because in terms of the Western schema God is an individual who knows and loves Himself as the *Logos* and the Spirit, rather than three (self-conscious) Persons subsisting in a communion of love. This argument appears to be more consistent with the official line. But then the Orthodox argue that Rahner's God is self-adoring, narcissistic[39] – as opposed to the God of love, who was revealed in His Image, the Crucified Son, who manifests the sacrificial nature of God's love by surrendering Himself to non-existence to bring us into His communion of love.[40] In contrast to Rahner's model, Bloom argues from the divine, self-sacrificial love of Christ on the cross to the intra-Trinitarian relations, which he describes in consciously anthropomorphic language:

---

[38] John F. McCarthy, *op.cit*, 6–7 and Gerald O'Collins *op.cit*, 135–136 also describe the Spirit in this manner

[39] See for example Anthony Bloom, *God and Man* (London: Darton, Longman & Todd, 1971/2004), 110

[40] Anthony Bloom, *op.cit*, 113–115

[…] in God we find the exulting joy of three persons who love in giving perfectly and receiving perfectly, but who being a Trinitarian relationship, if I may put it in this form of speech, are not in the way of each other, in which each of them accepts every single moment not to exist for the two others to be face to face – the miracle of total communion, fusion and oneness. […] The three simultaneously give, the three simultaneously place themselves in such a situation that the others are alone with each other. But that means death because self-annihilation, self-nothing, sacrifice, mean death and the cross is inscribed in the mystery of the Holy Trinity. […] And this is Trinitarian theology – the vision of three Persons whose love is such that they lay down their lives and they are caught up into eternal life, into life that can no longer be taken from them because they have given their lives and others have granted them eternity.[41]

Significantly, Hilberath[42] describes the Spirit in exactly the same way, while in Bloom's thought the principle of self-sacrificial love is common to all three. Bloom's emphasis appears to be more consistent with the biblical revelation: the Spirit reveals this love by remaining personally elusive while sharing His communion with the Father and Son *in us*; the Son reveals the same self-sacrificing love in a different way – for us as an objective image – by belittling Himself and laying down His life in loving obedience to the Father, both to glorify the Father and for us, so that we too might receive the Spirit and so participate in the intra-Trinitarian communion of love.

The Father similarly "makes Himself nothing" by revealing Himself only in the Son and the Spirit, thus glorifying the other two Persons. It is with such a vision of the Trinity in mind that Photius speaks of the Holy Spirit:

---

[41] *Ibid* 113; see also John Zizioulas, *Being as Communion*, 49
[42] In David Coffey, *op.cit*, 17

Everywhere He [the Saviour] preserves the Spirit's equality of essence and equality of nature and dignity of equal rank absolutely perfect and unadulterated. Accordingly it is said that He shares the common essence-above-essence of the more-than-glorious Trinity, in which each *hypostasis* glorifies each other *hypostasis* mutually with ineffable words.[43]

Thus linking notions of personhood and the paradigm of love clarifies the issues: in order to love in a self-transcendent, self-annihilating way, one must first have a "self" to transcend and "die to" in favour of another; it is therefore imperative to the Orthodox that each Person be seen as an "aware centre of interpersonal relations" if we are to speak of a Trinitarian communion of love, although the elusiveness of the Persons in their self-annihilating hiddenness makes it impossible to define what constitutes the distinctive "I-ness" of each Person.

In short, from an Eastern perspective, to differentiate the Spirit from the other two Persons by identifying Him as love seems to confuse Him with a common attribute and thus depersonalise Him. On the other hand, the Eastern personalistic conception evokes a counter-accusation of tritheism from the West.

2.iv. Western objections to the Orthodox model

Rahner ends his essay on the Divine Persons with an implicit dig at the Orthodox by saying his explanation is aimed at:

[…] overcoming the false opinion that what is meant by "person", especially within the doctrine of the Trinity, is clearly evident. He who starts with this false opinion may verbally protest to the contrary, may emphasise the mysterious character of the Trinity, may know of the logical difficulties […] Despite all

---

[43] *Myst.* 27

this he will have great difficulty avoiding a *hidden* pre-reflective tritheism.[44] (italics in original).

Furthermore, the derivation emphasis in Orthodox thought elicits the criticisms that the East subordinates the Son and Spirit, as opposed to only the Spirit[45] and does not show a proper relation between the Son and the Spirit.[46] In terms of this schema, the Father is identified with the One God of the Old Testament because He is the one unoriginate Person[47] in the Trinity who is the sole cause of the other two Persons and thus the sole beginning of the Godhead. If I might simplify: we know the Son and Spirit as Divine Persons through the economy. While Old Testament writers seem to have seen the Spirit as the presence and power of God in His interaction with creation,[48] the personal way in which Jesus spoke of Him, the activities ascribed to Him in the New Testament and mystical experience enable us to see Him as a Person. Because He is *of* God (the Father) He is, moreover, divine; ergo He is a Divine Person, which is the same as saying He is also God, i.e. His divinity is *derivative*.

The eternal divine Son was revealed in the Incarnation, though Christians have uncovered implicit references to Him in the Old Testament in hindsight. The revelation of His divinity – that is, as one who pre-existed in and with the Father (i.e. eternally) – was delivered verbally by Jesus Himself (such as Jn 8:58: "before Abraham was, I am" and Jn 10:30: "the Father and I are one"), was confirmed by the resurrection and mystically perceived in the Spirit following Pentecost. It was precisely His claim to be the Son of God in a pre-temporal and intimate sense that elicited the accusa-

---

[44] Karl Rahner, *op.cit*, 381; Gerald O'Collins (*op.cit*, 155–156) appears to agree with Rahner

[45] See for example M.A. Pugliese, *op.cit*, 162–163 and Gerald O'Collins, *op.cit*, 132–133

[46] For example, John F. McCarthy, *op.cit*, 7–8

[47] A perception dating back to at least St Justin Martyr (d. ca. 165) – see Gerald O'Collins, *op.cit*, 87

[48] Alasdair Heron, *op.cit*, 19

tions of blasphemy that led to His crucifixion. Notably, the content of these accusations was that He implicitly claimed to be equal with God (the Father) by virtue of claiming to be His Son (Jn 5:18), not that He claimed to be God "as such" As I understand it, the Orthodox have retained this sense of the Son's divinity – He is Divine by virtue of being *of* the Father, i.e. His divinity is derivative,[49] but He is properly divine because the Father eternally shares everything He is with the Son,[50] including the reality of being a Person. Ergo, there is one God, the Father, who imparts His divinity – and everything He is other than being Father – eternally to the Son and the Spirit in causing their existence.

We shall address the Western objections to this schema in the next few chapters. For now I would like to establish the thought that underpins them. O'Collins' reflection is rather telling in this respect. He does not explicitly mention Orthodox thought in his discussion of tritheism when he warns against describing the Divine Persons as "three autonomous subjects living and working together in a quasi-social unity",[51] but his argument is illustrative of Western view of tritheism in relation to notions of personhood. The heart of the matter, I believe, is that the West uses the word "person" as a synonym for individual in the Aristotelian sense of the word.

Thus, when Westerners say that the Three are not really persons, they wish to convey that the Divine Persons are not individuals. Thus O'Collins begins his discussion of divine personhood by summarising a particular post-modern conception of the human person as being "conscious (or minded), free and relational (or persons-in-community)"[52] and posits that the last characteristic curbs "any desire to picture persons as autonomous, self-sufficient cen-

---

[49] Here the classic distinction between what is ultimate or primary (God) and that which is dependent and derivative (creatures) is set aside as the Son and Spirit are *eternally* derivative and dependent on the Father; there is no way around this.

[50] This would follow the pattern of Jn 1:1: "[…] the Word was *with* God and the Word *was* God."

[51] Gerald O'Collins, *op.cit*, 155–156

[52] *Ibid* 177

tres of consciousness and free activity, or even as self-absorbed individuals".[53] He emphasises that authentic personhood is realised in interpersonal relationships: "Being a person does not precede interpersonal relations, as if we were first persons and then in relationship. A newborn baby (and even more an unborn baby) never exists without being related to its mother, father and others."[54] He then draws a sharp line between human and divine personhood, stripping away all the existential aspects of personhood except relationality:

> In the case of the Trinity, the relational aspect is both unique and crucial; otherwise one can slip into talk of three distinct centres of consciousness and decision-making, an interpretation of the divine persons that seems to abandon monotheism and finish up with three gods in perfect dialogue among themselves. In other words, an individualistic conception of the fully personal, when applied to the tripersonal God, leads one to picture three independent, fully divine minds and wills, which could even slip into inadvertent conflict. Such a conception could hardly ward off tritheism or the idea of three self-sufficient subjects who enjoy a separate existence, always act together as a closely meshed community of individuals, but do not constitute one God.[55]

O'Collins links "self-consciousness", a term he associates with the existentialist ego and modern psychology, with having a separate mind and will.[56] Thus he argues:

> Here the distinction between divine and human persons (and the distinction between divine and human relationships) comes into sharp focus. In the case of the tripersonal God, the dis-

---

[53] *Ibid*

[54] *Ibid*

[55] *Ibid*

[56] *Ibid* 176

tinctness of interrelated persons is not constituted by a separation of consciousness and free subjectivities. A threefold subsistence does not entail three consciousnesses and three wills, as if three persons, each with their own separate characteristics, constituted a kind of divine committee. One consciousness subsists in a threefold way and is shared by all three persons, albeit by each of them distinctively. [...] Each person must be seen to be identical with the divine nature or the substance of the godhead. Otherwise the distinction of the three persons will be upheld at the expense of the real, divine oneness; the divine unity will be recognised only after the distinct and separate constitution of the three persons.[57]

The difficulty is that he evaluates the idea of consciousness through the lens of the conception of the person as an individual in the Aristotelian-Thomist sense – a "distinct subsistent in a rational nature";[58] i.e. a person is conscious as a function of having his or her own separate nature with its own mind, will, etc. However, as we have seen, this is not what the Orthodox mean by Person. As we have noted, Eastern thinkers such as the Cappadocians did use the word "individual" illustratively in their expositions of the Divine Persons, but they did not use the word in the way that the West understood or understands it. They certainly did not mean three individual decision-makers with their own separate natures, minds and wills, but rather three ineffable "Subjectivities" that transcend and constitute the divine nature.

By contrast, in the Thomist definition the human person is a person only by virtue of subsisting in a distinctive rational nature. That is, the person is only person by virtue of natural distinction; ergo, personhood is a function of nature. Also, the person's nature is specifically a rational nature; therefore to be a person one has to have one's own mind. In this context self-consciousness is seen as an attribute that differentiates an individual person by nature. As

---

[57] *Ibid* 178
[58] *S.Th.* 1a.30.3 ad 4 in Gerald O'Collins, *op.cit*, 176

we shall see below, this was essentially the difficulty St Augustine faced in the 4th century.

Because personhood is seen as a function of nature in Western thought and because the Divine Persons share one nature, there cannot be three real (subjective) Persons as we have come to understand the word existentially; there can be only one Subject or Self subsisting in three subsistents, as Rahner claims. This seems Modalistic to the Orthodox as it compromises the ontological personal existence of the Divine Persons.[59] Or, as O'Collins puts it, "there are three person-constituting relations".[60] This again would seem anomalous to the Eastern mind; how can a relationship constitute a person? And later: "[…] being a person in God is defined only through relationship to the other persons. […] The divine persons are mutually distinct only through their relations of origin. […] Thus the (subsistent) relations account for what differentiates (and unites) the one Trinitarian reality" and "[…] The persons are who they distinctly are because of their relations with each other".[61] This logic is directly responsible for the formulation of the *filioque* because if the relations are the only way to distinguish the Persons, they must be shown to have diverse relations, as we saw at the beginning of this research paper and as O'Collins goes on to explain.

Notably, as with Coffey and Hilberath, O'Collins speaks of the relations as if there were three conscious "Subjectivities" in relation. For example, he describes *perichoresis* as "a blissful mutual presence, a reciprocal coinherence and participation in each other".[62] O'Collins even posits this intra-Trinitarian communion as "the ultimate ground and goal of all other relations in communion […] Because the divine life is one of total self-giving and unconditional sharing, human beings, because they are made in the divine

---

[59] Alasdair Heron, *op.cit*, 94; cf. Gerald O'Collins, *op.cit*, 137

[60] Gerald O'Collins, *op.cit*, 179

[61] *Ibid* 178; O'Collins (*op.cit*, 122) reads this notion of the person as an individual self into the Niceno-Constantinopolitan Creed. He seems to believe this is what the Fathers meant and says it provides "a 'genetic' approach to the Tri-personal God, with the divinity streaming from the Father to the Son and to the Spirit".

[62] *Ibid* 179

image and likeness (Genesis 1:26), are invited to exist in a communion and loving solidarity with one another and with the divine persons […]."[63]

But this is an anomaly: if Rahner's exposition, with which O'Collins seems to agree, reflects the official understanding of the Trinity and there is only one "self-consciousness" in the Trinity then, from an Eastern perspective, this implies that there is only one "self"; thus there are no distinct "Subjectivities" to be in relation. On the other hand, if the Divine Persons are three "Subjectivities", then from a Western perspective we arrive at tritheism. Resolving these questions is fundamental to resolving the impasse.

2.V. SUMMARY

A brief examination of Orthodox polemic against the *filioque* and the Western Clarification demonstrates that the two traditions have been arguing at cross-purposes, resulting in an unmanageable tangle of arguments that often appear contradictory, depending on the perspective from which one approaches the arguments. We noted above that some of the Orthodox polemic against the Latin model of the Trinity seems to be rooted in the misconception that in Western thought essence (ontologically) precedes personhood in the Godhead, while in fact the West identifies the Father with the One God, as in the East.

The real problem seems to relate to what is meant by the identification of the Father with the One God; in the East this is connected to the Father's identity as the sole personal originator of the Son and Spirit, who are two real Persons; in the West it means that the Father's essence is the substratum of the Son and Spirit, who are seen as two relations, which in turn necessitates the *filioque*, or alternately that the Father is the whole essence and the Son and Spirit are subsistent self-expressions of the Father.

Either way, to Easterners this schema distorts the identity of the Father as the personal cause of two real Persons, depersonalises

---

[63] *Ibid* 178–179

the Son and Spirit, subordinates the Spirit and implies that the Spirit is a composite.

Conversely, the Eastern schema seems to Westerners to confuse the identities of the Son and the Spirit. Also, the West's perception that the idea of three self-conscious Persons leads to tritheism is rooted in a misconception that this would imply three individuals in God. This misconception is due to the fact that the West uses the word individual as a synonym for (human) person in the Thomist sense of "distinct subsistent in a rational nature" or the existentialist perceiving mind, while the East in fact posits three unique divine personal Subjects who constitute one nature. These differing ideas of personhood have resulted in opposing explications of how God can be one and yet three. A vital point of divergences is that in the Orthodox model the Persons constitute the nature, while in the West personhood is seen as a function of nature; thus the term "person" cannot be properly ascribed to the Divine Persons. In Eastern thought the relations of origin distinguish the (real) Persons, while in the West the relations define and constitute the Persons, which appears Modalistic to the East.

3 THE EASTERN APPROACH TO TRUTH

So far I have focussed on different understanding of the words "Person" and "essence" in the context of Trinitarian thought; but another underlying difficulty seems to be that the East reads Western thought through the lens of an experiential faith, while the West reads Eastern thought as if it were purely rational, philosophical argumentation. The latter can be seen, for example, in Rahner's charge of logical inconsistencies and pre-reflective tritheism.[1] And in his outline of the thought of the Cappadocian Fathers, Maurice Wiles states: "Gregory [of Nyssa] was a thorough-going Platonist. For the Platonist the universal is more real than the particular. Strictly speaking, Gregory says, we should not speak of three men, but of three participants in the one, unique 'idea of man', the single, real 'humanity'."[2] Anthony Meredith's book *The Cappadocians* (1995) is also punctuated with "demonstrations" that these saints were Platonists.[3]

Orthodox writers such as Hierotheos insist that this is untrue; these saints might have used philosophical language in their writings – often in opposition to the way it was commonly understood – but Hellenic philosophy did not inform the content of their thought.[4]

Most alarming is O'Collins' comment when, summarising the post-Chalcedon (451 A.D.) evolution of the meaning of the word person in the West, he asserts that Aquinas' description of person as a "distinct subsistent in a rational nature" (*S.Th.* 1a.30.3 ad 4) "goes beyond *hypostasis* because individual dogs and oak trees rank

---

[1] See 2.iv above

[2] Maurice Wiles, *The Christian Fathers* (London: SCM Press, 1977), 47

[3] I shall provide examples of this as we proceed – in footnotes so as not to break the flow of the argument.

[4] Hierotheos (Vlachos), *The Person in the Orthodox Tradition,* 163

as *hypostases* or distinct subsistents".[5] This statement is indicative of a Western tendency to interpret the word *hypostasis*, as used at Constantinople I, to denote only its surface philosophical meaning.

These difficulties highlight a dire need for further clarification of the Eastern position, in which, as noted earlier, the Orthodox are permitted to explain their own tradition so as not to read Western assumptions into Eastern thought. This task needs to be handled on several fronts: we need to clarify (a) the criteria of truth that underpinned the patristic Eastern conception; (b) the relationship between theology and philosophy in Eastern thought; (c) what the Eastern Fathers meant by the words *"Hypostasis"* and *"Person"* in their Trinitarian thought; and, consequently, (d) what they understood by the Trinitarian formula of one *ousia*, three *Hypostases*.

In this chapter I shall sketch an outline of the Cappadocians' approach to truth in relation to Greek philosophy as the Orthodox explain it. In the following three chapters I shall return to the Eastern conception of the Person and how this fits into (a) the Eastern notion of truth and (b) the Eastern conception of the Trinity. Lastly, I shall draw out the implications for the *filioque* impasse.

3.1. ANCIENT PHILOSOPHY AND THE *LOGOS* APPROACH

The ancient Greek philosopher saw truth as being, which was equated with the realm of rational ideas that could be apprehended by the mind.[6] This approach originated with Parmenides (c. 500 B.C.), who insisted that reality could be appropriated only by reason, while sensible experience belonged to the realm of appearance and therefore to non-being. He also held that "to be" means to exist eternally, fully and completely; thus anything transitory is less than real.[7] This evolved, by the time of Plato, into the idea that only reason/intelligence was real (his world of Forms), while the illu-

---

[5] Gerald O'Collins, *op.cit*, 176

[6] Hierotheos (Vlachos), *The Person in the Orthodox Tradition*, 30–31

[7] Diogenes Allen and Eric Springsted, *Philosophy for Understanding Theology* (Atlanta: John Knox Press, 2007, 15; Hierotheos (Vlachos), *The Person in the Orthodox Tradition, op.cit*, 29

sory temporal sphere "participated" in this reality. Thus, in opposition to the Stoic's materialistic philosophy of immanence, in which spirit/*Logos* was understood as a diffuse sort of matter present in all things, Platonism was a philosophy of transcendence, in which the world of ideas, or "ideal forms", was considered more real than the material world.[8] In both the Platonic and Aristotelian schemas, truth was seen as unchanging and transcending history and the link between being and temporal reality was the perceiving mind. Moreover, truth and being were linked to unity and harmony. Anything that did not conform to this monistic harmony had no ontological claim to existence or truth. This effectively meant that the disharmonious mess of history, with all its change and decay, had to be either explained away or imbued with transcendent meaning.[9]

By contrast, there was general agreement in the Christian community that Christ was the truth (John 14:6).[10] Moreover, the Christian notion of truth arose out of human experience of a personal God, who revealed Himself to the Jewish prophets in history and in the Incarnation, and continued to do so mystically in the Holy Spirit.[11] The Jews also understood truth to be identical with God's activity in history, but it remained historically and eschatologically oriented in a schema of promise and fulfilment. The Jews were satisfied that God is and is "on our side" because He had made Himself known historically and had proved His faithfulness. They were not interested in the ontology of truth and tended to equate truth with doing or *praxis*.[12]

Thus when St Paul preached a radical theology of the cross in contradistinction to the Jewish preoccupation with signs and Greek wisdom (1 Cor 1:22; 2 Cor. 2:4–8; Ja 3:15), he was consciously debunking both the Greek and Jewish approaches to truth. The Christian assertion that Christ, an historical figure who had, more-

---

[8] Maurice Wiles, *op.cit*, 15–16

[9] John Zizioulas, *Being as Communion*, 8–69)

[10] *Ibid* 7

[11] Hierotheos (Vlachos), *The Person in the Orthodox Tradition*, 32; 166ff; 231

[12] John Zizioulas, *Being as Communion*, 68; Allen & Springsted, *op.cit*, xvii)

over, suffered an ignoble death, was the Truth and that the eschatological promises had been realised within history would have
been as problematic to the Jews, with their practical, eschatological
notion of truth, as to the Greek philosopher with his cosmological,
rational and ontological idea of truth.

However, by the 4th century the Church's interaction with
Greek philosophy had radically affected the Christian conception
of Christ as the truth.[13] Two particular aspects of ancient Hellenic
thought are relevant to our subject:

First, in terms of the Platonic schema, the passionless Good
or the One emanated and stood at the apex of the world of Forms
(an ideal world of changeless patterns of reality). This One was
seen as a unity without parts, differentiation or difference of any
kind.[14] As Wiles indicates, the Bible's idea of oneness was the oneness of God in contradistinction to the idea of many gods in a polytheistic milieu, not the undifferentiated unity of pagan Greek philosophy.[15] Yet, Wiles argues, some Christian apologists such as Irenaeus of Lyons (c. 180 A.D.), Clement of Alexandria (c. 200 A.D.)
and Origen used this concept of the One in their attempts to explain the Christian God to the pagan Greek thinkers of their time.[16]
As we shall see, the way in which this concept was used in East and
West came to differ radically. Second, in order to reconcile the
Christian conception of God with the One of Greek philosophy
and the Hellenic notion of truth with the Christian belief that
Christ was the truth, apologists such as St Justin Martyr, Origen
and Tertullian argued that Christ was the true *logos* (reason) of God
– so seeming to give their stamp of approval to the notion that
rational knowledge is truth and that truth is a cosmological rather
than a historical reality.[17]

---

[13] *Ibid* 69–71)
[14] Maurice Wiles, *op.cit*, 16; Anthony Meredith, *op.cit*, 11
[15] Maurice Wiles, *op.cit*, 18–19; Gregory of Nyssa makes the same
point in his *Letter to Ablabius* 4
[16] *Ibid* 16; 18
[17] John Zizioulas, *Being as Communion*, 72–74; St Maximus the Confessor was later to resurrect the notion that Christ is the logos of creation
and can be found in the *logoi* of all created things – but reinterpreted the

Wiles argues that this development is traceable to the Gospel of John. He argues that the fourth evangelist used the Stoic concept of *Logos*[18] in the way that it had been adapted for use by Platonists and theists such as Philo alike to describe the eternal Son of God.[19] The Platonists, he explains, identified the *Logos* with the world of Forms, while Philo used the word to denote the reason of a transcendent God. Both uses were intended to explain the inherent rationality in the world. Hierotheos disagrees. He argues that the writer of the Gospel of John in fact used the word "*Logos*" to contradict ancient Greek philosophy by indicating that Christ, an historical Person, was the *Logos* of God because He revealed the will and purpose of the Father.[20] It seems likely that this perspective informed St Irenaeus' (c. 130 – c. 200) assertion that the *Logos* of God was the Yahweh who had interacted with the Jewish Patriarchs.[21] Wiles does not cite original sources, but Hierotheos confirms that it was customary for the early Christians to refer to the Son as Yahweh (the revealed God) and to the Father as Elohim (the hidden God), seeing the Son as the one who revealed Himself without flesh in the Old Testament.[22] By the time of Irenaeus, the description of the Son as a word emitted from the mind of the Father and as a word from His lips also seems to have become common.[23] Wiles argues that later Fathers used this image, together with the *Logos* motif, to show how a passionless God could interact with the world without suffering change: "As a word going out from the mind of a man does not deprive the speaker of the mean-

---

logos as the (personal) love that holds the created universe in being; he thus reconciled the (person) of the historical Christ with ontology and posited that existence depends on love – see *ibid* 97

[18] An idea dating back to Heraclitus (about 500 B.C.), who saw logos/fire as the principle of balance between opposite forces, bringing order to the universe and principle of life in human beings – see Allen & Springsted, *op.cit*, 12–13

[19] Maurice Wiles, *op.cit*, 26; see also Gerald O'Collins, *op.cit*, 92 and Allen & Springsted, *op.cit*, 49

[20] Hierotheos (Vlachos), *The Person in the Orthodox Tradition*, 192

[21] Maurice Wiles, *op.cit*, 27

[22] Hierotheos (Vlachos), *The Person in the Orthodox Tradition*, 192

[23] Irenaeus, *Against Heresies* 2.28.6 in Gerald O'Collins, *op.cit*, 98–99

ing it expresses, no more need the outgoing activity of the *Logos* of God in creation affect in any way the changelessness of God and his inherent *Logos*."[24]

In my view Wiles overstates the case. He too readily assumes that all the Fathers who used this terminology used it in the same way as the Hellenic philosophers. However, Eastern thinkers do seem to agree with Wiles that a tendency to equate Christ as Truth with rational truth can be witnessed in the writings of philosopher and Christian apologist St Justin Martyr (c. 100 – c.165).

3.i.a. Justin Martyr

In his reply to accusations of preaching two Gods, Justin used the *Logos* analogy to illustrate that the Son was eternally begotten of the Father without being separated from Him.[25] This in itself raises no objections. What was problematic, from an Eastern perspective, was Justin's identification of the Son with Reason. To reconcile faith in Christ as the only path to salvation with the difficulty that men and women of great sanctity had lived before the Incarnation, Justin used the philosophical idea that reason in each of us exists by virtue of the fact that we participate in universal reason. He argued that "Christ is the *Logos* of whom every race of man are partakers and those who, like Socrates, have lived in accordance with that *Logos* are Christians, even though they may have been regarded as atheists".[26]

Zizioulas asserts that this development in Christian apologetics had serious consequences for the notion of truth as it was understood in the Church. By using the *logos* motif in this way to communicate that Christ was the truth, Justin implicitly gave the Platonic notion of truth his stamp of approval: God, as ultimate rational truth, is understood to be "he who is always the same in himself and in relation to all things"[27] and who is "known only

---

[24] *Ibid* 26; see also Gerald O'Collins, *op.cit*, 92
[25] *Ibid* 27–28
[26] *1st Apology* 46 in *ibid* 28
[27] *Dialogues* 3.5 in John Zizioulas, *Being as Communion*, 73

through the mind".[28] Justin understood the latter to be given to us "in order to contemplate that same being who is the cause of all intelligent beings".[29]

Like the Platonists, Justin also attributed error to the presence of things of the senses and especially to the body, bringing a distinctive dualism into Christian thought, as well as an ontologically necessary link between God and the sensible world, located in the mind. "Christ, as *logos* of God, thus becomes the ontological link between God and the mind, and the truth of philosophy is nothing less than part of this *logos*," Zizioulas[30] writes. This approach therefore favoured the monistic ancient Greek concept of being and did not adequately convey the otherness of God's being asserted in Biblical revelation.[31]

3.i.b. Origen (c. 185–254)

Zizioulas continues that Justin never made any official claim for philosophy in the life of the Church. It was Clement of Alexandria and Origen who set this trend in motion in the 3rd century. Clement conceived of truth as the "nature" of being; thus nature is equivalent to the truth of things. He then defined spirit as nature. We thus have the equation truth = nature = spirit, which in the Hellenic context was the equivalent of asserting that spiritual was a synonym for rational. Origen developed this idea into the notion that spirit is God's corporeal substance and used this idea in his attempt to explain tradition in a philosophical manner.[32]

The result was twofold: First, he argued within the paradigms of Hellenic philosophy, but reinterpreted Hellenic schemas in light of the Christian faith. For example, the Middle Platonists (about 100 B.C. to 200 A.D.) had collapsed Plato's unknowable "father" or intelligence or mind into his idea of the One or Form of the Good, and posited a remote Supreme Mind at the head of a hierar-

---

[28] *Dialogues* 4.1 in *ibid*
[29] *Dialogues* 4.2 in *ibid*
[30] *Being as Communion*, 74
[31] *Ibid* 93
[32] *Ibid* 75; 93

chy of beings. In an attempt to reconcile Plato and Aristotle, they made use of Aristotle's "unmoved mover", a mind that is involved in eternal contemplation such that it is wholly unaware of the world, affecting that which is outside itself through intermediaries.[33]

As Wiles notes, later Platonism had attempted to explain more convincingly than Plato the relationship between the transcendent realm and the world, and to distinguish clearly between the multiplicity and unity within that realm by positing three ranks within the transcendent realm: the supreme existent, an ineffable, truly transcendent One at the top; the divine Mind that emanated from it and contained within itself the ideal Forms; and on the next level the World Soul that emanated from the divine Mind and mediated between it and the world. Neoplatonist philosopher Plotinus, Origen's younger contemporary, exemplified this schema with his three *hypostases* in descending rank (the One, Mind and the World Soul).[34]

Origen, who shared the same intellectual milieu as Plotinus,[35] also reworked this schema. Unlike Plotinus, for the Father he seems to have retained the Middle Platonist reinterpretation of Plato's unknowable "father" or intelligence or Mind at the head of a hierarchy of beings. Origen thus describes the Father, the "one true God" of John 17:3, as an incorporeal, spiritual and fully actualised Mind, characterised by the fundamental Hellenic criterion of truth, perfect unity[36] and the Son with the Reason or Wisdom (*Logos*) of God. Finally, in contrast to the Neoplatonic World Soul that generates time, the third entity at the bottom of the hierarchy is the

---

[33] Allen & Springsted, *op.cit*, 47

[34] Maurice Wiles, *op.cit*, 33–34

[35] Edward Moore, "Origen of Alexandria" in *Internet Encyclopedia of Philosophy*, 2005 (online). http://iep.utm.edu/origen-of-alexandria/ (accessed 10/28/2011), n.pag; Moore notes that Origen was taught for a while by Plotinus' teacher Ammonius Saccas and drew on the works of Jewish Platonist Philo of Alexandria and Neophyagorean philosopher Numenius of Apamea.

[36] See for example *On First Principles* 1.1.6

Spirit that sanctifies.[37] As in Neoplatonic thought, the Father's power is universal and imparts existence to each one from His own existence, the Son's lesser power is rational and universal and the Spirit's is related to sanctity alone, reaching only the saints.[38] It is against this backdrop that Origen makes the connection between the Son as the *Logos* or Reason of God and the human mind, as with Justin Martyr. In *On First Principles* 1.7 he writes: "[...] the mind bears a certain relationship to God, of whom the mind itself is an intellectual image, that by means of this it may come to some knowledge of the nature of divinity, especially if purified and separated from bodily matter". Augustine was later to adopt this same schema, with a slightly different emphasis, although, like the Eastern Fathers, he rejected the idea of a descending order of being in the Trinity because it subordinated the Son and the Spirit.

As with Justin, Origen emphasised the unbegotten nature of the Father, stressing His ungenerate, underived existence against the derived existence of the Son and the Spirit – an emphasis the Cappadocians were to retain in a qualified sense,[39] while rejecting Origin's idea that the Son and Spirit were "gods", not God.[40] O'Collins and Wiles indicate that it was Origen who first posited, as a function of his schema of three descending *hypostases*, that the Spirit "came into being through the Word, the Word being anterior

---

[37] See for example *On First Principles* 1.3.8 and 1.8.3

[38] *Ibid* 1.3.3, 5–7

[39] It is possible that one reason Westerners consider the Eastern conception subordinationist is that Western thinkers tend to overemphasise Origen's influence on the Cappadocians. For example Anthony Meredith (*op.cit*, 106) describes Basil's conception as the Son and Spirit "descending" from the Father. See also pp. 13–17; 34; 42–43; 46–47; 54ff. The Cappadocians were in fact critical of Origen – see Basil, *De Spiritu Sancto* 73 – and retained only that in his thought that was consistent with their own vision. Meredith seems to assume too readily that a shared conceptual category necessarily implies an identical perspective. In particular, while Meredith notes departures from Origen's thought in the writings of the Cappadocians (*ibid* 35; 105–106), he radically underestimates their profoundly divergent approach and vision, and posits a litany of demonstrations of Origenistic, Platonic and other "influences" on their thought. He sums up his findings on p. 118ff.

[40] Maurice Wiles, *op.cit*, 35-36; Gerald O'Collins, *op.cit*, 110

to the Spirit",[41] which he qualified to mean an eternal coming into being. However, his older contemporary Tertullian (c. 155/160–c. 225) had also posited a precursor of the *filioque* in the same descending schema,[42] albeit in the sense of *per filium* and in the context of a corporeal idea of a Trinity in the Stoic sense of a refined, spiritual matter[43] that was identified with the economy.[44] This seems to suggest that such thinking was fairly common in the early 3rd century.

Notably in Origin's thought, the Father Son and Spirit were seen as three divine *hypostases* in the sense of three individual subjects, but not three substances[45] – another notion the Cappadocians were to retain and refine, while also rejecting the idea of a descending order of divine being.

Origen's conception was ultimately denounced by the Church, partly due to his notion of a descending order in the Trinity that subordinated the Son and the Spirit and because he believed all rational beings existed eternally, deriving their existence from the Father through the Son.[46]

The second consequence of his philosophical mindset, as Zizioulas[47] indicates, is that Origen's conception of the unbreakable link between Christ as the mind/*logos* of God and the *logoi* of created men retained both the pagan Greek monistic view of reality and its idea of truth. While stressing that the goal of the Christian life is union with God in a relationship of love, Origin also emphasised the transcendent meaning of the historical events described in the Bible; these are the truth known by those who are "spiritual", while the "somatic" gospel is only for the uneducated. Even the cross becomes a symbol and loses its ontological value as truth

---

[41] *Ibid*; see Origen, *Comm. in Ioannem*, 2.10

[42] *Against Prexeas* 4–5; 9; 13; 19

[43] *Ibid* 15–16

[44] *Ibid* 5; 7; 11; 19; 22

[45] Gerald O'Collins *op.cit*, 110; Maurice Wiles, *op.cit*, 35–36; Anthony Meredith, *op.cit*, 13

[46] Maurice Wiles, *op.cit*, 36–37

[47] *Being as Communion*, 77

once the meaning has been extrapolated.[48] Thus the *meaning* is the truth rather than the actuality of the historical reality. The idea that the historical Christ *is* truth (John 14:6) has effectively been explained away.[49] This seemed to indicate, Zizioulas insists, that the Christ event does not realise truth, but only reveals a pre-existing truth that is singular and comprehensive. He thus remarks: "If an interest in truth as revelation eclipses an interest in truth as history, it inevitably results in the human mind becoming the ground of truth, the crucial bond between truth and creation".[50]

In short, Christian thinkers such as Origen who appropriated the *Logos* model for use within the pre-existing Hellenic conceptual system were unable to arrive at a synthesis between the biblical and Hellenic approaches to truth, as both history and being, and subordinated the Christian gospel to the pagan Greek notion of truth.[51] This meant that the experiential truth preached by the Apostles was in danger of being conceptually secularised. Zizioulas argues that St Athanasius and the Cappadocians opposed this trend.

3.II. TRUTH AS COMMUNION

Zizioulas stresses that the Cappadocians and their older contemporary Athanasius, by contrast, saw truth as life, which they equated with communion, in line with an experiential sense of truth that had been present in the Church from the beginning. They saw knowing God as a mystical knowing, actualised intimately in communion, rather than as cognitive knowing.[52] Gregory of Nyssa says this explicitly: "The man who thinks God can be known [cognitively] does not truly have life; for he has been falsely diverted from true Being to something devised by his own imagination. For true

---

[48] Origen argued that Christ became "one with the Word and the true revelation of the Father only on the cross – see *Commentary on John* 1.231, 10.25 and 32.359; c.f. Anthony Meredith, *op.cit*, 85

[49] *Ibid* 75–77

[50] *Ibid* 78; c.f. Anthony Meredith, *op.cit*, 16–17; Meredith also notes that for Origen the great desire is for illumination of the mind – see p. 79

[51] *Ibid*

[52] *Ibid* 78–80

Being is true Life and cannot be known by us".[53] This sense of
truth was grounded both in the private mystical experiences of the
saints and the communal experience of communion with Christ in
the Eucharistic gathering. Hierotheos emphasises the first, Zizioulas the second.

3.ii.a. The mystical, apophatic approach

Testimony to direct experience of God in His self-manifestation in
the Holy Spirit can be found throughout Scripture. During the Incarnation it was experienced as an illumination of the divinity of
Christ,[54] but took on a particular emphasis after Pentecost.[55]

This supernatural dimension of revelation, which mystics insist cannot be accurately articulated in creaturely categories of
thought, evolved into the *apophatic*[56] approach to truth in the monastic movement that developed in the East in the latter part of the
3rd century, in terms of which the disciple opens him or herself up
to a direct encounter with God through a process of purification,
withdrawing the mind from its entanglement in the world (including from logic) and rooting his or her consciousness in the heart.[57]

---

[53] *Life of Moses*, P.G. 44.404 A–D in MC Steenberg, *Gregory of Nyssa:
Luminous Darkness*, 2000–2009 [online]. http://www.monachos.net/-
content/patristics/studies-fathers/60-gregory-of-nyssa-luminous-darkness
(accessed 20/05/2009), n.pag,

[54] Such as the transfiguration (Lk 9:28ff) and Peter's "You are the
Christ…" (Mt 16:13ff)

[55] See for example St Gregory of Nazianzus, *4th Theological Oration* 26
in Anthony Meredith, *op.cit*, 45

[56] The word *apophatic* derives from the words "away" and "say", indicating that we avoid defining, while *cataphatic* derives from the word "*ka-
ta*" to say, meaning I define something – see Hierotheos (Vlachos), *The
Person in the Orthodox Tradition*, 204. He emphasises that while one might
make certain *cataphatic* assertions about God, one arrives at one's
knowledge of God *apophatically* – see pp. 144–145

57 Hierotheos (Vlachos), *The Person in the Orthodox Tradition*, 34; 86ff;
166ff; although this was to be clearly defined by St Gregory Palamas in
the 14th century, this approach had underpinned monastic consciousness

A sharp distinction was made between the rational mind and the *nous*, the inner "intuitive" faculty that was perceived to be the "organ" most suited to receiving divine revelation.[58] This process must be seen as distinct from Neoplatonism, in which the mind was understood to be capable of being united with the Good because our higher intellect perfectly conforms to it on the level of mind and is thus made like it. The Eastern knowing of God is not a cerebral knowledge of archetypes, but intimate knowing through participation in the energies of God by grace, which is bestowed on the receptive soul.[59]

Hierotheos insists that St Athanasius and the Cappadocians belonged to this stream (contrary to Wiles and Meredith's assertion that Gregory of Nyssa was a thoroughgoing Platonist). Although they had studied philosophy (Gregory of Nyssa is thought to have been taught philosophy by his brother Basil),[60] they were not philosophers but mystics who theologised from the perspective of mystical encounters with God. Thus Hierotheos asserts: "The holy Fathers, as we can see in all their writings, attained experience of God, saw God in His glory, they lived Pentecost".[61]

---

from as early as the 3rd century; see also Hilarion Alfeyev, *The Mystery of Faith* (London: Darton, Longman & Todd, 2002), 184ff and MC Steenberg, *op.cit*, n.pag, p. 4 of A4 printout

[58] Hierotheos (Vlachos), *The Person in the Orthodox Tradition*, 28

[59] *Ibid* 166–168; as Sophrony says: "Consumed with love, man feels himself joined with his beloved God. Through this union he knows God, and thus love and cognition merge into a single act." – from *His Life is Mine* (p. 44) in *ibid* 80; John Zizioulas, *Being as Communion*, 16 thus emphasises that the being of God can be known only through personal communion.

[60] See Anthony Meredith, *op.cit*, 52, who interprets Gregory's talk of "higher learning" as a reference to philosophy.

[61] Hierotheos (Vlachos), *The Person in the Orthodox Tradition,* 164; see also pp. 27; 34; 41; 57; 163; 169; 172; 199. It is thus a mistake to assume that the asceticism of the Eastern Fathers was strongly influenced (through Origen) by Platonic ascetic ideals, as Anthony Meredith (*op.cit*, 12, 33–34; 43; 47; 55–56) does, following Andrew Louth. He interprets the Cappadocians' use of the phrase "enlightenment of the mind" in the Platonic sense rather than as a mystical knowing – a confusion caused by the fact that the Cappadocians imbued the language of illumination with

Athanasius' experience of the ascetic life and its mystical fruit are reflected in his *Life of Antony*. Gregory of Nyssa describes the ascetic journey in his *Life of Moses*.[62] In n46 of his prologue to this work, he states: "[…] the one who is going to associate intimately with God must go beyond all that is visible and – lifting up his own mind, as to a mountaintop, to the invisible and incomprehensible – believe that the divine is there where the understanding does not reach." Although he uses the word "mind", the emphasis on the incomprehensibility of God indicates he does not imply simply a cerebral illumination. Perhaps "mind" would be better rendered "consciousness" to accommodate post-modern nuancing. Commenting on this text, Steenberg asserts:

> That knowledge is cognitive is perhaps the first assumption with which one must do away, if he is to properly understand St Gregory of Nyssa's concept of the divine darkness. Yet it is an assumption so basic to modern thought that its influence is hardly given any consideration […]. Yet it is this very idea that Gregory addresses: the entire way of knowing with which we approach God. His is a knowing that goes beyond the confines and limitations of cognition, with its inherent inability to comprehend the transcendent.[63]

St Gregory Nazianzus' position, expounded in his *1st Theological Oration*, was that only a person who has attained the vision of God could rightly be called a theologian. In his *5th Theological Oration*, n13, he calls those who do not theologise from this perspective "praters".[64] A fundamental tenet of his theologising was that

---

new content. Meredith does note Gregory of Nyssa's departure from Platonic Origenism in his stress on God's infinity and strong insistence on what Meredith terms "moral virtue", although he links this to an intellectual shift in response to polemical needs rather than to Gregory's spirituality – see for example Anthony Meredith, *op.cit*, 78–79

[62] Hierotheos (Vlachos), *The Person in the Orthodox Tradition*, 167

[63] MC Steenberg, *op.cit*, n.pag

[64] Hierotheos (Vlachos), *The Person in the Orthodox Tradition*, 47

God could not be conceived or known by conjecture, but only by experience and revelation, saying that "it is impossible to express God and even more impossible to conceive Him".[65] Of one such experience, he writes: "I was running to lay hold on God, and thus I went up into the Mount, and drew aside the curtain of the Cloud and entered away from matter and material things, and as far as I could I withdrew within myself. And then when I looked up I scarcely saw the back parts of God".[66] Here he characteristically uses the biblical words from Moses' Sinai encounter (Ex 33:23) to denote the fact that he did not see God in Himself, but in His energies (manifestation).

St Basil says: "The worship of God is born of the knowledge of God and knowledge of God comes from participation[67] in His energies."[68] And in his *De Spiritu Sancto* 9.23: "How indeed could there be a corporeal approach to the incorporeal? This association results from the withdrawal of the passions which [....] have alienated it from its close relationship with God." In a letter to Gregory of Nazianzus, Basil describes his repentance, following the *apophatic* way of purification of the heart: "Making the heart ready for it [the grace of God] means the unlearning of the teachings which already possess it, derived from evil habits".[69] In the same letter he speaks of the soul's ascent to God:

> […] it [the soul] becomes forgetful even of its own nature; no longer able to drag the soul down to thought of sustenance or to concern for the body's covering, but enjoying leisure from

---

[65] *2ⁿᵈ Theological Oration*, 4 in Hierotheos (Vlachos), *The Person in the Orthodox Tradition*, 48; see also St Basil, *De Spiritu Sancto*, n53

[66] *2ⁿᵈ Theological Oration* Hierotheos (Vlachos), *The Person in the Orthodox Tradition*, 52

[67] Basil uses the word "participation", not in the Platonic sense of rational participation, but in the sense of intimate communion with God.

[68] *Letter 235, to Amphilochios* in Hierotheos (Vlachos), *The Person in the Orthodox Tradition*, 202

[69] In Hierotheos (Vlachos), *The Person in the Orthodox Tradition*, 43

earthly cares, it transfers all its interests to the acquisition of the eternal good.[70]

And elsewhere:

Utterly inexpressible and indescribable are the lightning flashes of divine beauty: word cannot put them forth, nor hearing receive them [...] This beauty is invisible to the eyes of flesh; it is perceptible only to the soul and the spirit, and those saints whom it has illuminated are left with the dart of unbearable longing.[71]

Words such as "utterly inexpressible" and "indescribable" come up repeatedly in the Fathers' references to mystical encounters with the Divine Persons. As Hierotheos says: "The Fathers speak of the fact that the saints see invisibly and hear inaudibly and participate unpartakingly and understand God 'unwittingly'."[72]

Coming from this stream, Athanasius and the Cappadocians opposed the rational conception of truth and consciously pitted the *apophatic* approach to truth against the Hellenic dialectical, discursive approach in order to encourage hearers to seek God experientially and thus come to know Him as life, rather than seeking to know about God.[73] Thus, in his letter to Eustathios, Basil speaks

---

[70] In *ibid* 44

[71] In *ibid* 44; Hierotheos cites *Ellines Pateres tis Ekklesia*, Thessaloniki, vol. 8:188

[72] *Ibid* 166

[73] *Ibid* 206; Anthony Meredith (*op.cit*, 30) misinterprets Basil when he says the saint's notion of true religion is linked to "truth about the object of worship [...] demanding not, as it did in the first centuries of the Church, surrender of life, but rather devotion to the truth" as enlightenment of the mind. This is a typical example of Eastern thought being read through the lens of the Western, rational approach. He similarly misrepresents Gregory of Nyssa when, speaking of the saint's *Life of Moses*, he says: "Everywhere the Platonic equation of truth and reality is evident" (see *ibid* 72ff). The point is subtle: Gregory certainly equates truth with reality but,

about the sorrow he feels about wasting his life in pursuit of "that wisdom made foolish by God"[74] – a reference to 1 Cor 1:20ff. Gregory of Nyssa refers to "knowledge falsely so called"[75] with respect to the philosophical arguments of his opponents. At the end of his *First Theological Oration*, Gregory of Nazianzus advises his hearers to discard Plato and Aristotle's ideas.

Hierotheos also notes the use of irony in Gregory's arguments against the philosophers when he shows up the absurdity of their questions. He speaks to the philosophers as if they were annoying children asking absurd questions about an ineffable reality that cannot be conceptualised. In answer to the question "how can the begetting of the Son be passionless?" he writes: "[...] because it is incorporeal. For if corporeal generation involves passion, incorporeal generation excludes it." He continues mockingly: "I marvel that you do not venture so far as to conceive of marriages and times of pregnancy and dangers of miscarriage".[76]

Hierotheos insists that one must not be misled by the fact that Eastern Fathers – true to their characteristic tendency to imbue the words of their opponents with different meanings – sometimes spoke positively about philosophy with a view to saying that the true philosophy was in fact *apophatic* theology. For example, in his *Philosophical Chapters*, John of Damascus gives six definitions of philosophy, ranging from science (which he calls natural philosophy) to "true philosophy": "Philosophy, again, is love of wisdom. But

---

as we shall see, reality for the Eastern Fathers was not Platonic rational being and its correlated meaning, but rather the subjective reality of an inter-personal God; thus Gregory's words: "It is truly the really real and knowledge of it is knowledge of the truth" (in *ibid* 73) should not be understood as Platonic mental enlightenment but as knowing truth intimately in living experience.

[74] In Hierotheos (Vlachos), *The Person in the Orthodox Tradition,* 41; Hierotheos also warns against taking Basil's *Homily to the young on how they could make use of Hellenic writings* to support the idea that he considered philosophy a means of arriving at truth; he urges them to associate with poets, prose writers and orators, but not to accept their life and philosophy.

[75] *Letter to Ablabius, On Not Three Gods*

[76] *3rd Theological Oration* in Hierotheos (Vlachos), *The Person in the Orthodox Tradition,* 49

true wisdom is God. Therefore the love of God is true philosophy."[77] Metaphysics is notably absent.[78]

The Fathers' mystical awareness of the inexpressible mystery of God led them to draw a sharp line between what could be positively said about God and what had to be consigned to the realm of mystery. In this context and as a polemic against the Eunomians, Basil asserted that we know God from His energies[79] but we do not know His essence. The Eunomians, who were extreme Arians, used Aristotelian logic to identify the essence of the Father with His unbegotteness, which is indivisible and therefore cannot be shared with other beings through generation; thus the Son must be of a "lesser essence" than the Father.[80] On this basis they also claimed that man knows the essence of God and therefore knows what God knows. (Notice how they identify knowing with ideas about God rather than experiential, relational knowing.) They therefore posed the question: "Do you worship what you know or what you do not know?"

If the Fathers answered that they did not know the essence, it would imply that they worshipped what they did not know, which would mean they were agnostics. If they answered that they knew what they worshipped, they would be asked to define the essence.[81] Basil therefore stressed the difference between knowing that God is and knowing what God is: "I do know that He exists, but what His substance is I consider beyond understanding".[82] He continued that to worship God does not imply that we have to comprehend

---

[77] Gregory of Nazianzus used the word "philosophy" in this way in his *Oration 20* on the ordination of bishops – see Hierotheos, *The Person in the Orthodox Tradition*, 53

[78] Hierotheos (Vlachos), *The Person in the Orthodox Tradition*, 61–63

[79] A distinction first made by Arius, who claimed the Son belonged to the energies of the Father, not the essence – see Hierotheos (Vlachos), *The Person in the Orthodox Tradition*, 164

[80] Hierotheos (Vlachos), *The Person in the Orthodox Tradition*, 200; 36ff; c.f. Meredith, *op.cit*, 30; 63–65

[81] *Ibid* 210

[82] *Letter 234, to Amphilochios*, in *ibid* 201; see also Athanasius, *Letter to Serapion* 1.18 in Khaled Anatolios, *op.cit*, 217

the essence of the object of worship; we only need to comprehend that this essence exists. Every essence has its energy and vice versa. Thus we recognise the essence through its energy (manifestation); a created essence has a created energy and an uncreated essence has an uncreated energy. Thus we recognise that the uncreated essence exists through the energies, but we do not comprehend what the uncreated essence is. By analogy, we can know the characters and qualities of another man without being able to define their essence.

This distinction between created and uncreated essence is vital to the Orthodox position on the economic and immanent Trinities: as God's essence is uncreated, it cannot be defined in created categories of thought.[83] The implication is that God Himself is Truth and He can only be known experientially in communion but not conceptually.[84] However, because the saints' experience of union with God is union in His energies, not His substance, communion with God does not enable the creature to comprehend the infinite divine reality. This is impossible; to comprehend this one would have to be infinite, which is possible only for God Himself.[85] Even mystical perception of the energies of God cannot be described accurately, because created language cannot accommodate it.[86]

This sense of the inexpressible mystery of God meant the emphasis of the Trinitarian dogmas of the 4th century, as worked out by the Eastern Fathers, was on what God wasn't in opposition to the logically deduced ideas of their opponents and to preserve this (mystical-historical) revelation, rather than an attempt to make detailed, positive (*cataphatic*) affirmations about the inexpressible reality of what God is in Himself.[87] As Dumitru Staniloae says,

---

[83] Hierotheos (Vlachos), *The Person in the Orthodox Tradition*, 204; 213

[84] *Ibid* 143–144; 175; 2 Cor 12:4

[85] *Ibid* 165

[86] Anthony Meredith (*op.cit*, 88–89) fails to grasp this aspect of Gregory of Nyssa's thought because he equates knowing God with conceptual knowing; thus while he rightly emphasises Gregory's emphasis on the incomprehensibility of God, he claims the saint limits knowledge of God to God's historical acts without taking the mystical dimension into account.

[87] *Ibid* 191; 197; 199; 212

dogmatic formulations "reveal the Truth in terms accessible to human intelligence [...] but they are not themselves the Truth".[88]

Grasping this mystical-polemical dimension of their theologising, along with the awareness that created language is not adequate to express eternal realities, is crucial to understanding the Eastern position.[89] This is why the Orthodox speak of the Trinity as an incomprehensible mystery while simultaneously formulating dogma against perceived heresy.[90] As Hierotheos puts it: "[...] the dogma expresses and formulates the experience of revelation, but the understanding of the dogma never means that the mystery of the Holy Trinity is also understood in parallel, for this mystery is inexpressible and incomprehensible even in its manifestations."[91]

Against this backdrop, Rahner's accusation of "pre-reflective tritheism" (2.iv above) would seems absurd to the Easterner, because his charge implies that mystically perceived truth must be made to conform to the rules of philosophical logic. This is impossible because (a) the Trinity transcends philosophical conceptual systems and (b) truth is not in any case a set of ideas arising from rational reflection but is God Himself, who is known experientially in personal communion. Thus *theo-logia* – words about God – are not deduced ideas based on a phenomenological view of the Incarnation, but testimony about mystically known Truth.

3.ii.b The Eucharistic approach

The Eucharistic gathering also informed the content of the Fathers' faith[92] and early on found expression in the saying *lex orandi, lex*

---

[88] Dumitru Staniloae, *Theology and the Church* (Crestwood: St Vladimir's Seminary Press, 1980), 73; cf. John Zizioulas, *Being as Communion*, 122

[89] Hierotheos (Vlachos), *The Person in the Orthodox Tradition*, 41; 164–166; see also Gregory of Nyssa, *Oration 28*; 2 Cor. 12:3–4

[90] *Ibid* 68; 72; 166; 223–224; *John Zizioulas, Being as Communion*, 116ff

[91] Hierotheos (Vlachos), *The Person in the Orthodox Tradition*, 166; see also Dumitru Staniloae, *op.cit*, 73; John Zizioulas, *Being as Communion*, 117

[92] Hierotheos (Vlachos), *The Person in the Orthodox Tradition*, 84

credendi (as we worship so we believe).[93] For example, Pomazansky cites Basil's quotations of doxologies that were handed down "from the Fathers" to support the notion of the Trinity: "Glory to the Father through the Son in the Holy Spirit" and the baptismal formulas given by the Lord Himself.[94] In particular, the Church had worshipped Christ from its conception; if He was not truly God then they were worshipping a creature.[95] Thus, while the worship was a spontaneous response to their experience of the crucified and risen Lord, it became crucial to demonstrate conceptually that He was divine only when the polemical need arose.

The experience of the Eucharist as communion with the Holy Trinity was equally important to the Fathers' notion of truth. Zizioulas traces the ecclesial aspect of the Cappadocians' thinking to St Ignatius of Antioch (c. 35 – c. 107), whose approach was informed by pastoral rather than philosophical concerns. Ignatius saw truth as life[96] – not in the Hebrew sense of *praxis* or the Aristotelian sense of life as a quality added to being, but rather in the sense that being *is* life, particularly being forever or incorruptibility (Eph 17:1; 20:2). This was in continuity with the Fourth Gospel's understanding of knowledge as knowing God, who *is* "eternal life" or true life (Jn 3:15, 36; 14:6; 17:3). Irenaeus also saw Christ as the truth, not of the mind (against Gnosticism),[97] but of the incorruptibility of being.[98]

Zizioulas argues that this perspective was informed by their experience of communion with God in Christ in the Eucharistic

---

[93] Gary LC Frank, *Christian Foundations 1: Community Life, KEA301-G/ KGE511-M (Tutorial letter 105)*, Pretoria: Unisa, 1997), 21

[94] Michael Pomazansky, *op.cit*, 78–79) Pomazansky does not cite original sources, but similar examples are found in *De Spiritu Sancto* 3, 13, 7, 16, 24, 28; see also Athanasius, *Letter to Serapion* 1.28

[95] Maurice Wiles, *op.cit*, 41

[96] John Zizioulas, *Being as Communion*, 78; he cites *Magn.* 1.2, *Eph.* 3.2, 7.2, 20.2 & *Sm* 4.1, etc.

[97] This was a complex, heterodox religio-philosophical movement that emphasised acquiring secret spiritual knowledge (*gnosis*) in the Platonic sense as the path to redemption. Its Christian form became prominent in the 2nd century – see Livingstone 1988: 215

[98] John Zizioulas, *Being as Communion*, 80

gathering – a theme that runs as a strong current throughout their expositions. Both men had to argue, Ignatius against Docetism[99] and Irenaeus against Gnosticism, that the Eucharist, which imparts life, is truly Christ in both a material and historical sense; thus truth had to become historical without ceasing to be ontological. There was also the understanding that the life of the Eucharist was the life of God Himself – not life that flows out mechanically from the interior of existence, as in Aristotelian thought, but the life of communion with God as it exists in the Trinity.[100]

Thus knowledge (of God) and communion are identical, as are being and (eternal) life. Incorruptibility is only possible in communion with God. But this can only be true if the life of God itself is communion, as the experience of the Eucharistic (and personal) communion suggests.[101]

Thus for Irenaeus creation and existence itself could only be founded on this living God of communion, implying that creation is an act of Father, Son and Holy Spirit.[102] While Irenaeus was concerned mainly with created being, this approach was to be vital in the formulation of Trinitarian theology in the 4th century.

3.ii.c Being as communion

Arius argued within the Origenistic *Logos* tradition and, in his fervour to maintain the monotheistic transcendence of the One God (the Father), posited that the Son was of a different substance to the Father (as in Origen's distinction between God and "gods")

---

[99] An early Church tendency to see Christ's suffering as illusory – see E.A. Livingstone, *op.cit*, 156

[100] John Zizioulas, *Being as Communion*, 80–81

[101] *Ibid*; c.f. Michael Pomazansky, *op.cit*, 74: "The dogma of the three Persons indicates the fullness of the mystical inward life in God, for God is love and the love of God cannot merely be extended to the world created by Him: in the Holy Trinity this love is directed within the Divine Life also."

[102] John Zizioulas, *Being as Communion*, 82; he cites *Ad Haer* 28.4; c.f. IV *Praef.* 4

and that "there was a time when the Son was not".[103] The latter was meant to denote that the Son was not eternal, like the Father, but nor was He created.[104] In order to distinguish between the Son and creation, Arius made a distinction between the essence and energies of God (it seems he was the first to do so) and argued that the Son is a product of the uncreated energies of God (the Father). In the estimation of the Fathers, Arius had gone too far with his relentless logic and this highlighted a need for a radical revision of Origen's teachings and the *Logos* approach to truth.[105]

Soteriological concerns were central to Athanasius' counter-argument: only a divine Saviour could impart to man a share in his own nature and so make them "partakers of the divine nature" (2 Peter 1:4), which was the essence of salvation[106] – an assertion that must be understood against the background of Irenaeus' doctrine of *theosis*, in terms of which the human being is deified through communion with God through the Son and in the Holy Spirit.[107]

In his refutation of the Tropici,[108] Athanasius affirmed the divinity of the Spirit in a parallel way: just as the Son can be seen to be divine through His creative and redemptive activity, so the Spirit's divinity is revealed by His recreative activity: "It is through the Spirit that we become partakers of God."[109]

Philosophically, Athanasius first made a clear distinction between substance and will[110] in order to assert that the being of the Son in relation to God was not the same as the being of the world in relation to God. The Son's being belongs to the substance of God, the world to His will. This enabled him to break with the

---

[103] *Ibid* 83; see also Alexander's *Deposition of Arius*; Kenneth Scott Latourette, *op.cit*, 152; Khaled Anatolios, *op.cit*, 7

[104] Maurice Wiles, *op.cit*, 37–40

[105] John Zizioulas, *Being as Communion*, 83; Hierotheos S Vlachos, *The Person in the Orthodox Tradition*, 164; c.f. Anthony Meredith, *op.cit*, 54;

[106] Maurice Wiles, *op.cit*, 41; *Against the Arians* 16; *Letter to Serapion* 1.23–25, 30 in Khaled Anatolios, *op.cit*, 222–225, 229

[107] Maurice Wiles, *op.cit*, 58

[108] A heterodox group that believed the Holy Spirit to be a superior rank of angelic being.

[109] *Letter to Serapion* 1.9,24 in Gerald O'Collins, *op.cit*, 130

[110] *Against the Arians* 1.29, 33

closed ontology of the Greeks, who saw the world as the lowest of a series of automatic emanations from the One. Thus to be is no longer the same as to will or to act.[111] Second, by connecting the Son's being to the very substance of God, he transformed the idea of substance.[112] "Has God ever existed without His own Son?" (or "without that which is proper to Him") he asks in *Against the Arians* 1.20.

By implication, Zizioulas asserts, Athanasius gives substance itself a relational character, which implies the idea of being as communion.[113] This is also implied in Athanasius' assertion that without the relationship between the Father and the Son "the perfectness and fullness of the Father's substance is depleted (or eliminated)".[114] This led Athanasius to make the extraordinary statement: "If the Son was not there before He was born there would be no truth in God,"[115] implying that the Father-Son relationship makes God to be the truth eternally in Himself.[116] Athanasius rejects any notion of a substance *per se* that is not qualified with the word Father (a relational term); such a notion of substance, he says, is the "thinking of the Greeks".[117]

"This is clearly the emergence of a new ontology," says Zizioulas.[118] He therefore argues that Athanasius' primary contribution to the development of a Christian ontology was the idea that communion does not belong to the level of will and action, but to that of substance. His distinction left a few questions unanswered, such as what then was the ontological basis of creation? Also, if the otherness of creation is due to it being a result of the will, how could one account for otherness within the being of God Himself?[119] The first question has still not been adequately answered,

---

[111] John Zizioulas, *Being as Communion*, 83–84
[112] *Ibid* 84
[113] *Ibid*
[114] *Against the Arians* 1.20 in *ibid*
[115] *Against the Arians* 1:20 in *ibid* 85
[116] John Zizioulas, *Being as Communion*, 85
[117] *De Synodis* 51 in *ibid*
[118] John Zizioulas, *Being as Communion*, 85
[119] *Ibid* 86–87

but the Cappadocians answered the second with their notion of personhood. Zizioulas adds in a footnote:

> The *homoousion* [formula] presupposes that *ousia* represents the ultimate ontological category. There seems to be no doubt that this is the view of Athanasius. If, however, we take into account the relational character of *ousia* in Athanasius, we can conclude that the Cappadocians do not depart from Athanasius' thought but simply draw out the consequences his theology had for the doctrine of God's being. Athanasius' relational notion of substance becomes through the creative work of the Cappadocians an ontology of personhood.[120]

Elements of Athanasius' *Discourse 1 Against the Arians* seem to support Zizioulas' view. Athanasius' primary concern in this text is to demonstrate the eternity of the Son against Arius' famous "there was a time when the Son was not". Athanasius argues that the Son is proper to the Father; therefore, because the Father is eternal, the Son must be eternal too.[121] To say that the Son was added in time would imply that the essence of the Father (i.e. the Father Himself) was imperfect prior to the Son's begetting.[122] It would also imply that God was first a Monad and became a Triad only with the begetting, again implying a deficiency in the Father and that He had to add something to His being.[123] Athanasius uses examples of designations attributed to the Son to demonstrate this point, such as Word and Wisdom,[124] Life and Truth – as in "I am the life, the truth [...]" of Jn 14:6,[125] Radiance[126] and Image.[127]

---

[120] *Ibid* 89
[121] *Against the Arians*, 1.14; see also 1.16, 19, 29
[122] *Ibid* 1.14
[123] *Ibid* 1.17
[124] *Ibid* 1.14, 17
[125] *Ibid* 1.19, 21
[126] *Ibid* 1.16, 20
[127] *Ibid* 1.21

He argues that none of these are foreign to the essence of the Father, any more than water is foreign to a spring[128] or the sun's radiance to the sun;[129] therefore, the Son, who is the Word, Wisdom, Life, Truth, Radiance and Image of the Father, are intrinsic to the Father's essence and therefore eternal.[130] To imply that they are not is to say that the Son, who is the Father's Word, Image, Truth, Life, etc., is external to and was added to God.[131] Athanasius argues that, while creatures participate in God's (i.e. the Father's) nature, the Son wholly participates in or partakes of the Father's essence (the Father Himself).[132] The relational element is emphasised when he argues that the Son/Word/Image who is begotten of the Father is also *with* the Father and is the One in whom the Father delights (he quotes Prov. 8:30). Athanasius then asks: "When did the Father not see Himself in His Image? Or when had He not delight?"[133]

Here we have the implication of a communion of interpersonal "others" – and the basis of salvation, understood as participation in the nature of God (2 Peter 1:4) – along the same lines that Irenaeus expounded it.[134] That is, salvation consists in knowing the Father in the Son by way of being in intimate communion with the Father in the Son. This is possible because the Son is (a) the Image of the Father by virtue of being one essence with Him and (b) Life because the Son's Life is the Father.[135]

But while the creature knows and experiences this by participation, the Son is this by essence.[136]

This idea of the common substance in turn implies that there are three personal Subjects in relation. However, at this juncture in history the word "*hypostasis*" (which was then used as a synonym

---

128 *Ibid* 1.19
129 *Ibid* 1.37
130 *Ibid* 1.19, 25
131 *Ibid* 1.20–21
132 *Ibid* 1.16
133 *Ibid* 1.20
134 See 3.ii.b above
135 *Ibid* 1.37–45
136 *Ibid* 1.39

for *ousia*) was not yet used to denote the Persons,[137] while the word "Person" was rarely used in relation to God because it was linked to Sabellianism – and the Arian party constantly accused the pro-Nicene party of this heresy.[138] Thus Athanasius simply used the Divine Names – Father, Son and Spirit – to indicate the self-evident experiential reality that the Three were what were later defined as *Hypostases*-Persons.

This is evident, for example, in his argument that the Son is not God by participation, as the Arians claimed: "For He is the expression of the Father's Person, and Light from Light, and Power, and very Image of the Father's essence".[139] This is one of the rare occasions that he uses the word Person. Later Athanasius' emphasis is on the fact that the Father is in the Son and the Son in the Father.[140] Thus sharing one essence is the same as being in one another. Further on Athanasius asks what it is that the Son participates in and argues that He participates directly in the Father.[141] He adds: "[...] it follows that what is partaken is not external to the Father, but from the essence of the Father".[142] One again gets the impression that it is a participation of one personal Subject in another personal Subject. On another point, Athanasius argues earlier that Christ is the Power of God, according to Scripture (1 Cor 1:24); thus the power is not the Father Himself or simply an attribute or energy of the Father's substance that is shared with the Son; this would imply, he argues, that the Son merely participates in the Father's power. Rather, Athanasius insists, the power is proper to the Son Himself (i.e. the Person) and the Son Himself is the Power of God (the Father).[143]

In other words, in both the Father and the Son, essence and personhood are indivisible and the attributes belong properly to the Persons. Thus when he says that "the Father is the origin of the

---

[137] John Zizioulas, *Being as Communion*, 37
[138] Kenneth Scott Latourette, *op.cit*, 157
[139] *Against the Arians* 1.9; c.f. St Basil, *De Spiritu Sancto* 21
[140] *Against the Arians* 1.61
[141] *Ibid*
[142] *Ibid*
[143] *Ibid* 1.11

Son"[144] and "the Son is the proper offspring of the Father's essence"[145] (an expression he uses often), he premises this on the awareness that the Father's essence is the Person of the Father; thus the Son is begotten as a distinct yet inseparable "Self" from the Father's "Self". He adds that any idea that this implies parts and divisions is "to have material thoughts about what is immaterial".[146] Thus the idea of incorporeal Persons who subsist without division and without being individuals is implicit in Athanasius, but it is not yet named.

3.III. SUMMARY

By the 4th century the appropriation of the pagan Greek notion of truth by certain Christian apologists was beginning to compromise the biblical notion of truth as experientially known reality. This resulted in the *Logos* imagery of the fourth evangelist being appropriated within Hellenic paradigms, rather than in contradistinction to them, and to a tendency to see truth as a rational affair. In particular, Origen had radically Hellenised the Christian conception of truth and Arius' relentless logic, following this approach, had highlighted the need to revisit the relationship between the ancient philosophical approach to truth and the Christian experience of revelation – both historical and mystical. Thus the 4th century Eastern Fathers affirmed the biblical, mystical and ecclesial Christian experience of God in contradistinction to the pagan Greek conception of truth as rational being that could be appropriated on the level of conceptual knowledge.

Athanasius posited the first step in this direction with an implicit assertion of the notion of being as communion – an interpretation that would certainly not be obvious unless viewed within the patristic experiential paradigm of knowledge of God being identical with communion with God. While Zizioulas tends to emphasise the ecclesial dimension of this awareness, I have chosen to place

---

[144] *Ibid* 1.14
[145] *Ibid* 1.15, 58
[146] *Ibid*

greater emphasis on the personal, mystical experience of the Fathers because, in my view, they would have read this perception back into their understanding of the Eucharistic celebration. Mystical experience of God in the Spirit also influenced the manner of the Fathers' theologising. First, it meant that they were keenly aware of the need to theologise in opposition to the philosophical conceptual system of their day. This fundamental approach to truth continues in the East to this day; the Orthodox reject logic and Hellenic philosophical presuppositions as criteria of truth, accepting only that which is known mystically and historically. The implication for our discussion about the *filioque* is that, inasmuch as the West argues its case philosophically, it is pitting philosophical criteria against non-philosophical criteria. Such argumentation, I believe, is counter-productive, as differing norms are at play.

Second, mystical experience imbued the Eastern Fathers with a keen sense of the incomprehensibility of the Trinity. This was made conceptually explicit in the distinction between the essence and energies of God that was used to assert, against the Eunomians, that we know God by His energies (His self-manifestation to creatures, the economic Trinity) but do not know His essence (God as He is in Himself – the immanent Trinity), which we cannot conceptualise – because God in His immanence is an eternal, incorporeal reality, which the created, temporal mind cannot grasp. This means it is fundamental to reach agreement on the line we draw between what we know through mystical and historical experience of God, and that which we have deduced philosophically with respect to Christian truth before we can answer the question: with respect to the *filioque*, has the West gone too far in its attempt to explain this sublime mystery? Or can the West demonstrate that the *filioque* falls within the category of mystical-historical revelation?

4   PERCEPTION AND CONCEPTION IN ORTHODOX THOUGHT

In this chapter I shall note (a) the sort of experiences the Cappadocians had; (b) how this mystical perception influenced their use of terminology; (c) how the Orthodox arrived at their conception of the person against the background of Hellenic philosophical thought and (d) how this completed the Orthodox conception of truth in contradistinction to the Hellenic notion.

This backdrop will enable us to address Western concerns about the Eastern conception and more comprehensively grasp the Orthodox position on the *filioque*.

4.I. MYSTICISM, POLEMICS AND LANGUAGE

4.i.a Direct encounters with God

I begin with a brief look at the content of mystical experience of the Trinity in the East to emphasise that this is the starting point for Orthodox theologising. We have noted that the Cappadocians wrote of mystical experiences of God, but did not describe them in detail. Alfeyev notes that this is due to the inexpressible nature of what is perceived in such encounters,[1] a point the Cappadocians emphasised. One could add that this is also due to a tradition among Orthodox monastics to keep their mystical experiences to themselves, both as an act of humility and to avoid arousing jealousy among fellow monastics who have not attained *theoria*. Hierotheos[2] therefore cites St Symeon the New Theologian (11th cen-

---

[1] Hilarion Alfeyev, *op.cit*, 187–188
[2] *The Person in the Orthodox Tradition*, 173ff

tury),[3] who is unique in the Orthodox tradition as he could be the only writer to describe his experience of the Trinity in detail. The assumption is that the content of the Cappadocians' experience was the same.[4] The following description, which I quote only in part, came about in response to a specific question for which the saint sought an answer in prayer. Metropolitan Stephen of Nicomedia, wanting to humiliate him, had asked: "How do you separate the Son from the Father, by a rational or real distinction?"[5]

> I see the Son, and I see the Father, the Father is seen as just like the Son, except that the one begets and the other is begotten. [...] Because they have the Spirit as their teacher they do not need learning from men, but illumined by the light of the Spirit they look at the Son, they see the Father and worship the Trinity of the Persons, the one God, inexpressibly united in nature. From the Father they receive the revelation that the Son is begotten without division, in a way which only he knows, for I am not able to say it. [...] The Father is Father because He begets unceasingly. And how is this eternal begetting produced? In that it does not at all separate from the Father and comes forth whole in an inexplicable manner and remains continually in the bosom of the Father. The Son is seen in the Father constantly. He is begotten but remains one with Him; and in the Son too one contemplates the Father, without distance or division or separation.[6]

Elsewhere in his *Hymns*, St Symeon speaks of three lights:

---

[3] Following Nazianzus' words in his *First Theological Oration*, the Orthodox give a person the title Theologian when they have attained the vision of God and spoken words (*logoi*) about God (*Theo*) from this perspective. It is for this reason that the mystic St Gregory of Nazianzus was given the title – a point Anthony Meredith (*op.cit*, 44) fails to grasp when he attributes the title to the saint's defence of the full humanity of Christ.

[4] Hilarion Alfeyev, *op.cit*, 88

[5] Hierotheos (Vlachos), *The Person in the Orthodox* Tradition, 174

[6] From *Hymns of Divine Love* in *ibid* 182–183

I see Christ […] Who humbles Himself and shows Himself to me, with the Father and the Spirit, thrice holy light, unique in the three and the three in one single light. Most certainly it is They Themselves who are the light and the Three are unique light which, more than the sun, enlightens my soul, and illumines my mind, in darkness until then […] For it is in the light of the Spirit that those who contemplate Him see Him, And those who see this light, it is the Son whom they contemplate, but the one who has been deemed worthy to see the Son sees the Father, And whoever contemplates the Father, assuredly sees Him with the Son. […] The light is inaccessible, the glory is unbearable.[7]

St Symeon does not describe the procession of the Spirit, which seems to be because He is *in* the Spirit, who reveals the Father and the Son to him; thus the Spirit is not an object of perception but the subjective ground of perception of the Son, in whom the Father is discerned. He does stress that three Persons can be clearly distinguished but that the manner of the Son and Spirit's origination cannot be grasped by the human mind.

The inexpressible and incomprehensible nature of the Divine Persons perceived in such an encounter means that any attempt to logically formulate ideas about the begetting and procession would be seen as trampling irreverently on Holy Ground. Thus Gregory of Nazianzus asserts: "The begetting of God must be honoured by silence."[8]

Gregory of Nyssa also spoke of an experience of God that transcended apparitions. In his *Life of Moses* he asserts that visual

---

[7] In Hilarion Alfeyev, *op.cit*, 188

[8] *3rd Theological Oration* in Hierotheos (Vlachos), *The Person in the Orthodox Tradition*, 51; one finds the same sort of affirmation in Irenaeus – see *Against Heresies*, 2.28.6 in Gerald O'Collins, *op.cit*, 98

encounters[9] are part of the mystic's early experience; one finally arrives at a sublime interior experience of God in darkness.[10]

The main points to note are that (a) the Orthodox claim that such mystical perceptions of God were not isolated cases, but have been experienced over and over again by the saints.

And (b) there is an assumption that the Fathers had the same experience as the Apostles, such as St Paul, who heard "inexpressible words" that "it is not lawful to for a man to utter" (2 Cor. 12:4).[11]

Also (c) the conviction is that the content of the Cappadocians' experience of God was the same as St Symeon describes and that in their theologising they drew out the conceptual, polemical implications of such encounters.

Such experiences are indicated, for example, in Basil's assertion that the Spirit will, "by the aid of your purified eye, show you in Himself the image of the invisible, and in the blessed spectacle of the image you shall behold the unspeakable beauty of the archetype".[12] And the correlation between such experience and theology can be seen in Gregory of Nazianzus' words:

> If, it is asserted, we use the word "God" three times, must there not be three Gods? […] We have one God, because there is a single Godhead. Though there are three objects of belief, they derive from the single whole and have reference to it. They do not have degrees of being God or degrees of priority over against one another. They are not sundered in will nor divided in power […] It is as if there were a single intermin-

---

[9] Namely apparitions, understood as manifestations (energies) of the Persons

[10] MC Steenberg, *op.cit*, n.pag

[11] Hierotheos (Vlachos), *The Person in the Orthodox Tradition*, 171–172; 199–200

[12] *De Spiritu Sancto* 23; see also n45; Anthony Meredith (*op.cit*, 60) interprets a similar text from Gregory of Nyssa to mean one sees God interiorly in one's *own* purified image (following Augustine), but in this context the Cappadocians usually used "archetype" to denote the Father and "image" to denote Christ

gling of light, which existed in three mutually connected Suns. When we look at the Godhead, the primal cause, the sole sovereignty, we have a mental picture of the single whole, certainly. But when we look at the three in Whom the Godhead exists, Who derive their timeless and equally glorious being from the primal cause, we have three objects of worship.[13]

This also means (d) that Scripture is read through the lens of this mystical perception. Thus for the Fathers Scriptural exegesis was not merely a philosophical or logical exercise, but a process of recognising the correlation between biblical events and sayings and mystically apprehended reality, and connecting the dots.

The assumption that the Fathers had the same mystical experience as the Apostles also implies (e) that they share the same doctrinal authority as the Apostles and their authority rests on the fact that they knew God directly[14] – which is consistent with the biblical notion of authority: the authority of the prophets and of Christ Himself (who spoke with authority because He spoke of what He knew intimately).

Thus Basil says: "Shall we not place among the Apostles and Prophets a man who has walked by the same Spirit as they?"[15]

Finally, (f) the words "Light from Light" in the Symbol of Faith are, notably, not analogous but a literal description of mystically perceived reality, as the above examples indicate, *contra* Meredith's claim that the Cappadocians' use of the word "light" in relation to divine reality comes from Plato and describes cerebral enlightenment.[16]

---

[13] *Letter to Ablabius* in Hilarion Alfeyev, *op.cit*, 39; notice that the Godhead exists in the Three, not the Three in the Godhead.

[14] Hierotheos (Vlachos), *The Person in the Orthodox Tradition*, 191; 232

[15] *De Spiritu Sancto* 74; he is referring to "the great Gregory" Thaumaturgos, (210/213–270/75), the "Apostle of Cappadocia" – see Anthony Meredith, *op.cit*, 3

[16] Anthony Meredith, *op.cit*, 43; 46

4.i.b Mysticism and polemics

Against this backdrop, it is vital to understand that, firstly, although the Greek Fathers applied their notion of *hypostasis*-person to the human person in certain instances, they developed it specifically with reference to God within the context of Trinitarian theology, not in order to develop a new anthropology or to expand philosophy. Thus their formulation cannot be understood with reference to human persons except in a qualified sense.[17] Hierotheos therefore cautions against confusing the created with uncreated, eternal and temporal person in the thought of the Fathers.[18] For humans beings the Fathers mostly used the word *anthropos* (man). But whether they spoke of human individuals as persons or man, they used the word *theologically*, not anthropologically or philosophically, and qualified it by saying that a *true* man or person is not simply a sentient biological entity, but one who is deified by participating in the life of God.[19]

We shall return to this theme at the end of this chapter. In the meantime, it is worth noting that O'Collins' assertion that Aquinas' description of person as a "distinct subsistent in a rational nature goes beyond *hypostasis* [as in the Chalcedonian formula] because individual dogs and oak trees rank as *hypostases* or distinct subsistents"[20] is misplaced in this context, as Aquinas' formula was posited with the human person in mind, while the Fathers were making a point about the Divine Persons.

Second, the Eastern Fathers' conception was worked out in a specific polemical situation.[21] Their formulation of three Persons-*Hypostases* was worked out in opposition to Sabellianism, which described the Persons as three modes of being – in the sense of three masks or roles or appearances of the one God[22] – and their predecessors the Patropaschites, who identified the Father with the

---

[17] Hierotheos (Vlachos), *The Person in the Orthodox Tradition*, 68; 75
[18] *Ibid* 157–158; 211–212
[19] *Ibid* 75–77
[20] Gerald O'Collins', *op.cit*, 176
[21] Hierotheos (Vlachos), *The Person in the Orthodox Tradition*, 68; 132–133; 158
[22] *Ibid* 116, 133; see St Basil, *Letter 52: To the Canonicae*

Son and affirmed that the Father suffered in the Son at the crucifixion, and the Adoptionists, who taught that Christ was a human
creature who was adopted by God.[23] It is noteworthy that the pro-
tagonists of these schools of thought all argued within the paradigms of ancient Greek philosophy, or at least made their starting
point conjecture and anthropocentric views.[24]

By contrast, the Cappadocians' wished to assert, quite simply,
that the Father, Son and Spirit were ontologically real personal Subjects without defining what the essence of Personhood was in God;
it was simply an assertion of an experienced reality.

4.i.c Implications for language

As mystics, the Cappadocians' were keenly aware of the distinction
between the uncreated and created, eternal and temporal, and the
inadequacy of created language to convey the reality of the Trinity.[25] Thus the fundamental difficulty was to find the words to articulate a sublime perception for which no terminology was available
in created categories of thought.[26] They had no option but to use
the language currency of their time, as inadequate as it was.

Hierotheos explains: "Having the experience of the revelation,
but knowing the terminology which philosophers and heretics were
using, they made God-inspired formulations with the available terminology, giving it a different content."[27] The words of St Gregory
of Palamas are particularly illustrative in this regard: "And if any of
the Fathers says the same thing as those outside, it is true only of
the words, but the meanings are far apart".[28]

The Eastern Fathers' use of the word "individual" in their explanations of divine personhood is indicative of this practice. For

---

[23] *Ibid* 69–70

[24] *Ibid* 40; 164–165

[25] *Ibid* 95; 199; Dumitru Staniloae, *op.cit*, 73

[26] John of Damascus, *Expositions* 1.8; Hilarion Alfeyev, *op.cit*, 37; Hierotheos (Vlachos), *The Person in the Orthodox Tradition*, 187

[27] Hierotheos (Vlachos), *The Person in the Orthodox Tradition*, 164; see
also pp. 26–27; 34; 68; 172

[28] *Triads* 1.1.11 in *ibid* 116

example, we earlier quoted Basil as saying, when explaining the meaning of *hypostasis*, that "each one of us partakes of being by the common notion of essence, but we are this man or that man by our own individuality".[29] And in his *Letter to Ablabius,* Gregory of Nyssa uses an example of three human individuals who are distinguished by their unique attributes – but he also emphasises the consubstantiality of humankind and reiterates several times that it is due to an "erroneous habit" that we speak of them as if they have separate natures".

It is with this perspective in mind that we should understand John of Damascus' statement that *hypostasis*, person and individual are the same thing.[30] Polemically, the Fathers had linked person to *hypostasis* to denote the fact that the Father, Son and Spirit are Persons in a subsistent sense, just as individuals are; person and individual are the same in terms of being unique, subsistent and subjective but the word "individual" was not meant in the sense that the Hellenic philosophers used the term.[31] One Western thinker who fails to grasp this is Lucian Turcescu,[32] who cites St Gregory's use of the word "individual" and his descriptions of the properties of the individual to refute Zizioulas' claim, made in his book *Being is Communion* and various articles, that the Cappadocian Fathers' conception of the Person was in contradistinction to the "Western" notion of the individual. Zizioulas makes the distinction to make explicit the fact that the Eastern Fathers did not mean that the three Divine Persons are individuated by nature, as human beings are, because the Three are one nature.

Turcescu further criticises Zizioulas for imposing postmodern categories of thought on the Cappadocians. There is a great deal of truth in this too, but what Turcescu fails to recognise

---

[29] *Letter 214 to Count Terentios* in George Barrois, *op. cit*, 128

[30] *Dialectics* 39–43 in Hierotheos (Vlachos), *The Person in the Orthodox Tradition*, 75; 150–151

[31] Hierotheos (Vlachos), *The Person in the Orthodox Tradition*, 74–75; 115–116

[32] "'Person' versus 'individual', and other modern misreadings of Gregory of Nyssa" in *Modern Theology*, (Oxford: Blackwell Publishing, October, 2002), 527ff

is that Zizioulas uses post-modern terminology to make explicit a mystical *awareness* that underpinned the thought of the Cappadocians, so as to make this underlying perception accessible to the postmodern reader. There is no way to do this other than by using current conceptual categories, as the Fathers did in their day.

To avoid such misunderstandings, one needs to bear in mind three tendencies that arise from the Eastern Fathers' creative use of language:

First, they used examples from created life *illustratively* to indicate a reality beyond that which they described.[33] Thus, as we have noted, in his *Letter to Ablabius*, Gregory of Nyssa uses an example of three human individuals who are distinguished by their unique attributes and St John of Damascus uses the Archangel Gabriel and St Paul the Apostle to illustrate the idea that a person is "one who by reason of his own operations and properties exhibits to us an appearance which is distinct and set off from those of the same nature as he" and that they "belonged to a particular species" but were at the same time a particular individual.[34] The Fathers used such examples to illustratively indicate the ontological uniqueness of the Divine Persons, who transcend all human notions of personhood, by appealing to our ability to recognise distinct personhood in creaturely reality.[35]

Second, the Fathers tended to use words *relatively*. In fact, the first eight chapters of St Basil's *De Spiritu Sancto* is premised on the assertion that the language of revelation is fluid and cannot be interpreted in terms of the rules of philosophy.[36] This is also true of the word "person". As the word was used theologically to denote the Divine Persons, it is used of human persons only relatively. Thus human persons are sometimes said to be not truly persons – relative to the perfect, uncreated personhood of the Divine Persons. But when human personhood is taken as the measure of per-

---

[33] See St Gregory of Palamas in Hierotheos (Vlachos), *The Person in the Orthodox Tradition*, 209–210

[34] *Dialectics* 39–43 in Hierotheos (Vlachos), *The Person in the Orthodox Tradition*, 74–75

[35] Hierotheos (Vlachos), *The Person in the Orthodox Tradition*, 76ff; 116

[36] See especially 2.5; 5.7; 6.13

sonhood, they might speak of the Divine Persons as being Persons in a superlative sense.[37]

Another example is the discussion about being. Speaking from a creaturely perspective, they might say *apophatically* that the Trinity is above being (against Hellenic monism) or speak of the supra-essential essence. But in another context, when speaking of the Trinity without reference to creation, the Fathers might speak *cataphatically* of the being of God while simultaneously affirming that it is above human comprehension and then qualify their statements by saying that these *cataphatic* statements clarify things about the nature of God but do not define the nature of God itself.[38] They similarly speak of the impossibility of seeing God and yet speak of mystical encounters with God, which can be confusing unless one places this in the context of their distinction between the essence and energies of God.

Here it is helpful to note that in the examples of mystical experience we have cited, the Father becomes visible in Christ, that is, as a result of the divine economy of the Son. Thus is it impossible to see God as He is in Himself, yet possible to see Him in His energies (self-manifestation) through the glorified Son in the Spirit.[39] As Irenaeus said: "The Father is the invisible of the Son, the Son is the visible of the Father."[40] Thus *cataphatic* statements generally refer to the energies (manifestations) of God.

Third, their choice of created terminology was informed by their *polemical* circumstances. Although keenly aware that philosophical categories of thought could not accommodate or express the sublime reality of God, the Fathers tended to use the same language as their opponents, but either qualified it or imbued it with new meaning. This means that one cannot assume that they used philosophical terminology as the ancients used it; one needs to rather grasp the *awareness* underpinning their thought.[41]

---

[37] Hierotheos (Vlachos), *The Person in the Orthodox Tradition*, 212ff

[38] *Ibid* 204–206; Hierotheos quotes John of Damascus, *The Orthodox Faith*, and St Maximus, *First Century on Theology* 4 to support this view

[39] Hilarion Alfeyev, *op.cit*, 184–187

[40] In *ibid* 187

[41] John Zizioulas, *Being as* Communion, 117–118

We have noted how they reinterpreted Arius' distinction between the energies and essence of God and how they imbued the word "philosophy" with new meaning, with true philosophy understood as "love of God". As we shall see shortly, the Eastern Fathers also reinterpreted the use of the term "unbegotten". Origen and Arius had used the word to express the substance of the Father, but the Cappadocians used it to denote a personal *hypostatic* property of the Father.

This is true also of the word Person. The Sabellian Modalists had used the word in the sense of "mask" and "mode of being" to say that the one God (one in *ousia-hypostasis* according to Nicaea I) revealed Himself in three modes or roles. The Cappadocians answered this by joining person to *hypostasis*, so giving the word person ontological content and using the expression "modes of being" to denote the subsistent modes of being (begetting and proceeding) that enable us to *recognise* and *distinguish* the three Persons-*hypostases* in the immanent Trinity. Thus at Nicaea I, where it was necessary to emphasise the consubstantiality of the Father and the Son against Arius, the word *hypostasis* was used as a synonym for *ousia*; but Sabellius' use of this definition to argue that the Persons are three "masks" or roles of the One God necessitated a change in terminology.[42]

Hierotheos insists that this did not imply a change in theology; the experiential perception of the Trinity remained the same but was more accurately defined in light of new needs.[43] Hierotheos also emphasises that the fluidity of human language means the Fathers made different use of the language of their day in every epoch (and this continues to be the case), but that once an ecumenical council has defined the meaning of specific terminology against a particular heresy it cannot be altered.[44] Nevertheless, a distinction is made in the Orthodox mind between the mystery of the Trinity (Truth in itself) and the language used to convey it, which is not

---

[42] Hierotheos (Vlachos), *The Person in the Orthodox Tradition*, 192–193; Hilarion Alfeyev, *op.cit*, 34

[43] Hierotheos (Vlachos), *The Person in the Orthodox Tradition*, 74; 164; 194–196

[44] *Ibid* 165

itself the truth.[45] It also cannot be emphasised enough that these definitions do not attempt to comprehensibly articulate the ineffable reality of the Trinity, which human conceptual systems cannot accommodate. They are merely pointers intended to give one a *sense* of the ineffable reality, using creaturely terminology, against the errors of heretics.[46] The only way to truly understand divine personhood is to experience the sublime reality oneself.[47] Thus Hierotheos stresses: "We cannot understand logically even the modes of being of the Persons, for they are beyond logic. For this reason theology as experience is beyond philosophy and philosophy cannot give an answer."[48] These considerations are crucial to understanding the Cappadocians' conception.

4.II. PATRISTIC ORIGINS OF THE ORTHODOX VIEW OF PERSONHOOD

4.ii.a Personhood and monism

Zizioulas provides a broad background to the difficulties the Cappadocians faced with regard to the word person, showing how ancient Graeco-Roman cosmology influenced the prevailing understanding of personhood in the 4th century, when the Trinitarian debates were raging – and how these Fathers rose above these categories in their endeavour to show, firstly, how the Trinity could be simultaneously one and three, and, secondly, the absolute ontological independence of God from the world, in line with the biblical faith in a transcendent Creator who is the cause of existence.

The problem was twofold: First, Greek ontology was fundamentally monistic: the being of God and the being of the world

---

[45] To identify dogma with the truth itself would be regarded as a Eunomian conception of truth.

[46] *Ibid* 199; 204; see also Athanasius, *Letter to Serapion* 17 in Khaled Anatolios, *op.cit*, 217

[47] *Ibid* 181

[48] *Ibid* 144; see also p. 165

formed an unbreakable unity.[49] By contrast, the biblical faith proclaimed that God was free of the world, a transcendent Other who created the world *ex nihilo*. Plato's (c. 428 – c. 347 B.C.), "creator" did not satisfy, as he simply crafted pre-existing matter, which limited divine freedom.[50] So the Cappadocians had to conceptualise an ontology that avoided Greek philosophical monism (and the "gulf" between God and the world taught by the Gnostics).[51] Second, in Platonic thought "the person as a concept is ontologically impossible because the soul, which ensures man's continuity, is not united permanently to the concrete, individual man".[52] Through a process of reincarnation it can be united to other concrete bodies, which in Plato's thought was the only means by which the soul could be individuated as a distinct personality (all souls are created alike).[53] With Aristotle, "the person proves to be a *logically* impossible concept precisely because the soul is indissolubly united with the concrete and 'individual'," which is dissolved at death.[54]

Thus in both models the human person has no enduring identity beyond biological existence. Personhood is effectively a function of biological existence. Zizioulas relates the ancient Greeks' inability to endow human individuality with permanence and ontology to the philosophical principle that "whatever exists is essen-

---

[49] John Zizioulas, *Being as Communion*, 16; c.f. Allen & Springsted, *op.cit*, xv; 58 and Fr Romanides in Hierotheos (Vlachos) (*The Person in the Orthodox Tradition*, 29), who writes that, according to the ancient philosophers, "creation is either a natural emanation of the essence of the one (pantheism) or a seeming or even fallen reflection of an unbegotten real world of basic ideas (idealism) or an indissoluble union of form and matter, according to which matter is the principle of multiplication of form, but without independent existence and without beginning (Aristotle)." This is typified by Aristotle's (384–322 B.C.) conception, in which the first cause or prime/unmoved mover was the most exalted being *in* the universe and Plotinus's One as the top story of reality – see Maurice Wiles, *op.cit*, 47

[50] John Zizioulas, *Being as Communion*, 16; see also Allen & Springsted, *op.cit*, 3ff; Hierotheos S Vlachos, *The Person in the Orthodox Tradition*, 32–33

[51] John Zizioulas, *Being as Communion*, 16

[52] *Ibid* 28

[53] *Ibid*; Zizioulas cites *Timaeus*, 41 D f, *Phaedo*, 249B & *Republic*, 618A

[54] *Ibid*

tially one and its 'reason' is 'common' for all those who are 'awake'".[55] Thus, Zizioulas continues, differentiation or accidence was seen as a tendency towards non-being, a deterioration or fall from being. Even the One was bound by this ontological monism, which was the basis from which the ancient Greeks, no matter the diversity of their interpretation of this schema, explained the harmony in the universe.[56] Zizioulas argues that "[...] in such a world it is impossible for the unforeseen to happen or for freedom to operate as an absolute and unrestricted claim to existence: whatever threatens cosmic harmony and is not explained by 'reason' (*logos*), which draws all things together and leads them to this harmony and unity, is rejected and condemned."[57]

In short, the many are subordinated to the One and exist for the sake of the One; the human being's value relates only to his or her usefulness to the whole. Against this backdrop, in ancient Greece the word person, which originally meant "the part of the head below the cranium" (i.e. where the eyes are situated), came to be identified with the mask used in the theatre – the arena in which "the conflicts between human freedom and the rational necessity of a unified and rational world [...] are worked out in dramatic form".[58] It is here that "man strives to become a 'person', to rise up against this harmonious unity which oppresses him as a moral necessity", but is ultimately punished for his *hubris*, confirming that "the world does not exist for the sake of man, but man exists for its sake", as Plato's Laws pronounced.[59]

---

[55] Heraclitus, *Frs.*, 89; 73 in *ibid* 29

[56] See also Allen & Springsted, *op.cit*, xvi

[57] John Zizioulas, *Being as Communion*, 30–31; for example, in Plato's *Timaeus* the individual is considered virtuous when they mirror in microcosm the virtues (i.e. human excellence) of the ideal, rationally organised city-state, which in turn is a reflection of an ordered natural world, which is in turn ordered as a copy of the world of eternal Forms – see Allen & Springsted, *op.cit*, 2–3; for the Neoplatonic version of this principle, see pp. 50–54

[58] *Ibid* 31–32 (The Sabellians used the word *prosopon* in this sense – see Hierotheos (Vlachos), *The Person in the Orthodox Tradition*, 68; 192)

[59] *Ibid* 32

Personhood here is nothing but a mask, with no relation to true *hypostasis*. But at the same time, because of the mask the actor has acquired a certain freedom to be himself, to be a true (free) identity, which is forbidden by the rational, moral harmony of his universe. Thus the mask is related to the person, but the relationship is tragic; to be a person meant having to add something to one's being. The person is not seen as a true *hypostasis*, which at this stage means "nature" or "substance".[60]

The ancient Roman word *persona* leaned more heavily than its Greek equivalent towards the idea of concrete individuality, but in its sociological and later legal use it maintained the theatrical sense of "role" – one's social role or legal relationships. Zizioulas relates this notion of the person to the Roman organisational and social mindset, which was not concerned with the ontology of the person, but with man's relationships. Thus, as in ancient Greece, as a role player, one's freedom is subordinated to the state, but this role-playing also provides an opportunity to be affirmed and thus taste the freedom of personal identity.[61]

Thus both the Greek *prosopon* and Roman *persona* implied a certain personal dimension, but the cosmological framework did not allow this dimension to be justified ontologically. As Zizioulas says: "*Prosopon* and *persona* remained pointers towards the person. But they *consciously* – and this is precisely what was demanded by the cosmological framework of a self-authenticating cosmic or state harmony – constituted a reminder that this personal dimension is not and *ought* never to be identical with the essence of things, with the true being of man".[62] (italics in original)

4.ii.b. The monarchy of the Father

Against this background we begin to appreciate the achievement of the Cappadocians, outlined in 1.iv.b above, with respect to giving the concept of personhood an ontological basis by joining the word "*hypostasis*" (in the sense of subsistence) to the word "person"

---

[60] *Ibid*
[61] *Ibid* 34–35
[62] *Ibid* 35

to denote the fact that personhood is an ontological reality – that is, uniting "the person with the being of man, with his permanent, enduring existence, with his genuine and absolute identity".[63] This constituted a revolution in Greek thought, Zizioulas says,[64] although it also caused a great deal of confusion during the Trinitarian disputes of the 4th century, because *hypostasis* had been used as a synonym for *ousia* at Nicaea I, while the word person was associated with Modalism.[65] But the positive significance of identifying *Hypostasis* with Person is that, firstly, "the person is no longer an adjunct to being, a category which we add to a concrete entity once we have established its ontological *hypostasis*. It is itself the *hypostasis* of being".[66] Second, being is not an absolute category in itself; it is the person that constitutes being, "that is, enables entities to be entities".[67]

In this way the Fathers demonstrated, in line with the creation *ex nihilo* doctrine, that the world was not ontologically necessary but was rather the product of the (personal) freedom of God. But, more importantly, the being of God was also identified with the Person; that is, the *hypostasis* of the Father is the ontological principle or the cause of the being and life of God.[68] Thus:

---

[63] John Zizioulas, *Being as Communion*, 35

[64] *Ibid* 36

[65] Hierotheos (Vlachos), *The Person in the Orthodox Tradition*, 193–194. John Zizioulas (*Being as Communion*, 37) adds that Tertullian's use of the word person in – *una substantia, tres personae* (in *Against Praxeas*, 11–12) did not meet with the approval of the East because the term person had not yet acquired ontological content and led towards Sabellianism. Basil later remarked that those who identify *hypostasis* with substance and fall back on using the word *prosopa* "fall into the Sabellian evil" (*Ep.* 236,6). Anthony Meredith (*op.cit*, 104) seems to miss the fact that Athanasius used *hypostasis* as a synonym for *ousia* when he asserts that the saint was indifferent to whether one said there was one *ousia* and three *hypostases* or one *ousia*, one *hypostasis*. He seems to think the saint used *"hypostasis"* to mean "person".

[66] John Zizioulas, *Being as Communion*, 39

[67] *Ibid*

[68] *Ibid* 39–40

By usurping the ontological character of *ousia*, the word per-
son/*hypostasis* became capable of signifying God's being in an
ultimate sense [...] the final assertion of ontology in God has to
be attached not to the unique *ousia* of God but to the Father,
that is, to a *hypostasis* or person.[69]

From here Zizioulas' argumentation is angled to address the
idea that the substance precedes the Persons in the Western conception of the Trinity, which seems to be a misconception.[70] I will
not repeat what has already been said on this issue, but I would like
to note the emphasis Zizioulas places on freedom. That is, God –
as essentially personal being – is absolutely free from any ontological necessity; God exists as a Trinity because the Father exists *hypostatically* (as Person) and perpetually confirms His free will to exist
by eternally constituting the Trinitarian existence by bringing forth
the Son and the Spirit.[71] Thus, *contra* O'Collins' assertion that the
person cannot precede relationality, the Orthodox assert that the
Person of the Father, as the originator of the communion and the
cause of the other two Persons, is the cause of being itself; He precedes relationality (ontologically, not temporally) and even being,
because, in Orthodox thought, being *is* communion and He is the
cause of the communion. Zizioulas summarises it as follows:

[...] the ultimate ontological category which makes something
really *be* is neither an impersonal and incommunicable "substance" nor a structure of communion existing by itself or imposed by necessity, but rather the *person*. The fact that God
owes His existence to the Father, that is, to a person, means (a)
that His "substance", His being, does not constrain Him (God

---

[69] *Ibid* 88
[70] Although it remains true, as we shall see and as John Zizioulas (*Being as Communion*, 40) says, that the West emphasises the one substance of
God as the principle of unity in God, this does not necessarily imply the
Greek monistic principle that God is first (ontologically) being and then
Trinity; the fact that the West also identifies the One God with the Father
means that the difficulty is more subtle than that.
[71] *Ibid* 40–41

does not exist because He cannot but exist), and (b) that communion is not a constraining structure for His existence (God is not in communion, does not love, because He cannot but be in communion and love). The fact that God exists because of the Father shows that His existence, His being, is the consequence of a free Person; which means, in the last analysis, that not only communion but also *freedom*, the free person, constitutes true being. True being comes only from the free person, from the person who loves freely – that is, who freely affirms His being, His identity, by means of an event of communion with other persons.[72] (Italics in original)

Thus personhood in God is not a function of having particular natural attributes (as in the Thomist description of the human person): the Father, who is ontologically prior as the cause of the Trinitarian communion, is pure subjectivity. It follows that for the nature (communion) to be, the Son and Spirit must also be ontologically prior to the common nature, because the communion is a function of Divine Personhood, and not vice versa. Thus O'Collins' statement that "the divine unity will be recognised only after the distinct and separate constitution of the three persons" (see 2.iv above) is correct, if one leaves out the "separate" and understands that Person means pure, incorporeal Subjectivity and not, as in Western thought, merely a "distinct subsistent" that is individuated by having its own rational nature – i.e. its own mind.

Also, his description of "person-constituting" relations sounds decidedly odd in light of this Eastern view of divine personhood. And when Zizioulas says the Divine Person is free of necessity, it has nothing to do with autonomy – an equation O'Collins[73] seems to make; he is saying a Person is not constrained by nature to be what He is.

In short, with their ontology of divine personhood the Cappadocians coined the language to affirm that the cause of created being is the Person of the Father, not a transcendent, rational Be-

---

[72] *Ibid* 17–18
[73] *Op.cit*, 177–178

ing from which creation automatically emanates. We know this because the Only Begotten, who subsists in an eternal communion in and with the Father, revealed it historically and calls us to share in this relationship by adoption, while the Spirit makes this known to us mystically as an interior reality. This brings us to the Eastern notion of truth as communion.

4.ii.c. Truth is the Person in communion

Another important aspect of the Cappadocians' disassociation of the word *hypostasis* from *ousia* and its identification with *prosopon* is that *prosopon* was a relational term. The implication is that "to be" and "to be in relation" are identical, i.e. being in itself (*hypostasis*) and being in relation (being a person). The Cappadocians arrived at this conception by arguing that no nature exists "in the nude" but always has its mode of existence.[74] In terms of the affirmation that Christ is the Truth, this development makes explicit that truth is not located in an ontology of rational being, but in a Person in communion:

> The essential thing about a person lies precisely in his being a revelation of truth, not as "substance" or "nature" but as a "mode of existence". This profound perception of the Cappadocian Fathers shows that true knowledge is not knowledge of the essence or the nature of things, but of how they are connected within the communion event. [...] While *ekstasis* [a communion of ecstatic, divine love] signifies that a person is a revelation of truth by the fact of being in communion, *hypostasis* signifies that in and through his communion a person affirms his own identity and his particularity; he "supports his own nature" in a particular and unique way.[75]

---

[74] For example Basil, *Ep.* 38:2 in John Zizioulas, *Being as Communion*, 88; see also Gregory of Nyssa, *Letter to Ablabius*
[75] John Zizioulas, *Being as Communion*, 106–107

This means that the Holy Trinity is truth as life by virtue of being Persons in communion: "The Holy Trinity is a primordial ontological concept and not a notion which is added to the divine substance, or rather which follows it [...] The substance of God, "God", has no ontological content, no true being, apart from communion," says Zizioulas.[76] Thus in the Trinity "love is the supreme ontological predicate of being"– not simply "raw existence", but rather being as fullness of life.[77] It also means that the Son is truth both eternally and historically by virtue of His eternal communion in the Father and the Spirit:

> When Christ says He is the truth and at the same time the life of the world, He introduces into truth a content carrying ontological implications. If the truth saves the world it is because it is life. The Christological mystery, as declared by the Chalcedonian definition, signifies that salvation as truth and life is possible only in and through a person who is ontologically *true*, i.e. something which creation cannot offer [...] The only way for a *true person* to exist is for being and communion to coincide. The triune God offers in Himself the only possibility for such an identification of being with communion; He is the revelation of true personhood.[78] (Italics in original)

In short, the *Logos* of God is not a divine idea; nor is He the Father's knowledge of Himself except in the sense that He is identical to the Father in essence so as to be His very image and thus the Person in whom the Father discovers His very self "imaged"; the Word is a Person, the one who says "*I* am the *life*, the *truth* and the way" (Jn 14:6):[79]

---

[76] *Ibid* 17
[77] *Ibid* 46
[78] *Ibid* 106–107; c.f. Dumitru Staniloae, *op.cit*, 74–75
[79] *Ibid* 100–101; see also Athanasius, *Contra Arianos*, 1.20–21; Hierotheos (Vlachos), *The Person in the Orthodox Tradition*, 135

"The incarnate Christ is so identical to the ultimate will of God's love that the meaning of created being and the purpose of history are simply the incarnate Christ. […] the incarnate Christ, is the truth because he represents the ultimate, unceasing will of the ecstatic love of God".[80]

This conception of the Truth being a Person is pivotal to our discussion because it encapsulates the central point the Eastern Fathers were making with the Person-*Hypostasis* formula of Constantinople I – a point the Western tradition seems to have wholly missed. This is evident in Edmund Hill's comment in his introduction to his translation of St Augustine's *On the Trinity:*

There was very surely a great danger of the Trinitarian revelation being interpreted by pagan converts in the primitive church as a modification of the stark Judaic monotheism in the direction of at least a philosophical polytheism. My guess is that it was to counter this danger that John introduced his concept of the *Logos* into his Trinitarian theology […] the anthropomorphism lurking in the terms "Father and "Son" needed neutralising by the introduction of impersonal terms.[81]

It is notable that Hill equates "personal" with "anthropomorphic" and thus interprets St John's *Logos* imagery in a diametrically opposed way to the Eastern interpretation, which is, in short, that by building on the experience that being/truth is life and life is communion, the Cappadocians posited an ontology of personhood that enabled them to conceptually reconcile the ancient Greek conception of truth as being with the Christian experience that an historical figure was the truth and therefore also the Hebrew notion of truth, which focused on God's actions in history. The emphasis on a communion of personal love was in direct contradistinction to

---

[80] *Ibid* 98–99, see also Hierotheos (Vlachos), *The Person in the Orthodox Tradition*, 160–161

[81] Edmund Hill, introduction to St Augustine, *The Trinity*, (New York: New York City Press, 2007), 33

the ancient Greek idea that truth as rational being can be apprehended by the mind due to an ontological link between mind and
being; communion implies that the bridge between the transcendent God and created persons is not an automatic Platonic emanation, but reciprocal love between others.[82] It also implies otherness
within the intra-Trinitarian communion – and that the non-
redeemed human being is not ontologically true.

4.ii.d Relationship between human and divine persons

In Orthodox thought, the Incarnate Son is the measure of what
human persons should become, because to be a true person means
to be a person who has eternal life in communion with God (the
Father).[83] As St John says of the Parousia: "We will be like Him
because we will see Him as He is" (1 Jn 3:2). Only in Christ do we
see human personhood perfectly actualised, because His mode of
being was not informed by his human nature, but wholly by His
communion with the Father in the Spirit. Thus one could say He
was a truly human person and therefore the icon of true human
personhood precisely by virtue of being divine. He is conversely
the perfect image of God for us by virtue of the fact that He is a
perfect man – that is, a perfect Person in communion.[84]

It is only in the Person of the Son that the eternal and created
are perfectly united.[85] "Thus," says Zizioulas, "patristic theology
considers the [human] person to be an 'image and likeness of God'.
It is not satisfied with a humanistic interpretation."[86] The *unredeemed*
(or non-deified) human being is not truly a person in the theologi-

---

[82] John Zizioulas, *Being as Communion*, 89–92
[83] Hierotheos (Vlachos), *The Person in the Orthodox Tradition*, 76–78;
135; 146; 213; Anthony Meredith, *op.cit*, 78ff
[84] John Zizioulas, *Being as Communion*, 54ff; Hierotheos (Vlachos), *The
Person in the Orthodox Tradition*, 78; 135; 160–161
[85] Hierotheos (Vlachos), *The Person in the Orthodox Tradition*, 227
[86] John Zizioulas, *Being as Communion*, 50

cal sense, because he or she, in the absence of communion with the triune God, is a biological entity enslaved by nature.[87] Post-modern writers distinguish between a deified and non-deified human being by distinguishing between a person and an individual, i.e. a subject in communion and a biologically constituted "rational animal".[88] So, speaking relatively, the non-redeemed human being is not truly a person. Thus Sophrony Sakharov says:

> God is Person and the man who has communion and union
> with God is a person. [...] Properly a man and a person is one
> who has passed from the image to the likeness. In the teaching
> of the holy Fathers, to be in the image is potentially to be in
> the likeness, and being in the likeness is actually the image. [...]
> ontologically all people can be regarded as persons, and even
> the devil himself is a person, but soteriologically we are not all
> persons, since we have not all attained the likeness.[89]

These soteriological affirmations should be understood against the backdrop of the doctrine of *theosis* (divinisation),[90] in

---

[87] Hierotheos (Vlachos), *The Person in the Orthodox Tradition*, 76; against this backdrop we can see the absurdity of Maurice Wiles' (*op.cit*, 47) statement that "Gregory [of Nyssa] was a thorough-going Platonist [...] Strictly speaking, Gregory says, we should not speak of three men, but of three participants in the one, unique 'idea of man', the single, real 'humanity'." Wiles does not quote his sources, but in is clear from corresponding arguments in Gregory's *Letter to Ablabius* (3ff; c.f. 1 Cor 12:12ff) that his perception was not informed by philosophy but by a mystical perspective in which humanity is viewed as a likeness of the Trinity. As the Divine Persons are consubstantial, so the mystic perceives the real consubstantiality of "man", who is made in the image of God. In the same letter Gregory reiterates several times that it is due to an "erroneous habit" that we speak of individuals as if they have separate natures. When he uses the expression "idea of man" he is referring to the *false* conception of humankind as many separated natures – a notion that he regards as "a customary abuse of language" (see n5).

[88] *Ibid* 79

[89] In *His Life is Mine* in *ibid* 80–81; see also pp. 96–97; 130–131; 148ff

[90] See for example St Basil, *De Spiritu Sancto* 23

terms of which human beings are called to participation in the life of God to become by adoption what the Son is in eternity,[91] as we have already seen in the thought of Irenaeus and Athanasius.

As Basil also says: "The dispensation of our God and Saviour concerning man is a recall from the fall and a return from the alienation caused by disobedience to close communion with God".[92] But the human person can only become like a Divine Person in a qualified sense because the Divine Persons are uncreated, while we will always be creatures.[93]

Zizioulas adds that it was due to this awareness that, in the "primitive" Church, human relationships were redefined in relation to God (our Father), the Church (our Mother – in which a rebirth takes place through baptism) and our brethren in Christ. Thus our relations are no longer defined by natural, biological origin but by the transcendent relation of communion in (the Body of) Christ; love of others is no longer a duty linked to biological relations, laws or necessity.[94]

In this transcendent, eschatological sense, as an "ecclesial *hypostasis*", as Zizioulas calls it,[95] the human person can be said to constitute his/her own nature, not as a biological entity (which is a given), but as a relational being. This is why the ascetic seeks to become free of his or her enslavement to biological necessity in cooperation with the triune God and so achieve the likeness and true image of God – i.e. enter into "the freedom of the sons of God" – and actualise true personhood born of divine grace in communion with the Trinity.[96] This is not a dualistic denial of the biological nature of human existence, but a denial of the biological *hypostasis* – i.e. to have one's mode of being determined by nature.[97]

[91] John Zizioulas, *Being as Communion*, 49–50

[92] *De Spiritu Sancto* 35

[93] Hierotheos (Vlachos), *The Person in the Orthodox Tradition*, 215

[94] John Zizioulas, *Being as Communion*, 56–59; 63

[95] *Ibid* 57ff

[96] *Ibid* 49–53; see also Hierotheos (Vlachos), *The Person in the Orthodox Tradition*, 86ff; 152; 213; c.f. John Meyendorff, *Byzantine Theology* 9–10

[97] John Zizioulas, *Being as Communion*, 63

4.III. SUMMARY

In short, the Cappadocians' conception is not premised on logical deduction or philosophical presuppositions, but on mystical experience. Thus the basis of the Eastern truth claim is that the distinct Persons are mystically recognised in direct encounters with the Persons in their self-manifestations, that they are ineffable and thus cannot be explained logically. There are several implications for our discussion:

First, the Eastern conception of the Person is a mystical-theological one relating to the Divine Persons that should not be read as a conception of either philosophical or anthropological truth. Second, the assumption that the Fathers had the same mystical experience as the Apostles and therefore share the same doctrinal authority as the Apostles means the Orthodox will reject logical arguments that are not premised on direct historical-mystical experience.

I have also stressed the Fathers' keen sense of the inexpressible, incomprehensible mystery of God and the otherness of the reality of God in contradistinction to creaturely realities. Their awareness of the inability of the human mind to conceive and human language to express infinite, incorporeal reality meant they used creaturely terminology illustratively and relatively to indicate that which is beyond words. This means their exposition is finely nuanced and can be easily misunderstood if not examined both in detail and in relation to the whole.

It is also important to examine their thought in relation to their polemical situation. We noted briefly the specific heresies they faced and how this influenced their choice of language. Polemically, they tended to use the language of their opponents and imbue it with new meaning. This means that one cannot assume that they used philosophical terms in the same way the ancients or their predecessors used them or that the use of such terminology implies that their thought was influenced by others who used such terminology.[98] The Cappadocians gave the word Person ontological con-

---

[98] As Anthony Meredith (*op.cit*) does; he assumes Platonic asceticism was an important influence on the Cappadocians' asceticism (p. 12), he links St Basil's communal monastic rule to the Pythagoreans of South

tent by joining it to the word *hypostasis* in order to coin the language needed to describe a personal God who is Creator and also three personal Subjects, that is, to accommodate Judeo-Christian revelation. They thereby conveyed, against both Sabellianism and the Greek view that personhood is an adjunct to being, (a) that the Divine Persons had ontological status and (b) affirmed the biblical, personal otherness of God the Father in contradistinction to the Greek monistic view of being and the world.

They thus established that the Father is the personal yet transcendent cause of being, who constitutes the Trinitarian existence as communion of love. It is unlikely that the West would have any difficulty with these assertions about the monarchy of the Father. But when one ascribes this conception of the Person to the other two Persons, there appears to be a fear in the West that this implies Tritheism – particularly if the definition of being a Person implies freedom, which to the Western mind seems to denote three wills in the Trinity.

I have also shown how the Fathers married their existential experience of truth and life as communion and their concept of Persons-*Hypostases* to arrive at the notion that Truth is the Person in communion, thereby giving conceptual content to the awareness that Christ is the truth in actuality, as against the rational *Logos* approach. By implication, Christ is both the revelation of Divine Personhood and the measure of what human persons should be. Thus the non-deified human person is not truly a person; true personhood can only be actualised in communion with the triune God. Post-modern Orthodox theologians distinguish these two states by using the word person for the deified human being and individual for the non-redeemed human being.

Italy (pp. 25–27), his sense of the social nature of the human being to Stoicism (p. 29) and his emphasis on the incomprehensibility of God's nature to Arius' assertion that the nature of the Father is incomprehensible, as well as to Plato (p. 22). In my view, the assumption that each strain of thought can be reduced to the influence of the ideas of other thinkers implies a denial that the Fathers' thought was a product of genuine experience of God.

5 THE INDIVISIBLE TRINITY

In this chapter I shall attempt to make explicit the Orthodox conception of the Trinity in relation to some Western concerns about elements of the Orthodox position. I shall angle this discussion on the problematic term "self-consciousness" as it seems key to the misconception that the Orthodox denote three individuals with a separate nature, mind and will in God.

5.1. THREE SELF-CONSCIOUS PERSONS?

O'Collins asserts that three self-conscious persons in the Trinity would compromise the oneness of God because "the divine unity will be recognised only after the distinct and separate constitution of the three persons."[1] Zizioulas also has qualms about applying the term "self" to the Divine Persons (although the Fathers used the term), because of its association with the individual and all that this denotes in Western thought.[2]

And Hierotheos doesn't like "consciousness" because of its association with the psychological and metaphysical conception of the human person, whose chief characteristics are considered to be consciousness, self-knowledge and reasoning abilities,[3] and with the psychological model of the Trinity proposed by Augustine, "who tried to interpret the dogma of the Trinity within Platonic anthropology. Using psychological interpretations, that is to say, starting from man, he characterised God as *nous*".[4]

Here we come up against the problems of language again; the fact is that any word one uses carries with it baggage from creature-

---

[1] Gerald O'Collins, *op.cit*, 178
[2] John Zizioulas, *Being as Communion*, 105–106
[3] *The Person in the Orthodox Tradition*, 118–119; 130–132; 150
[4] *Ibid* 131

ly associations; for the West the word person also has associations that militate against applying it properly to the Father, Son and Spirit. It is all a matter of how a word is used and what these writers are attempting to indicate. Orthodox thinkers who are true to patristic thought and yet apply terms such as "consciousness" and "self-consciousness" to the Divine Persons do not use it in the way that Augustine did: (a) they do not posit only one Self in God and (b) they use available post-modern language *illustratively* and *relatively*, as the Fathers did, to make the patristic Orthodox perspective accessible to the post-modern mind.

The reality is that, as real Persons, the Divine Persons cannot be unconscious but should rather be understood to be conscious in a superlative sense. With this in mind, I think such language is useful provided, as Hierotheos emphasises, that one (a) properly qualifies one's meaning to bring out the difference between personhood in God and personhood as we experience it in our creaturely mode of being,[5] and (b) to always bear in mind that the Orthodox conception was worked out with respect to the Divine Persons, not human persons.

Against the backdrop of Orthodox Trinitarian theology as a whole, I think one can safely assume that Eastern theologians who use the term "self-consciousness" do not intend to indicate Aristotelian individuality in the Divine Persons; their conception has to be understood in the context of a perception of being, personhood and relationality that transcends anything found in creaturely reality. With this in mind I shall use terms such as Person, Self, an "I" a "Subjectivity" or "personal Subject" with reference to the Divine Persons, with the understanding that in the context of Eastern Trinitarian theology these terms denote a transcendent meaning to that understood with reference to human personhood. Another point to take into consideration is that different Orthodox thinkers, in emphasising different aspects of the Orthodox conception, sometimes seem to contradict one another. So if one takes one

---

[5] *Ibid* 207; 212; St Gregory of Nyssa does this consistently in his *Letter to Ablabius*, constantly drawing parallels between divine and human personhood and then making distinctions.

emphasis as the whole picture this will also lead to misunderstanding. For example Zizioulas says the divine nature is communion; Lossky says the Persons are the nature. Each theologian is bringing out a different aspect of the fundamental idea that the Trinity is three Persons in perfect communion; the Persons and common nature are therefore indivisible. Thus both statements accurately represent different aspects of the same conception. I shall attempt to unpack the whole picture here, which is not easy because each piece of the puzzle requires understanding it within the context of the whole. I shall try to build up the picture one piece at a time.

5.II. THE MEANING OF PERSONHOOD

Our very first difficulty lies in getting at what the Orthodox actually mean by "Person". While arguing that the Person is an ontological reality, the Orthodox will simultaneously say *theologically* and *apophatically* that the Person cannot be defined. The person, this unrepeatable identity, to paraphrase Lossky,[6] cannot be identified with nature or any natural attributes or qualities that are shared with others by nature, but transcends it. It eludes every definition. It is the unique, wholly other that cannot be conceptualised; it can only be recognised. Thus Hierotheos says: "No one can define the person philosophically, but it is an object of revelation. And this revelation happens in the heart."[7] Personhood is thus a subjectively known truth/reality that cannot be apprehended or defined objectively; the eternal, subjective "I am" can be identified only subjectively by another I; there is a correlation between the form of knowing and the subject known.

By implication, from an Eastern perspective, philosophy, which is by nature "objective" and abstract, is not a suitable tool for uncovering the reality of God. This is extremely important, because I suspect that the brevity of the Eastern Fathers' communication of their position to the West following Constantinople I can be attributed to an assumption that the Western brethren would

---

[6] *Op.cit*, 42–43
[7] Hierotheos (Vlachos), *The Person in the Orthodox Tradition*, 86; see also pp. 93ff

recognise as self-evident what was meant by the person-*hypostasis* terminology because it was merely an articulation of "the true faith", "the ancient faith", "the faith of our baptism"[8] that was known experientially. A common experience would have been assumed. This assumption could well have been the cause of Photius' disbelief that the *filioque* originated with such an esteemed saint as Augustine,[9] because his reputation would have led the Eastern Church to believe he was a mystic who enjoyed the same perception as the Eastern saints.

Simply put, there is no creaturely terminology to make the meaning of divine personhood accessible. If one were to be absolutely true to the *apophatic* approach, as Hierotheos is, one would not be able to say anything at all to make the patristic perception of the Person accessible to the Western mind. So, if I may, I shall use a qualified creaturely analogy to illustrate how I understand what the Orthodox mean: The ineffable person is known in both human and divine persons by recognition, the former empathetically and the latter mystically.

The human person is that distinctive "you" that is recognisable as distinctly, incommunicably him- or herself; if you look into a baby's eyes you will recognise a distinct "you-ness" (whatever you name the child) that cannot be ascribed to another baby; if you meet twins who are identical in every aspect of nature, mannerisms, way of speaking, character traits, style of dress, activities, etc., you might confuse them at first; but once you get to know them you see past the natural and learn to recognise the essential, unique "I" that is exclusive to that one – so even if you meet them separately, you will know which unique person is before you. Or let us say you meet, say, Harry, as a child and then 60 years later, when age has radically changed his nature, you will still recognise that distinctive, ineffable person you know as Harry, more mature and perhaps even radically changed in character and personality, but still essentially unchanged in *who* he is. It is the distinctive other who is no longer looking back at you when he or she has passed on.

---

[8] *Synod of Constantinople A.D 382: Synodical Letter*
[9] *Myst.* 72–73

That, I believe, is what the Orthodox label "person" when they make a distinction between "person" and "individual" as the words are used today because, philosophically, the term "individual" encompasses the created nature as well. However, while human persons are biologically constituted and in a state of becoming true persons, the Divine Persons are incorporeal, eternal and wholly communion, that is, their being is their communion.[10] This point is fundamental to the Orthodox perspective. This reality is subjectively recognised in mystical experience, but cannot be objectified or explained logically. Therefore this assertion is made in conscious defiance of logic. It falls under the category of testimony.

Thus, just as the three Persons share an ineffable common nature that is not some spiritual substance, but an incomprehensible essence that we recognise and describe in terms of the divine attributes, or "essential energies", as Hierotheos calls them,[11] such as love, holiness, intelligence, freedom, peace, eternity, etc.,[12] a point on which East and West agree,[13] so in Orthodox thought, the Persons are recognised as unique, subjective *hypostases* (a) historically in their diverse functions in the economy and (b) mystically because the common energies are expressed in unique *hypostatic* ways.

In terms of the Persons' unique roles in history, the Three share one goal – to unite humankind to the Father in love. Thus the Father remains transcendent that we might be raised up to Him, the Son (the eternal image) becomes for us the incarnate image of the Father and the Spirit becomes a subjective presence in

---

[10] John Zizioulas, *Being as Communion*, 107–108; Hierotheos and Zizioulas agree that Heidigger's *"da sein"*, translated variously by his students, comes close to the Orthodox sense of personhood as being if it is translated as "being present" in contradistinction to *"sein"* (raw being), because it gives priority to existence "with others and thus approaches the sense of being as communion. Hierotheos argues that *da sein* would best be translated as *hypostasis*, with the sense of existence as presence – see Hierotheos (Vlachos), *The Person in the Orthodox Tradition*, 121–125.

[11] Hierotheos (Vlachos), *The Person in the Orthodox Tradition*, 218–219; see also Gregory of Nyssa, *Letter to Ablabius* 6

[12] Vladimir Lossky, *op.cit*, 43; Gerald O'Collins, *op.cit*, 119; 148; Hierotheos (Vlachos), *The Person in the Orthodox Tradition*, 204; 218

[13] See for example Richard Cross, *op.cit*, 470

our subjectivity, making present for us the Father and the Son, thus dehistoricising Christ (as truth) and bringing us into relationship with the Father through Christ (as life).[14] The Spirit is thus the Spirit of *Truth* and *Life* because He binds creatures to the Father and Son as communion.[15] In short, each one acts according to the common will with respect to creatures, but in differing *hypostatic* ways or modes, indicating three distinct Persons.[16] Sophrony Sakharov provides a post-modern example of mystical experience in which one recognises the subjectivity of each Person:

> The light that appears in man when he believes in Christ testifies to His Divinity. Our spirit accepts the Lord Jesus as immutable Truth, authentically Holy. And this eternal Light begets testimony within us identical with the teaching of Christ. In this Light we contemplate the Father. We apprehend this Light as the Holy Spirit. In it we see Christ as the only-begotten Son of the Father. In it we perceive the Oneness of the Three. Praying to this God, we live (sic) the One being of the three Persons. But we apprehend and relate to this Oneness variously: I approach the Father in one fashion; I pray otherwise to the Holy Spirit; I turn to Christ in a different manner. An especial spiritual feeling is associated with each that in no way detracts from their Oneness of being, with each *Hypostasis* of

---

[14] Dumitru Staniloae, *op.cit*, 75; John Zizioulas, *Being as Communion*, 129–130

[15] Dumitru Staniloae, *op.cit*, 97; see also Basil, *De Spiritu Sancto*, 47; 64

[16] John Zizioulas, *Being as Communion*, 110–113; it is against this backdrop that one needs to assess the validity of Rahner's argument, cited above, against "the false opinion that what is meant by 'person', especially within the doctrine of the Trinity, is clearly evident". Rahner's objection is that this idea poses logical difficulties, but the Orthodox are merely coining the terminology to express what they know experientially; logic is not their criterion of truth.

the Holy Trinity we have to a certain extent a different relationship.[17]

Sophrony perceives the common essence and particularity of
each Person, but also speaks of having a relationship with each
one; one can only enter into relationship with a subjective entity,
which implies each One is subjective. The Orthodox argue that
three distinct Subjects can be recognised by the fact that the essential energies or attributes are *enhypostatic;* that is, they are expressed
through the Persons and the essence is seen through the particular
hypostatic qualities.[18]

So, for example, there is one love (the primary ontological attribute of the essence), but we experience that the Father loves in a
paternal way, the Son in a filial way and the Spirit in His particular
way, which is less easily defined because the Spirit is known as the
One who reveals and shares His mode of loving the Father and
Son *in* us rather than as an object of perception.

But the fundamental point is that each person is distinguished
as a unique Subject because we can distinguish each Person's
unique way of loving, which indicates His unique identify. But as
these are expressions of the personal being of each One rather than
the inner core of the Person Himself, this remains an objective description of the Persons – of their energies or self-manifestation;
we are not able to penetrate conceptually the subjective Selves who
are manifest in these energies. We might come face to face with the
Son in a mystical apparition, for example, but no mystic has ever
been able to describe the "who" that they encountered; they can
only describe His holiness, His love, His beauty... in short, the
attributes He shares with the other two Persons by virtue of the
common essence – and add that He manifests Himself Son.

Nor can one logically explain how the Persons are constituted
as subjective entities without being individuals because this is
above human conceptual categories. Still, the question remains:

---

[17] From *We shall See Him as He is* in Hierotheos (Vlachos), *The Person
in the Orthodox Tradition*, 95
[18] Hierotheos (Vlachos), *The Person in the Orthodox Tradition*, 218–219

how can one know that what one perceives is three subjective Persons rather than one subjective consciousness experienced in a threefold way? Here one can argue logically that it would be difficult to speak of the triune God as love unless there were three Subjectivities in the Trinity.

5.III. THE PARADIGM OF LOVE

We know from human experience that we cannot speak of love unless there is at very least a subject who loves and another who is loved. For that love to be realised in relationship, one would need one or more *others* to be in relationship. In human experience, a person whose love is inwardly directed towards oneself would be considered narcissistic. The same would apply to God, as we observed earlier.[19] Also, if there was only one Subjectivity in God, whose love is directed only towards creation, then His love would be contingent and have a beginning, and would therefore not be essential in God.[20] Thus if God is love, eternally and independently of creation, there must be another (or others) who freely receive and reciprocate that love; thus the revelation that God is love implies subjective otherness within the Trinity. As Zizioulas says: "The being of God is relational being: without the concept of communion there would be no way of speaking about the being of God."[21] Thus, *contra* the Western notion that the Divine Persons are relations of origin, the Orthodox make the rather obvious point that there could be no relationality unless there was also a distinct ontological reality to be in relation.[22] Staniloae thus asserts:

> We are aware that the most perfect and most meaningful unity is unity in love, that is, unity between persons who retain their own individual identities. Any other unity is devoid of meaning

---

[19] See also Hilarion Alfeyev, *op.cit*, 37; Dumitru Staniloae, *op.cit*, 77

[20] Dumitru Staniloae, *op.cit*, 79

[21] John Zizioulas, *Being as Communion*, 17; see also Hilarion Alfeyev, *op.cit*, 38

[22] John Zizioulas, *Being as Communion*, 88

and spiritual life. Hence the expressions "one in being" and "three Persons" must not lead us to contemplate the divine being in itself as distinct from the Persons and from their mutual love, but rather as the love existing in Persons and between Persons.[23]

This would be impossible if each Person did not have consciousness. Thus, while both traditions agree that that which is common to all three Persons belongs to the nature, which would include consciousness, the question, I think, is: how can each Person share the common consciousness unless each Person is a subjective "I"? The alternative – that one Subject experiences Himself in a threefold way – would be a form of Modalism. In order to preserve the revelation of three Divine Persons or "Subjectivities" who are equally love, it is therefore imperative to show that the Three have self-awareness. In fact, many Orthodox seem to identify divine personhood in this way. For example, Pomazansky says:

"Because God in His very Essence is wholly consciousness and thought and self-awareness, each of these three eternal manifestations of Himself by the one God has self-awareness, and therefore each one is a Person. And these Persons are not simply forms or isolated manifestations or attributes or activities; rather, the Three Persons are contained in the very Unity of God's essence."[24]

In his *Letter to Ablabius*, Gregory of Nyssa uses a similar argument, arguing from the economy, to affirm that one nature is operational in three distinct Persons. He posits that while the operation of seeing or beholding (all things) belongs to the one nature, "Scripture attributes the act of seeing equally to the Father, Son and Holy Spirit". Does this necessarily mean three minds in God

---

[23] Dumitru Staniloae, *op.cit*, 76; see also John Zizioulas, *Being as Communion*, 18

[24] Michael Pomazansky, *op.cit*, 75

and therefore three individuals, as O'Collins claims? If this were true, this would be tritheism, as he adds.

However, in Orthodox thought the form of relationality in God precludes individuality on the level of "mindedness" because the communion of the Divine Persons and relations between human individuals are fundamentally different.

5.IV. THREE MINDS?

Easterners who describe the Divine Persons as self-conscious do not mean it in the same way that human beings experience self-consciousness, which affirms the human person as a separate, individual entity. One has to bear in mind that when the Orthodox borrow from creaturely terminology, they are thinking of the human person *theologically* as the image and likeness of a Divine Person in communion, not in Aristotelian terms. This is clear in Hierotheos' précis of Christo Yannaris' philosophical-theological description of the human person, in which he uses creaturely self-awareness illustratively as his starting point:

> We all understand that what differentiates personal existence from every other form of existence is self-consciousness and otherness. We call the awareness of our own existence "self-consciousness, the certainty I have that I exist and that it is I who exist, a being with identity, an identity which differentiates me from every other being. And this differentiation is an absolute otherness, a unique, distinct and unrepeatable character which defines my existence". But since this self-knowledge and otherness are not products of thought but of many factors which are being investigated by contemporary psychology as well, therefore the way in which the ego is formed and matures "is nothing other than the relationship, reference. It is the potential that constitutes man, the potential to be opposite someone or something, to have one's face-toward someone or something, to be a 'person' (pros-opon)". Thus "we use the

word person to define a relational reality. The person is defined as a reference and relationship and it defines a reference
and a relationship".[25]

The underlying theology is basically what we discussed in the
previous chapter. But notice how Yannaris uses "self-
consciousness": it is simply "awareness of our own existence" and
is related to a "relationship of reference [...] to have one's face to-
ward someone or something, to be a person" – i.e. a being in
communion. As an image of Divine Personhood, this description
indicates that the Divine Persons' self-awareness should not be
understood as an inward-looking sense of self in opposition to others, but as consciousness that is wholly immersed in the other two
as a consciousness of the others, as Staniloae affirms:

> Each divine "I" puts a "Thou" in place of Himself. Each sees
> Himself only in relation to the other two. The Father sees
> Himself only as the subject of the Son's love, forgetting Him-
> self in every other aspect [...] But the "I" of the Father is not
> lost because of this, for it is affirmed by the Son who in His
> turn knows Himself and loves Himself only as He who loves
> the Father. [...] They are three, yet each regards only the oth-
> ers and experiences only the others.[26]

Nor is this self-awareness a product of thought as in the Cartesian "I think therefore I am". Perhaps comparison with a fundamental tenet of Kantian epistemology will be helpful here: according to Cooper, Kant points out that our self-awareness is a result of
perceiving other objects passing before us in time – i.e. we are
aware of ourselves as spatio-temporal beings-in-relation prior to

---

[25] *The Person and Eros* (Athens: 1976), 19 in Hierotheos (Vlachos), *The Person in the Orthodox Tradition*, 82–83
[26] Dumitru Staniloae, *op.cit*, 88

cognitive processes.[27] By contrast, the Orthodox do not speak of time, space or objects in the Trinity, but of an eternal awareness of the other Two as two inter-subjectivities within His own subjectivity. Thus Staniloae says:

> God is pure subject. But the character of being a pure subject is experienced only by one who in no way experiences himself as object of the other, or who does not experience the other as he experiences himself, that is, as his own object. Otherwise this would create a certain opposition between subjects, and every "I" would also experience himself as the object of the other. The divine "I", as pure subject, must be experienced as such by another divine "I" and must also experience the other divine "I" as pure subject. [28]

---

[27] D.E. Cooper, *World Philosophies, An Historical Introduction* (Oxford & Cambridge: Blackwell, 2003), 342

[28] Dumitru Staniloae, *op.cit*, 76; this distinction between subject and object throws light, I believe, on Gregory of Nyssa's concept of divine darkness. Steenberg (*op.cit*) quotes a verse from *Gregory's Commentary on the Canticle of Canticles*: "Moses' vision of God began with light; afterwards God spoke to him in a cloud. But when Moses rose higher and became more perfect, he saw God in darkness." Earlier we cited examples of visions of God as light; this would be consistent with the first stage of Moses' journey, which we observed is actually an apparition of the triune God in the glorified Christ, i.e. an accommodation to creaturely perceptual needs: one first perceives God as an *object* of perception. But if one considers the incorporeality and pure *subjectivity* of the Divine Persons, a deeper experience of the triune God would properly entail no visual content but rather be an experience of pure *subjective* communion. It is a darkness that is full of sublime content. By contrast, Anthony Meredith (*op.cit*, 70ff), reading Gregory's *Life of Moses* through the lens of the Western mindset, interprets this concept in Gregory as referring to the darkness of faith, or "conviction", as he puts it. Moreover, he interprets Gregory's allegorical account of Moses' spiritual ascent as a progression of *ideas* and moral virtue rather than as a progression in relationship with God.

It is this superlative sense of consciousness that some post-modern Orthodox thinkers wish to emphasise with respect to the Divine Persons, without implying individuality. They would therefore agree with Zizioulas[29] that: "Being a Person is fundamentally different from being an individual or a 'personality', for a person cannot be imagined in himself but only within his relationships."[30] Thus one way of describing a person is as a "subjectivity in relation". The existential description of the person as an "interpersonal centre of consciousness" is probably the closest Western definition of personhood to the Eastern perception of the Divine Persons, except that this expression is used in the West in respect of individuals who first exist independently and then come together in relationship. I think the most important point to emphasise is that, in Eastern thought, the Divine Persons experience relationship in a non-creaturely way, as Hierotheos[31] emphasises. As Basil says:

> For the Father is in the Son and the Son is in the Father; [...] and herein is the unity. So that according to the distinction of Persons, they are one and one; according to the community of Nature, one. [...] in the case of the divine and uncompounded nature, the union consists in the communion of the Godhead. One, moreover, is the Holy Spirit, and we speak of Him singly, conjoined as He is to the one Father through the one Son, and through Himself completing the adorable and blessed Trinity; of Him the intimate relationship to the Father and the Son is sufficiently declared by the fact of His not being ranked in the plurality of the creation, but being spoken of singly; for He is not one of many, but One. [...] He is in such wise united to the Father and to the Son as unit is to unit.[32]

---

[29] *Being as Communion*, 105
[30] See also Hierotheos (Vlachos), *The Person in the Orthodox Tradition*, 158
[31] *Ibid* 99ff
[32] *De Spiritu Sancto*, 45

Or, as Staniloae puts it, "these 'I's' do not encounter one another from the outside, as with human 'I's'. From eternity they are completely interior to one another".[33] Thus while relationship between human individuals is mediated via the created nature, in which two or more separate people act in a certain way to facilitate a relationship, in the Trinity the Persons in communion *are* the nature; there is no division between them, as there is between human individuals.[34] Or, as Staniloae frames it: "Persons are in the first place interior 'I's', non-composite (simple) and indissoluble. They are able to unite in their entirety as interior unities without losing their character as unities."[35] Staniloae spells it out thus:

> The content of the divine "I" must consist not in opposed subjects and objects, but in other subjects interior to itself in an internal intersubjectivity. Because they do not each individually possess natures, the divine "I's" can be perfectly interior to themselves. Inasmuch as a divine Person does not possess the other Persons as if they were "contents", properly so called, the relation of the divine "I's" must be conceived as a communion so perfect that each subject must experience Himself as a triune subject [...] yet without changing his own proper position. The Father experiences Himself as Father, but he simultaneously experiences, as Father, all the subjectivity of the Son. The subjectivity of the Son is interior to Him, but as to a Father [...] In the same way the Son experiences the paternity of the Father, but precisely in His character as Son.[36]

Ergo, the three Persons are not individuals (distinguished by nature) who are related in a communion of love; they rather *are* one another in every way except in their distinct properties. Thus Jesus

---

[33] Dumitru Staniloae, *op.cit*, 87; see also Hierotheos (Vlachos), *The Person in the Orthodox Tradition*, 216–217

[34] Hierotheos (Vlachos), *The Person in the Orthodox Tradition*, 101ff; 214–216

[35] Dumitru Staniloae, *op.cit*, 86

[36] *Ibid* 77

could say: "He that has seen Me has seen the Father" (Jn 14:9), but not, as Basil explains, "in the express image, nor yet the form, for the divine nature does not admit of combination; but the goodness of the will, which, being concurrent with the essence, is beheld as like and equal, or rather the same".[37] In other words, He is the image by nature, while being a distinct Person.

So, to return to O'Collins' concerns, of course each Person would have to be "minded" if mind is understood to be the faculty by which one is conscious and knows. However, when he asserts that this would indicate three individuals, he is thinking in terms of biologically constituted persons and therefore of a creaturely, non-redeemed mode of knowing and loving.[38] Zizioulas[39] argues that this sort of thinking is rooted in the Western conception of being preceding communion (i.e. we first exist and then enter into communion) and therefore a conception of the truth of being preceding the truth of communion. This is a function of our non-redeemed state and also the cause of our sense of individuality, in terms of which other objects have to be recognised as objects and given meaning before we can relate to them (as in Kantian epistemology). Thus the idea that we need to intellectually know something or someone in order to love them is a function of our fallen state that is rooted in our refusal to make being dependent on communion. In this context he criticises the Augustinian-Thomist idea that the Spirit, as the love of God, is a function of God's knowledge of Himself, as this notion is informed by our fallen state of consciousness that implies a separation between person and nature and between thought and action.[40]

This criticism needs to be understood in light of the mystical perception of Orthodox ascetics, who continue to have a profound

---

[37] *De Spiritu Sancto* 21

[38] A point Hierotheos consistently stresses with respect to the Western position in *The Person in the Orthodox Tradition*; see for example p. 218

[39] *Being as Communion*, 102–103

[40] See also Dumitru Staniloae, *op.cit*, 82–85; Staniloae, following Sts Maximus and Gregory Palamas, does allow the analogy, albeit interpreted in a different way, as we shall see below.

influence on Orthodox thought. As an anonymous *gerondas*[41] on Mount Athos explains to Hierotheos,[42] the human soul, made in the image of God, is threefold, having three powers – the *nous*, heart and will. In the non-fallen or redeemed human person the *nous*, heart and will are united in God; in the fallen person the three become disunited and pull in different directions; the *nous* comes to ignore God, the heart comes to love creatures independently of the Creator and the will comes to be enslaved by the passions.

Thus the point is subtle: Augustine uses a mind-knowledge-love/will analogy to demonstrate the threeness yet oneness in God, as we shall see, but the way he uses this imagery – to distinguish the Persons – implies a separation in God reminiscent of the fallen state of being as it is described by Orthodox ascetics.

The "powers" are no longer united but reflect the human person's approach to both God and human persons: we must first learn to know (of) Him before we can love Him precisely because we have fallen away from communion with Him.[43] However, in God such an ordering would be unnecessary because in God the three Persons are eternally in perfect communion.

Thus, because in Orthodox thought each Divine Person knows the other two wholly in a perfect intersubjectivity, they are not minded in the Cartesian sense of being self-aware by a process of cognition and do not make decisions discursively as human beings do. Thus the Orthodox are not talking of some "pseudo-divine committee", as O'Collins[44] describes it. O'Collins is quite right when he says: "It is as if God realises the dream expressed by the saying of people who are very much in love: 'They are of one mind and one heart'"[45] – but not as separately constituted individuals united in love, because in God the Three are one by nature and the nature is the Persons, who contain one another in a commun-

---

[41] An ascetic who has arrived at a state of grace and has disciples

[42] *A Night in the Desert of the Holy Mountain* (Levadia-Hellis: Birth of the Theotokos Monastery, 1991/1998) 54–55

[43] Augustine, *Confessions*, 10.20.29; c.f. John Zizioulas *Lectures in Christian Dogmatics*, 77; 79

[44] Gerald O'Collins, *op.cit*, 177

[45] *Ibid* 178

ion of love; there is no spatial difference between them. As Stanilo-ae says: "Pure divine subjectivity is experienced in the perfect communion of certain "I's" united in a unique subjectivity. Thus we speak of one God (a unique subject) and of three "I's" (three subjects)."[46]

So one could say that one consciousness is experienced in a threefold way, with Rahner, or that three consciousnesses are experienced as one consciousness, provided one understands that we are speaking of three ineffable Persons. Because the Persons are incorporeal and live within each other in perfect inter-subjectivity, their "mindedness" is not a function of individually constituted natures and thus does not denote three individuals.

In this sense the Orthodox are in agreement with O'Collins when he says: "Unless we accept that all the divine essential or natural properties (like knowing, willing and acting) are identical with and shared in common by the three persons of the Trinity, it is very difficult to see how we can salvage monotheism."[47] However, as Staniloae puts it, rather strongly: "It is the sin of individualism that hinders us from understanding fully that the Holy Trinity is a complete identification of "I's" without their disappearance or destruction."[48]

One can summarise it like this: the Thomist definition of the *human* person as (a) distinct, (b) subsistent and (c) possesses a rational nature might be a useful way of differentiating human beings from animals, but it cannot be applied to the Divine Persons. In Orthodox thought, (a) and (b) would apply to Divine Persons, but not (c) – it would also not apply to the true human person, at least soteriologically. In Eastern thought, in the Trinity (tri-unity) "mindedness" or consciousness is not a function of possessing a rational nature; a person is not a person because they have a mind, i.e. a rational nature; rather a person is "minded" or conscious because they are a person. But in their intersubjectivity the Divine Persons are wholly one-minded. Ergo, the Persons tri-mutually

---

[46] Dumitru Staniloae, *op.cit*, 76
[47] Gerald O'Collins, *op.cit*, 179
[48] Dumitru Staniloae, *op.cit*, 89

constitute the *hypostatic*-personal attribute of one-mindedness in their communion of love.

The implications for our debate are that the two traditions agree that in bringing forth the Son and Spirit the Father wholly shares Himself and all that He is with the Son and Spirit,[49] except being Father, and that the Father is essentially a personal Subject – i.e. the incomprehensible essence *is* the "I" of the Father. However, in the Western conception the Father is the only "I" and therefore the whole essence of the Trinity, while in the East, in the begetting and procession, the Father eternally brings forth two other unique, ineffable and ontologically real "I's" who share His subjectivity and essential energies, and each one experiences and manifests the common energies (including consciousness) in a particular *hypostatic* and subjective way because they come forth from Him without being separated from Him.[50] Thus the Son and the Spirit share the whole nature of the Father wholly[51] in a subjective way, including His subjectivity *and the subjectivity of the other Person*, because all that is in the Father – the Father Himself and the Other Person, is present in each One.

In light of the Eastern emphasis on inter-subjective communion, we see that McCarthy's criticism that the Orthodox conception shows no relation between the Son and the Spirit, is false. In his 1996 response to the Clarification, McCarthy[52] draws diagrams that represent the Eastern view as a bottomless triangle, with the Son and Spirit as separate points at the bottom, and the Western view as a complete triangle by virtue of the *filioque*, because in this version a line can be drawn across the bottom from the Son to the Spirit.

---

[49] See for example Vladimir Lossky, *op.cit*, 44; Hierotheos (Vlachos), *The Person in the Orthodox Tradition*, 140

[50] Dumitru Staniloae, *op.cit*, 92

[51] Hilarion Alfeyev, *op.cit*, 35, Alfeyev adds: "The three *Hypostases* do not divide the one nature into three essences, neither does one essence merge or mix the three *Hypostases* into one." See also Hierotheos (Vlachos), *The Person in the Orthodox Tradition*, 140

[52] *Op.cit*, 7-8

In actual fact, because the Persons live inside one another, the Orthodox diagram should be drawn as a complete triangle, with each Person representing a triangle that is entirely filled by the other two. The difference is that it is not a causal relation, but a mutual indwelling, in which the Spirit and the Son are eternally within one another in the Father.[53] This perception of the Trinity comes through participation in the divine communion in which the mystic experiences three subjective Presences in his or her own subjectivity: in sharing His communion with the Father and Son with human persons, the Spirit engages our own loving, filial consciousness; we thus love the Father personally in the Spirit without our freedom being compromised.[54] This can only be possible if it is how the Persons subsist eternally.

But does this personal freedom not imply three wills?

5.V. THREE WILLS?

As O'Collins[55] rightly says, the will is a property of the nature, not of the Person, both in the human person and in the Trinity, while the Person directs the will, as Constantinople III (680–81) affirmed.[56] The conciliar formula posited two wills in the incarnate Christ by virtue of His two natures; in the Trinity we have three Persons in one nature, as O'Collins[57] indicates. So, he asks how do three Persons direct one nature or, specifically, the one will? Well, this is a false question, in terms of Eastern thought, because the Persons – who are the ontological ground of being – *are* the nature

---

[53] See St Basil, *De Spiritu Sancto*, 63–64; he qualifies this by saying it is more correct to say that the Spirit is *with* the Father and Son to denote the inseparable fellowship of distinct *Hypostases*, but it is also true that we mystically perceive the Father to be in the Son and the Son in the Spirit.

[54] Dumitru Staniloae, *op.cit*, 103–104; see also St Athanasius, *Letter to Serapion* 1.19–20 in Khaled Anatolios, *op.cit*, 218–219

[55] *Op.cit*, 178

[56] See for example Hierotheos (Vlachos), *The Person in the Orthodox Tradition*, 134

[57] *Op.cit*, 179

as Persons in communion, as I have indicated.[58] Thus you cannot speak independently of the Persons and the nature. Staniloae brings out this perception clearly:

> We must see the divine essence simultaneously as a relation-unity or conversely as a unity-relation. Unity must not be destroyed on behalf of relation, nor relation abolished in favour of unity. Relation or reciprocal reference is act, and this act belongs to God's essence. Reference is common to God, although each Person has His own position in this common act of reference. [59]

It might be helpful to place this in the context of Zizioulas' emphasis on being as communion and put that together with Athanasius' distinction that, in God, communion does not belong to the level of will and action, but to that of substance. In terms of the paradigm of love in Orthodox thought, love is not an act of the will but is the ontological content of the substance of God.

If I understand the Eastern perspective correctly, the Persons *are* the substance. Thus *each* person *is* love, but because the Persons *are* the nature, the one nature is *personal* love. Ergo, the Persons do not love by will, as human individuals do, but by nature. Therefore freedom cannot be associated with the will in the Trinity.

As Hierotheos says: "For in human facts freedom is taken for a will of choice, whereas we cannot speak of a will of choice in the Persons of the Holy Trinity, but rather of a natural will which is common to the Holy Trinity because it is linked with nature."[60] And later: "I cannot conceive that each Person acts freely, with the

---

[58] See also Allen & Springsted *op.cit*, 69–71 & cf. Vladimir Lossky *op.cit*, 41

[59] Dumitru Staniloae, *op.cit*, 80

[60] Hierotheos (Vlachos), *The Person in the Orthodox Tradition*, 220; in this context Hierotheos takes a swipe at scholasticism as the "attempt to adapt the way of being of the Holy Trinity to human facts and interpersonal relations" – see also pp. 221; 104–105 & 134

common essence which they have, for in that case we would end with God having a moral will rather than a natural one".[61]

He therefore says *apophatically*: "God's love is not personal, but it is His *enhypostatic* energy." The distinction between creaturely and divine love is crucial. In the fallen creaturely condition, where there is an absence of or opposition to love, love is an act of the will. In the Trinity there is no absence and no opposition. God exercises His will only in respect of creation because He is a bringing something new out of nothing. So, properly speaking, one cannot speak of a will with respect to the intra-Trinitarian relations but only with respect to the triune God's relationship to creation, where the Three act with one loving intentionality.[62] Hierotheos brings this out in his convenient précis of Zizioulas' three distinctive characteristics of the Person:

> One is freedom. Indeed when we speak of freedom we do not mean it in the ethical and philosophical sense of the possibility of choice, but are referring to the lack of commitment to any given, even the given of existence [in the monistic sense of being]. It appertains to the uncreated. The second element of the person is love, since 'the only exercise of freedom in an ontological manner is love'. The third distinctive mark is the 'concrete, singular, and unrepeatable entity'. [...] even these three distinguishing features [...] exist only in God, since only God is self-existent, has real love and is singular.[63]

---

[61] *Ibid* 219–220

[62] See St Basil, *De Spiritu Sancto*, 20–21. In *his Letter to Ablabious* 9ff, St Gregory of Nyssa cites the commonality of the operation of the three Persons in the economy – as "one motion and disposition of the good will"– in which each Person acts inseparably with the other Two, as a demonstration of the Oneness of the Persons. Gregory also cites this lack of common intentionality among human beings as grounds for properly thinking of "men" in the plural, despite their natural consubstantiality.

[63] Hierotheos (Vlachos), *The Person in the Orthodox Tradition*, 83; see also John Zizioulas, *Being as Communion*, 42ff

Thus in the indivisible Trinity love *is* freedom. It is not something the Three *do*, but what they *are*.[64] Therefore freedom does not imply individual autonomy or separate wills.[65] The same argument applies to the issue of subordination: the Son and Spirit are not subordinate to the will of the Father because their origination is not an act of will.

5.VI. SUBORDINATION OF THE SON AND THE SPIRIT?

We have touched on the fact that the Cappadocians used the term "mode of being" to combat Eunomius who, following Aristotelian logic, asserted that the Father's unbegotteness was His essence, which is indivisible; therefore the Son and Spirit cannot share the Father's essence, which means they are of a "lesser essence" and therefore created. Eunomius cited Christ's words "the Father is greater than I" (Jn 14:28) to support his argument.[66] Basil answered by citing several texts that indicate the equality of the Son and asserting that the above text could therefore apply to only origin: "So what remains of what we said about the greater is the mode, that is to say, of the source and origin".[67] Thus the Father's mode of being is His unbegotteness, the Son's mode of being and reason for being is His begotteness, the Spirit's His procession. Because origin and existence are one in the eternal Trinity, this simply means this is the

---

[64] John Zizioulas, *Being as Communion*, 120–121

[65] Meredith's (*op.cit*, 56–57:97) assertion that, for Gregory of Nyssa, "the root of the image of God in us" lies in "the freedom of will" is a good example of how Eastern thought is misunderstood when read through the lens of Western presuppositions. For the Westerner "freedom" means free will, but for Easterners this is not the case.

[66] See for example Hierotheos (Vlachos), *The Person in the Orthodox Tradition*, 137–138; 200–201; Anthony Meredith, *op.cit*, 63–65; Athanasius, *Against the Arians* 1:30ff

[67] *De Spiritu Sancto* 20; see also St John of Damascus in Hierotheos (Vlachos), *The Person in the Orthodox Tradition*, 139; Tertullian made the same point in *Against Praxeas* 9

way in which each one exists; so these are considered distinctive *hypostatic* characteristics.[68]

Zizioulas notes that by identifying the manner of origin with the *hypostases* rather than the essence, the Fathers accepted a certain subordination of the Son and Spirit – an inescapable consequence of being caused by the Father, but without downgrading the Son or Spirit to the level of created being, because their distinctions were founded on the common substance; thus the three Persons could still be shown to be equal in rank and honour.[69]

Staniloae explains further that the begetting of the Son and the procession of the Spirit are not acts of the Father's will but rather in accordance with His will, that is, in accordance with the divine freedom and goodness. The Son comes forth "from the being of the Father" not, as in the case of creatures, from His will. As God is pure subject, the begetting of the Son cannot be seen as the action of one subject upon another as this would make the latter an object of the former. The Son is also said to take His birth from the Father.[70] The terms birth and begetting therefore "express only the unchanged positions of the two Persons and the unity between them".[71]

Basil argues similarly that we must not "regard the economy through the Son as a compulsory and subordinate ministration [...] but rather the voluntary solicitude working effectively for His own creation in goodness and pity, according to the will of God the Father".[72] Similarly, the Spirit proceeds from the Father but the Father also causes Him to proceed. Thus there is no passivity in either the begetting or proceeding on the part of either the Father or the other Person. "The act of the Son's begetting and the act of the Spirit's procession are acts of a pure, common subjectivity, the first proper to the Father and the Son, the second to the Father and the Spirit".[73] Thus, while the Father is the cause of the Trinitarian ex-

---

[68] Hierotheos (Vlachos), *The Person in the Orthodox Tradition*, 138
[69] John Zizioulas, *Being as Communion*, 89
[70] Dumitru Staniloae, *op.cit*, 90
[71] *Ibid* 77
[72] *De Spiritu Sancto* 18
[73] Dumitru Staniloae, *op.cit*, 77

istence, the three subsist wholly as a mutual self-giving and receiving in love. In this way each one freely affirms His own identity as Father, Son and Spirit: "The Father therefore establishes the Son in existence from all eternity by his integral self-giving while the Son continually affirms the Father as Father by the fact that He both accepts His own coming into existence through the Father and gives Himself to the Father as Son".[74] However, this does not mean the exercise of three independent wills, but infers the way in which each one exercises the common will as a common self-giving.[75]

The equality of the Divine Persons is, paradoxically, therefore a function of the sublime humility of the essential but *enhypostatic* self-sacrificial love Bloom describes[76] in which, as Staniloae puts it: "Each divine 'I' puts a 'Thou' in place of Himself. Each sees Himself only in relation to the other. [...] They are three, yet each regards only the others and experiences only the others."[77] This is manifested concretely in the economy by each one hiding Himself and revealing the other Two and the Two revealing themselves in the other One. Thus Basil writes: "You see, consequently, that sometimes the Father reveals the Son, sometimes the Son reveals the Father [...] hence the whole divinity addresses itself to you at one time in the Father, at other times in the Son and in the Spirit".[78] The "*I* am" is always one yet three.

Again, all the works of the Father are effected in and by the Son and vice versa. As Athanasius says: "Then because the Father [...] is the only one who is wise, the Son is His wisdom".[79] Gregory of Nyssa writes: "But he who sees the Son, sees the Father, the Father has begotten another Self of His own, not by going outside Himself, but by revealing Himself wholly in this other".[80] This "initiative of the Father of considering Himself represented by another

---

[74] *Ibid* 78

[75] *Ibid* 79–80

[76] See 2.iii above

[77] Dumitru Staniloae, *op.cit*, 88

[78] *Adversus Eunomium* in *ibid* 88–89

[79] *Letter I to Serapion* in Dumitru Staniloae, *op.cit*, 89

[80] *Contra Eunomium* in *ibid*; note Gregory's use of the word "Self".

'I' is implied in the act which is known as the begetting of the Son from the Father".[81]

This brings us to the contentious issue of the modes of being, which goes hand-in-hand with the relation between the economic and immanent Trinities. Due to space considerations I shall carry this discussion over to the next chapter.

5.VII. SUMMARY

In this chapter we have seen that the perception of three subjectively aware Persons is fundamental to the Orthodox conception of the Trinity. While the 4th century Fathers might not have had the terminology at their disposal to define a Person as a subjectively conscious being-in-communion, post-modern Orthodox thinkers are convinced that this is the awareness they intended to preserve in their formulation of one *ousia*, three Persons-*Hypostases*. This conviction is born of the fact that modern and post-modern mystics enjoy the same sort of mystical encounters with the Divine Persons that the Fathers enjoyed and therefore testify to the same reality, albeit making certain different terminological distinctions to cater to the post-modern mind. In such mystical encounters the Three are recognised as distinct personal Subjects through their *enhypostatic* energies.

This perception in turn throws light on how the East interprets the historical economy and specifically what the distinct activities of the Three in the economy reveal about the inter-Trinitarian relationships: the Three assume differing functions in the economy, although acting according to the common will; each Person acts in a particular way with a view to including humanity in the divine communion of love, indicating that each one is a real Person. This constitutes the context in which all the objections to the *filioque* that we outlined earlier must be understood.

But it is a mistake to conclude that the East thereby implies three individuals in the Trinity. This misconception arises from the fact that in the West human personhood is the measure of what it

---

[81] Dumitru Staniloae, *op.cit*, 89

is to be a person. Westerners therefore assume creaturely norms, in terms of which human persons are seen as rational beings individuated by nature. Thus the West concludes that the Divine Persons are not real Persons.

By contrast, the Orthodox emphasise, theologically, the incorporeality of the Divine Persons, who subsist in a perfect, intersubjective communion. Thus the Persons and nature are indivisibly Persons in communion. Because the Three subsist as a communion of love, this means each one has to be subjectively conscious as a fundamental characteristic of being a person. But as the Persons and nature are an indivisible intersubjectivity, we cannot speak of three individuals with separate minds and wills. Nor can we speak of the subordination of the Son and the Spirit to the will of the Father, as the inter-Trinitarian life is a common expression of the tri-subjective love. It is also false to say that in the Eastern conception there is no relation between the Son and the Spirit; it is simply a different sort of relation, in which the Spirit and the Son are eternally within one another in the Father.

It is also noteworthy that on the surface there is a great deal of agreement between East and West, but there is enormous divergence in the "subtext" due to the differing notions of personhood. For example, the East would agree with the Augustinian-Thomist philosophical definition, "there cannot be in the Godhead any other relations than relations of origin"[82] because origin and existence are one in the eternal Trinity, but would mean it differently to how the West means it. In Western thought this implies that the Persons can be distinguished only by causal relations, necessitating the *filioque*, while in Eastern thought causality is referred to the Father and the consequent modes of being relate to inter-subjective relationality.

East and West agree that the Persons and shared essence are indivisible, but the two traditions arrive at this conclusion via a different route, with the West differentiating the Persons *within* the one nature (i.e. one Self) and the East emphasising that the nature is contained in the Persons, meaning the attributes or essential en-

---

[82] John F. McCarthy, *op.cit*, 7-8

ergies of the nature are personal-*hypostatic* attributes shared in common by all three but experienced and manifested in differing subsistent personal-*hypostatic* ways or modes.

Both traditions also agree that the divine essence is incomprehensible, but the East would add that this is because the Persons *are* the nature and *they* are ineffable. In terms of the fundamental notion that that which is common to all three Persons belongs to the nature, while the individual, peculiar properties belong to the Persons, the East also agrees that consciousness is an element of the nature. Thus, while Rahner and O'Collins argue that in the Trinity one consciousness is experienced in a threefold way and many Orthodox argue that three consciousnesses are experienced as one consciousness, the East might use either formulation to emphasise different aspects of the indivisible Trinity. But, again, the Orthodox understand these words in a radically different way to the West.

Orthodox thinkers who speak of three self-consciousnesses are simply trying to emphasise that in Eastern thought each of the Persons experience consciousness as a unique "I", though no attempt is made to explain how the Persons are constituted as personal Subjects. This falls into the category of incomprehensibility.

By contrast, the Western conception seems to suggest there is only one "I" in the Trinity, an idea that seems to go hand-in-hand with the notion that what cannot be explained logically cannot be true – an approach that is foreign to Eastern thought.

6 THE PROCESSION OF THE SPIRIT

In this chapter I shall outline how the Eastern approach to truth and conception of personhood relates to the Eastern notion of the divine modes of being and the relationship between the economic Trinity and immanent Trinity. I shall then discuss the Eastern conception of the procession of the Spirit in relation to assertions that elements of Eastern patristic thought are harmonious with the Western position. Finally, I shall comment on the reasonableness of the Orthodox objections to the *filioque* in light of the Eastern perception of the Trinity.

6.1. ECONOMIC AND IMMANENT TRINITY

It is not the case that the Orthodox deny any relation between the immanent and economic Trinity. As we have seen, quite a lot has been said *cataphatically* about the inter-Trinitarian life, particularly with respect to the inter-subjective relationality of the Persons. It is simply that the Orthodox limit positive affirmations about the Divine Persons to that which we can know from experience.

Over and above the stress on experience, three logical points are posited for this limitation, the first being the issue of time and eternity. Our knowledge of the Trinity is gained through participation in the divine energies, that is, by the Persons' self-manifestation in the economy (historically and mystically).

But, as Staniloae says, these are experiences of the "saving activity that God exercises upon us and within us. He is revealed to us as an economic Trinity."[1] Pomazansky adds: "When [...] we speak of the Tri-Unity of God, we speak of the mystical, inward life hidden in the depths of the Divinity, revealed to the world *in*

---

[1] Dumitru Staniloae, *op.cit*, 75

145

time" (italics in original).[2] As the origins of the Son and Spirit are eternal realities, we cannot know the mechanics of these from our experience of the Divine Persons in time.

Thus, about two centuries before the Cappadocians, Irenaeus emphasised the indefinable mystery of the begetting on this basis.[3] Basil echoes this when, after speaking of the Spirit's sanctifying operation in the economy, he asks: "How shall we form a conception of what extends beyond the ages? What were His operations before that creation whereof we can conceive?"[4]

And: "He existed; He pre-existed; He co-existed with the Father and the Son before the ages. If follows that, even if you can conceive of anything beyond the ages, you will find the Spirit yet further above and beyond."[5]

The implication is that, as God is eternal, the creaturely mind cannot fully grasp God as He is in Himself. To do so one would have to be eternal, like God. In fact, one would have to *be* God. Thus God's self-revelation is always an accommodation to human perceptual limitations.[6]

Second, the immanent God is incorporeal.[7] As the Creator of spatio-temporal reality, the immanent Trinity transcends created spatio-temporal perceptual and conceptual categories. The only way in which we can know the Trinity is by entering into communion with God. However, this knowing is not cerebral but experiential and cannot be explained.

As Gregory of Nyssa states in his *Life of Moses*:

---

[2] Michael Pomazansky, *op.cit*, 75; see also Hierotheos (Vlachos), *The Person in the Orthodox Tradition*, 128

[3] See *Against Heresies*, 2.28.6; 3.18.1 in Gerald O'Collins, *op.cit*, 98

[4] *De Spiritu Sancto* 49; see also n1; Meredith (*op.cit*, 105) does not seem to appreciate the distinction between the economic and immanent Trinities when he criticises St Basil for not defining the Spirit's "role" in the intra-Trinitarian life, indicating a utilitarian mindset.

[5] *De Spiritu Sancto* 49

[6] Hierotheos (Vlachos), *The Person in the Orthodox Tradition*, 211–213; Gregory of Nyssa, *Letter to Ablabius* 2

[7] See for example St Basil, *De Spiritu Sancto* 15

[…] the sacred text is teaching here that spiritual knowledge first occurs as illumination […] But as the soul makes progress […] so much the more does it see that the divine nature is invisible. It thus leaves all surface appearances, not only those that can be grasped by the senses but also those which the mind itself seems to see, and it keeps on going deeper until by the operation of the spirit it penetrates the invisible and incomprehensible, and it is there that it sees God. The true vision and the true knowledge of what we seek consists precisely in not seeing, in an awareness that our goal transcends all knowledge and is everywhere cut off from us by the darkness and incomprehensibility.[8]

The third point relates to the ineffability of the Persons: the Orthodox argue *that* we can know from the *enhypostatic* energies (personal manifestations) and the distinct functions of the Divine Persons in the economy that they are incorporeal, sentient "Subjectivities" but we cannot explain *how* it is possible to be a consciously aware Person without having a separate nature.

The same argument applies to the modes of being. We know from divine revelation that the mode or manner of communion is that Son is eternally begotten and that the Spirit proceeds from the Father. But as the manner of origin belongs to the eternal, immanent being of God, we cannot know how the Son is begotten or how the Spirit proceeds.[9]

The Cappadocians therefore insisted that we can assert *that* God is, but not *how* God is; the relations of origin can be perceived mystically through the economic Trinity only "as through a glass darkly", but we cannot know how these come about.[10]

---

[8] In Jean Daniélou, *From Glory to Glory: Texts from Gregory of Nyssa's Mystical Writings* (New York, St Vladimir's Seminary Press, 1961/1995), 118

[9] Hierotheos (Vlachos), *The Person in the Orthodox Tradition*, 202, 211ff, 220–221; Michael Pomazansky, *op.cit*, 83–84

[10] Hierotheos (Vlachos), *The Person in the Orthodox Tradition*, 202–203; he cites Basil's *Letter 235 to Amphilochios* and Gregory of Nazianzus' *Third Theological Oration;* c.f. John of Damascus, *Orthodox Faith*, 1.4

The biblical expressions "begotten" (the one who was incarnate) and "proceeding" (the one who was not) can be verified in mystical experience, but the causality of these relations cannot be explained.[11] This is the point at which the Orthodox fall silent.[12]

To know this would be to know how a "Subjectivity" is caused in an eternal becoming.

6.II. MODES OF BEING

We have noted that, just as a human person cannot be defined, but can only be recognised in personal relationship, so in the Trinity one can recognise the Divine Persons in mystical encounters. This constitutes the *subjective* aspect of knowing. The mode of being provides us with a subjectively recognised but also conceptually objective way of distinguishing the Persons.[13]

One can illustrate this from human experience: I (the human person) *have* a mind and a will, which are attributes of my nature and which I direct. That is, I have nature, but I am not my nature. I cannot be uniquely distinguished by anything I share in common with others, such as having a certain form and qualities such as the ability to love or think and so on. I can be distinguished *objectively* from other persons by the manner in which I direct my mind and will *gnomically*, and thus by my actions; this constitutes my mode of being.[14]

However, while this objectively distinguishes me from others, it does not enable anyone to know my inner *hypostatic* being, which

---

[11] *Ibid* 169–170

[12] *Ibid* 143

[13] The biblical record would constitute an *objective* criterion of truth, but mystical experience of the reality to which it testifies enables one to understand its meaning subjectively.

[14] Andrew Louth, *Maximus the Confessor* (London & New York: Routledge, 1996), 58ff; this is a précis of the "Cappadocian logic" worked out later by St Maximus the Confessor.

is ineffable.[15] You can only know me, the true, inner me, to the degree that I reveal myself to you – and even this is partial, because to know me fully you would have to *be* me (or God).[16]

In contrast to creaturely modes of being, in the Trinity the Persons and nature are wholly personal and indivisible, and the manner of origin of the Son and Spirit and their mode of being are one and the same thing because they are eternal and are therefore related to each other in an eternal, subsistent manner.[17] But similarly to creaturely experience, while one can distinguish the Persons by their *hypostatic* modes of being, which is the same thing as their mode of origin, neither the inner reality of the Persons nor the how of the begetting and proceeding can be known or conceptualised. To do so one would have to *be* God, i.e. eternal and incorporeal. Thus the modes of being merely indicate the subsistent relations of real Persons.

Hierotheos therefore emphasises that these *hypostatic* characteristics of the Persons (modes of being) must not be confused with the *Hypostases* themselves.[18] He traces this error to the erroneous idea that the modes of being relate to the nature, not the *Hypostases*, which would be Sabellianism.

In the thought of the Eastern Fathers the *Hypostasis* is the essence with its particular characteristics; thus the Three are *essentially* one but *hypostatically* three (i.e. three "I's") and we know this because each one subsists in a particular way; thus each Person possesses that which is common to the three and that which belongs individually to the Person. But one cannot say that the essence has

---

[15] Vladimir Lossky, *op.cit*, 42; 48–49; c.f. Hierotheos (Vlachos), *The Person in the Orthodox Tradition*, 201–202, summarising Basil; Dumitru Staniloae, *op.cit*, 75

[16] See Sophrony in Hierotheos (Vlachos), *The Person in the Orthodox Tradition*, 86

[17] Hierotheos (Vlachos), *The Person in the Orthodox Tradition*, 214–215

[18] *Ibid* 140–141; Meredith (*op.cit*, 105) seems to make precisely this mistake, saying that in St Basil's conception of the one *ousia*, three *hypostases* "each person of the Trinity can be thought of as a union of the general divine nature and an individual characteristic, sometimes referred to as a *tropos hyparxeōs* or way of existing. So the Father is as it were a compound of divinity + Fatherhood, and so on".

characteristics, and therefore modes of being, because essence does not have *hypostatic* (personal) characteristics. Nor can one say that the Person is His characteristics; these rather indicate the presence of a distinct Person. Thus the mode of being indicates a personal *Hypostasis* – a subjective presence – and must not be confused with the *Hypostasis* itself. To say that the Persons are the relations is the same as saying the Persons are the modes of being and therefore not real Persons, which would be Sabellianism.

6.iii. The procession of the Spirit

We noted in 1.iv.b above that Basil speaks of the Spirit proceeding from the Father "not by generation, like the Son, but as Breath of His mouth".[19] To answer those who say that the single procession does not demonstrate any proper relation between the Son and the Spirit,[20] he speaks of the Spirit as sharing the "natural communion" of the Father and the Son and of being "one nature" with them by virtue of proceeding from the Father in conjunction with the Word.[21] He adds: "He is moreover called 'Spirit of Christ' as being by nature closely related to Him".[22] Thus "the Holy Spirit is insepa-rable and wholly incapable of being parted from the Father and the Son".[23]

Thus, in the Orthodox conception the Son and the Spirit are seen as coming forth from the Father together, within one another and within the Father. Staniloae elaborates on this idea within the context of his understanding of inter-subjective communion be-tween the Divine Persons. In so doing he goes beyond the Cappa-docians to work out the implications of their thought for the post-modern mind. Interestingly, he uses Ss Maximus and Gregory Palamas' exposition of the mind-knowledge-love analogy to explain

---

[19] *De Spiritu Sancto* 46; 38; 48
[20] As McCarthy (*op.cit*, 7–8) does
[21] *De Spiritu Sancto* 46
[22] *Ibid* 46; see also n63
[23] *Ibid* 37

his position – the same analogy that Hierotheos and Zizioulas are so scathing about.

However, because (a) these saints understood the Persons to be real Persons and (b) they made a distinction between the economic and immanent Trinity, they used the analogy in a different way to Augustine. In fact, instead of arriving at the *filioque*, Palamas used it to demonstrate the Orthodox understanding of *per filium*, which seems to be how his predecessor St Maximus understood the *filioque* and which is why he condoned it.[24] Wishing to defend the Western Church, Maximus held that, with the words "from the Son", Westerners intended to say that that the Spirit is given to creatures through the Son, that He is manifested and sent by the Son, but not that the Spirit has His existence from the Son.[25] He seems to have assumed that Westerners had the same presuppositions as the East.

In Palamas' case, he was familiar with the *filioque*, argued against it and showed how St Maximus' in fact differs from the West.[26]

The following exposition will therefore demonstrate several things at once: (a) that it is not so much the words or images used that are important, but the way in which they are used; (b) the Eastern interpretation of the expression "through the Son"; (c) that sayings from the Eastern Fathers cannot be used to demonstrate harmony with the Western interpretation because the two traditions are working with differing presuppositions; and (d) my central contention that the fundamental point of divergence lies in our differing understanding of the word "person".

The first point that must be emphasised is that, as Staniloae stresses, the mind-knowledge-love analogy as it is used in the East belongs properly to the revelatory (economic) Trinity.[27] We have noted that he affirms that the Father remains transcendent that we might be raised up to Him, the Son becomes for us the incarnate

---

[24] Hierotheos (Vlachos), *The Person in the Orthodox Tradition*, 132

[25] Michael Pomazansky, *op.cit*, 90; John Zizioulas, *Lectures in Christian Dogmatics*, 80–81

[26] Michael Pomazansky, *op.cit*, 91

[27] Dumitru Staniloae, *op.cit*, 75

image of the Father and the Spirit (who leads us into all truth – Jn 16:13) reveals Himself as a subjective presence in our subjectivity, making present for us the Father and the Son.

In this revelatory context Staniloae uses the mind to denote the transcendent Father, knowledge as the Son who is for us the "subjective-objective" revelation of the Father and love as a metaphor for Spirit, who is the one who subjectively reveals to us the intra-Trinitarian communion of love. As Basil says:

> Hence He [the Spirit] alone glorifies the Lord, for, it is said, "He shall glorify me" (Jn 16:14), not as the creature, but as the Spirit of Truth (Jn 14:17) clearly showing forth the truth in Himself, and, as the Spirit of Wisdom, in His own greatness revealing Christ as the Power of God and the Wisdom of God (1 Cor 1:24). And as [another] Paraclete He expresses in Himself the goodness of the Paraclete who sent Him, and in His own dignity manifests the majesty of Him from whom He proceeded.[28]

The way in which the Spirit reveals the truth is important, because this demonstrates the Eastern patristic perspective of the biblical text: "What things soever He [the Spirit] shall hear, He shall speak; [...] He shall receive of mine and show it to you. All things whatsoever the Father has are mine" (John 16:13–15). Basil explains that the Son is the image of the Father (as Person) in the incarnation by virtue of manifesting their common nature, particularly the common will, and that it is by virtue of the common nature that all that the Father has belongs to the Son.[29] He argues, in parallel, that the Spirit also reveals and shares that which is common to the three Persons by nature, not, of course, as an incarnate Person, but precisely as Spirit. On this account the Spirit's "proper and peculiar title is Holy Spirit, which is a name especially appro-

---

[28] *De Spiritu Sancto* 46; see also Jn 14:15
[29] *Ibid* 18–21; 36

priate to everything that is incorporeal, purely immaterial and indi-visible".[30]

He continues that it is by virtue of the shared nature that the Spirit shares names in common with the Father and the Son, such as His peculiar title of Spirit (as in "God is Spirit" – Jn 4:24), Para-clete, Truth, Righteousness and Wisdom – because of His close relationship with the other two Persons.[31] Because the Son and Spirit have all things in common from the Father, "that which is mine" belongs to all three except for the *hypostatic* characteristics. And, of course, the Orthodox argue that the characteristic of being an originator of *hypostases* is a *hypostatic* characteristic of the Father; thus this is precisely the one thing the Son cannot share with the Father. In this context, although Basil does not describe the Spirit as love, the analogy is fitting as a description of the Spirit's revela-tory mode, because He reveals the common nature of the Trinity and the manner of knowing the Father and Son is a communion of love in the Spirit.[32] Thus Staniloae says: "The mode of the 'Image' or of the 'Truth' and the mode of 'Love' are particularly necessary to reveal the Father [the "abyss of the mind"] in whom the fathom-less depth of the Godhead is an unoriginate mode which is itself at the origin of other revelatory modes."[33]

However, while Basil seems to have limited the expression "through the Son" to this economic activity of the Spirit,[34] Stanilo-ae asserts that these economic relationships also indicate the posi-tions of three Persons in the structure of divine love, and these positions must be understood in the context of the self-effacing intersubjectivity of the Divine Persons, in which each One knows Himself only in the other two.[35] He thus explains the mind-knowledge-love analogy – the Father thinking Himself or begetting

---

[30] *Ibid* 22

[31] *Ibid 22*; 48

[32] *Ibid* 8, 49; thus speaking of the Spirit as communion is appropriate only in terms of His economic function, in that He shares with us His own communion in and with the Father and the Son

[33] Dumitru Staniloae, *op.cit*, 97

[34] *De Spiritu Sancto* 16–18

[35] Dumitru Staniloae, *op.cit*, 92

His image, and loving Himself or His image – in terms of a communion of three "I's": consciousness can occur only when there is relation, that is, where there is a content that is different from the "I" but which is ontologically bound up with it. And when there is relation, each sees the other two directly and Himself only indirectly – and in this lies the supreme humility of divine love. But it is not the case that the Son first exists and is then known by the Father (in order of precedence). Here we see how relations of origin and the inter-subjective relations are one:

> It is clear that in the "truly existing existence" of God every act[36] is substantial and shares in existence. In God thinking is not one thing and existence another. By thinking Himself, the Father duplicates Himself *hypostatically* yet without becoming two in being. By thinking Himself, He knows Himself both as thinker and as the one who is thought and known by Himself. He beholds the Son, the *hypostatic* "Truth", that is, Himself as another "I", and simultaneously knows Himself as the source of this His personal image.[37]

It is in this personal sense that the Eastern Fathers intended the analogy of the Son as the thought/Word that the Father thinks/speaks about Himself. However, a communion of two would not be a fullness of existence; by loving the Son in the Spirit, that is, because of the presence of a third "I", this is a generous love between three rather than a greedy (erotic) love between two, in which each adores Himself in the Other. It is because there is a Third that the Two are one, not through the reciprocity of their love alone, but also through their self-forgetfulness in favour of a Third, thus making the Three equal in love and causing the love to be generous and diffusive. Thus the Spirit can be said to unite the Father and Son in Himself in the sense that the Two transcend

---

[36] Here he uses the word "act" in the sense that act and being are one: "Love is the being of God; it is His substantial act" – see p. 79
[37] *Ibid* 91

their common subjectivity in the Third and this manifests the full-ness of existence and therefore of truth:

> We can say that if the Two do not meet in a Third, their sub-jectivity is not truly a common subjectivity (because Two would both lose themselves passionately in the Other as ob-jects and lose their distinctness). It becomes a common subjec-tivity, true and objective, by this meeting of the Two in their common 'object', which is the Third.[38]

At the same time, the threefold intersubjectivity makes possi-ble the personal distinction of each one precisely by the inclusion of the third. Staniloae explains that existence confirmed as truth is experienced not by only one subject or by many isolated subjects, but only by two in relation to a third: "Truth can then be defined as existence experienced in common, that is to say, among three."[39] The third represents all that can exist over and above the other two, so any other subjectivities brought into this communion would not be internally necessary and are comprehended within this structure of three.[40] As Gregory of Nazianzus says: "A com-plete Trinity is formed from three perfect elements, for the monad is in motion because of its richness, but it transcends the dyad for it is beyond matter and form from which bodies arise and defines itself as trinity (for this is the first [stage] of synthesis beyond duali-ty) in order that the divinity might not be too restricted, nor over-flow to infinity."[41]

It is in this sense that certain Eastern Fathers, such as St Max-imus and St Gregory Palamas spoke of the Spirit as the life, love, bridge or bond between the Father and the Son.[42] The Father knows Himself in the other Two in the modes of Image and Love

---

[38] *Ibid* 94

[39] *Ibid* 95

[40] *Ibid* 95–96

[41] From *Oration 23* in *ibid* 101

[42] Dumitru Staniloae, *op.cit*, 96; he cites St Maximus, *Quaestiones ad Thalassium* 13; 28; John of Damascus, *The Orthodox Faith*, 1.12

– a notion that is underpinned by the perception that love is the proper mode of knowing the truth.[43] Thus the Son as image is one mode of knowing Himself, the Spirit as love another mode. "But it is a mode that reveals the Father as completely as His image reveals Him."[44] "And each of these *hypostatic* modes carries in itself, together with the entire divine being, the other modes as well."[45] Inasmuch as the Spirit exists for sake of the Son in a particular generosity of love that the Fathers observed about the Spirit, He is called Love, because love always exists for the sake of another, never for its own sake.[46]

Inasmuch as the Spirit radiates from the Father as light[47] for the sake of the Son and abides in and radiates from the Son, the Fathers sometimes add the clause "through the Son". The Fathers perceived the Spirit, as the Third Person, as the atmosphere of infinite love and life in whom the "I-Thou" relationship of the Father and Son is bathed. It is in this *revelatory* way that Palamas' "through the Son" must be understood.[48] There is no indication that these Fathers use the "through the Son" as an approximation of "from" or "by" the Son with respect to the eternal procession, as the Clarification asserts. The same is true of the third last paragraph of Gregory of Nyssa's *Letter to Ablabius*, which Meredith quotes to support the *filioque*:

> That is the only way we distinguish one person from another.
> By believing that is, that one is the cause and the other depends on the cause. Again, we recognise another distinction,

---

[43] *Ibid* 97

[44] *Ibid* 96

[45] *Ibid*

[46] *Ibid* 98; Staniloae cites St Athanasius, *Contra Arianos* 3;15; *Ad Serapionem*, 1.18–19; St Basil, *De Spiritu Sancto* 26; 64; the central idea is that we only know the Son because the Spirit illumines Him and makes us capable of understanding Him, but (in His humility and love) the Spirit never reveals Himself.

[47] Notably, in the mystical experiences outlined in 4.i.a. above, the Spirit was identified as the light in whom the Son was bathed.

[48] *Ibid* 98

with regard to that which depends on the cause. There is that [sc. the Son] which depends on the first cause [sc. The Father], and there is that [sc. The Holy Spirit] which derives from the first cause through the second.[49]

Zizioulas explains that in this text Gregory is careful to preserve the Spirit's direct relation with the Father while at the same time distinguishing the Son from the Spirit by affirming the Son's mediatory role of "through the Son", without positing the Son as a cause of another *hypostasis*. This is fundamental to Gregory's argument, which rests on the fact that we distinguish between the Persons by recognising one as the Cause (Father and therefore One God) and those who are caused.[50] It should also be noted, as Pomazansky stresses, that the Orthodox have not dogmatised the expression "through the Son"; it is simply an explanatory expression used by some Fathers.[51] But the pivotal point remains that if the Persons are real Persons, then the revelatory modes of being (described as knowledge and love) of the Son and Spirit should not be confused with the Persons themselves.

Staniloae makes a further distinction that clarifies the issue a little more: the Spirit, as a Person, also has a relation to the Son: the Spirit does not proceed in order to stand alongside the Son. He rests or abides eternally in the Son and is the one in whom the Son loves also the Father. Nor does He exist solely for the sake of the Son. But in the mutual personal love of the Father and the Spirit for the Son, the Son is the "goal" of the procession from the Father, who comes to rest upon the Son through His Love, and goes no farther than the Son. This abiding in the Son (a) distinguishes the Spirit from the Son, because the Son does not come to rest in any Person, and (b) denotes the special position of the Spirit in the divine structure of love, as is reflected in the economy.[52]

It is in this sense (and not in the sense that the Clarification quotes him) that St John of Damascus said that the Spirit is eternal-

---

[49] In Anthony Meredith, *op.cit*, 109
[50] John Zizioulas, *Lectures in Christian Dogmatics*, 79–81
[51] Michael Pomazansky, *op.cit*, 91
[52] Dumitru Staniloae, *op.cit*, 100

ly "between" the Father and the Son. Any progress of the Spirit beyond the Son, through the Son would make it impossible to explain why the divine processions stop with the Spirit, as Photius argued (see 2.i above), because this introduces the idea that one who is caused could also become a cause of other *hypostases*[53] and leads to "the disorder of infinite plurality", resulting in a continuous dilution arising from increasing remoteness from the unoriginate cause of existence (as in Platonic hierarchies). By contrast, the Son and Spirit originate directly in the Father and therefore share directly and eternally in His "unoriginateness".[54]

In order to reconcile the idea that the Spirit, as Love, proceeds from the Father alone but is also reciprocated by the Son, Palamas explained that the Son "avails Himself of the Spirit" but possesses the Spirit "as one who has come forth together with Him from the Father and abides in Him (the Son) through the unity of nature".[55] Both the Father and Son rejoice in the Spirit, says Palamas, "for this joy of the Father and the Son [...] is the Holy Spirit who is common to both in what concerns their inner association; this also explains why the Spirit is sent forth by both, but why He is of the Father alone in what concerns His existence, and therefore proceeds from the Father alone with respect to His existence".[56]

The love of the Spirit is in turn reflected back to the Father as a responsive, personal love – i.e. through the Son.[57] Thus the Son loves the Father as an active subject in and through the Spirit and the Spirit of the Father is ceaselessly the Spirit of the Son as well.[58] "Consequently," Staniloae writes, "the fact that the Word of the Father, which is also the Word (spoken) to the Father, or better, the response to the Father, is a Word or response full of the Spirit;

---

[53] *Ibid* 199–101; thus a creature who participates in the intra-Trinitarian communion does so by virtue of being in the Son in communion with the Spirit.

[54] *Ibid* 102

[55] *Capita Physica Theologica*, 36, PG150, 1145 A–B in *ibid* 102; see also p. 106

[56] *Capita Physica Theologica* 36, PG180, 1145 A–B in *ibid* 102

[57] Dumitru Staniloae, *op.cit*, 102; 105

[58] *Ibid* 103–104

it is the Word of the Spirit."[59] This non-causal reciprocity resembles a kind of passage of the Spirit through the Son and vice versa, in which the one contains the Other in Himself.[60]

This intimate union of the Son and the Spirit is reflected in the activity of Divine Persons on human Persons: we cannot possess the Spirit apart from Christ or Christ apart from the Spirit. We have the Spirit of Sonship because the Spirit of the Son becomes our Spirit too and we are thereby placed in direct relation with the Father, just like the Son.[61] Thus by sharing with human persons His own communion with and in the Father and the Son, the Spirit engages our own loving, filial consciousness "and attunes our souls to the spiritual life beyond";[62] we thus love the Father personally in the Spirit without our freedom being compromised and the Spirit becomes our Spirit of sonship (but we do not thereby cause the Spirit).

Staniloae argues that the alternative way of explaining the expression "Spirit of the Son" would be one of two forms of the *filioque*: either that the love of the Son for the Father is other than the love of the Father for the Son, meaning that the Spirit has two Fathers, or, as in the official Catholic version, that the Spirit proceeds from the Father and the Son as from a single principle.[63]

This would imply, he asserts, that the Spirit is an overflow of the common essence that is not directed from one Person to another, but towards something else, which would confuse the Persons and make the essence a source of personal being.

In consequence of both explanations, the Spirit loses His character as the Spirit of the Son received from the Father and the Son loses His character as Son in the manifestation of the Spirit within Him, since the Son becomes the source and therefore the Father of the Spirit. The Spirit would therefore not be the Spirit of the Son, but the Spirit of another Father. "It follows that the Son

---

[59] *Ibid* 105

[60] *Ibid*

[61] *Ibid* 106

[62] *Ibid* 103–104; c.f. St Basil, *De Spiritu Sancto* 23, 61; Rom 8:16; Gal 6:4

[63] *Ibid* 104

would no longer find Himself in filial relation to the Father through the Spirit."[64]

Here he echoes Athanasius' answer to the taunt that if the Son is the Image of the Father, then He must also beget a Son, just as the Father does. In *Against the Arians*, the saint argues that this would imply an endless multiplication of begettings, as in creaturely reality, which introduces time into the Triad. Thus the Son would become a Father to another Son who in turn becomes another Father, and so on. He continues:

> Hence, in such instances, there is not, properly speaking, either father or son, nor do the father and son stay in their respective characters [...] Thus it belongs properly to the Godhead alone, that the Father is properly Father, and the Son properly Son, and in Them, and Them only, does it hold that the Father is ever Father and the Son ever Son.[65]

In line with this thinking, Staniloae insists that Orthodox teaching preserves the position and personal distinction of each Person in the inter-Trinitarian communion:

> At the basis of this teaching we find a reciprocity between Son and Spirit that is not due to the fact that one has taken His origin from the other, but is due to the simple fact that both come forth from the Father and that there is a certain connecting link between them.[66]

Thus if we view the Divine Persons as real Persons who subsist in an eternal inter-subjective communion of love, we cannot use the sayings of the Fathers as they were used in the Clarification to support the Western position: because the divine origins relate

---

[64] *Ibid* 104

[65] *Against the Arians* 1.21; he repeats the same argument in *Letter to Serapion* 1.16

[66] Dumitru Staniloae, *op.cit*, 104

to the coming forth as distinct Persons, (a) the expression "through the Son" when used in respect of the immanent Trinity must be understood as a coming forth as Person in conjunction with the Son, although it usually relates the radiance of the Spirit from the Son as perceived mystically or the giving of the Spirit in the economy, and (b) the mind-knowledge-love analogy, when used by the Eastern Fathers, has an entirely different meaning to the Western meaning and must be interpreted as a description of the modes of being of the Persons as revealed in the economy, which cannot be confused with the Persons themselves.

That is, the Son's immanent identity cannot be defined as knowledge, nor the Spirit's immanent identity as love, as these modes simply describe the revelatory position of each in the economy and indicate their positions in the inter-Trinitarian communion.

One should add that the same argument applies to the "Trinitarian order" that the Clarification speaks of. In the thought of the Eastern Fathers, this is related to the revelatory, economic modes of the divine Persons, not the relations of origin. Basil sets this out clearly in *De Spiritu Sancto* 41 against those who introduce the idea of "sub-numeration" into the Trinity, which he calls a "palpable absurdity":[67]

No man knows the Father save the Son and so no man can say that Jesus is the Lord but by the Holy Spirit (1 Cor. 12:3). […] as it is written: "In your light we shall see light," namely, by the illumination of the Spirit, the true light that lights every man comes into the world (Jn 1:9). It results that in Himself He shows the glory of the Only-Begotten, and on true worshippers He Himself bestows the knowledge of God. Thus *the way of knowledge* of God lies from One Spirit through the One Son to the One Father, and conversely the natural Goodness and the inherent Holiness and the royal Dignity extend from the Father *through* the Only-Begotten to the Spirit. Thus there is

---

[67] St Gregory Nazianzus similarly emphasises the monarchy of the Father – see Anthony Meredith, *op.cit*, 106

both acknowledgement of the *hypostases* and the true doctrine of the Monarchy is not lost.[68] (Italics mine)

It is particularly notable that Basil describes the functions of the Persons in respect of God's movement towards creatures and the process of gathering them up into His own communion, not of the immanent relations.[69] With respect to the immanent Trinity, he asserts that the word "co-numeration is appropriate to subjects of equal dignity".[70] Once again, the stress is on the fact that the modes of being and functions in the economy indicate real Persons, but cannot be confused with the Persons themselves.

In terms of the procession of the Spirit, the bottom line is that in Eastern thought the Spirit is understood to come forth from the Father as Person, that is, as a personal "Subjectivity", together with and in the Son. The expression "through the Son" is usually understood to relate to the Spirit's economic manifestation.

6.IV. SUMMARY

The Orthodox meaning of "through the Son" takes on an entirely different meaning to the Western sense of *per filium* on account of being premised on a notion of divine personhood that is rooted in historical-mystical experience rather than philosophy. The Eastern Fathers simply affirmed that which is perceived mystically and verified by the biblical witness – polemically and dogmatically against Sabellianism, and in contradistinction to ancient Hellenic philosophical categories of thought – that divine personhood is *hypostatic*.

The Cappadocians posited three ineffable yet real personal Subjects whose existence cannot be explained rationally but who indivisibly constitute the one essence in perfect, inter-subjective communion. Thus the divine unity, while caused by the Father by

---

[68] *De Spiritu Sancto* 47
[69] Meredith again (*op.cit*, 106) misinterprets the Eastern notion of the structure of love in the Trinity as a hierarchical descent from the Father.
[70] *De Spiritu Sancto* 42

virtue of the Father being the cause of the other two Persons, is in itself a communion of love. While affirming that the sublime reality of the Persons is beyond human conception, they used Arius' essence/energies distinction to affirm that the energies (manifestations) indicate the presence of real Persons-*Hypostases*, in which each Person manifests the common attributes in an *enhypostatic* way, indicating both the common ineffable essence and unique ineffable identities. Similarly, they argued that the Sabellian "modes of being" – the modes of being Father, Son and Spirit – indicate the reality of subsistent Persons in inter-subjective relations, which in turn indicate three subsistent relational identities.

Thus the self-manifestation of the only begotten Son in His mode of Sonship indicates a distinct, subsistent Person who is eternally and ontologically the Son of the Father, while the Spirit's revelatory mode indicates an ineffable Person who eternally shares the inter-subjective communion of the Father and Son by nature. Because the modes of being indicate subsistent relations, they also indicate the manner of origin – that the Son comes forth as Son but that the Spirit does not – but not the how of the origin. Thus while both the Persons and immanent relations are recognised in each Person's mode of being, both the Persons and the divine processions remain ineffable.

In this context, on the rare occasions that the expression "through the Son" is used by the Eastern Fathers in relation to the immanent Trinity it is understood within the context of the Son and Spirit eternally coming forth from the Father together as real Persons in inter-subjective communion. Thus "through the Son" would mean "with and in" the Son, not "from" the Son.

However, the expression is usually understood to relate to the Persons' revelatory modes of being. In this context, the underlying sense seems to be that a distinction is made between the Persons themselves and their "acts" or manifestation or energies. Thus the subsistent relations, or modes of being, which indicate that the Father, Son and Spirit are real Persons in communion in three modes, should not be confused with the Persons themselves. To say that the Person *are* the relations revealed in the economy would imply that they cannot but act in the way they do in history, which would in turn undermine the perception that they are really three Persons who act in the freedom of love.

We have seen that the Western objections to the Eastern conception are not warranted in light of these paradigms and that the West has tended to misunderstand Orthodox thought because Westerners tend to read Eastern expositions as if they were an exercise in philosophical deduction. I have cited some comments from Rahner, Wiles, O'Collins and Meredith as examples of this problem, mostly in footnotes so as not to disrupt the flow of the argument. Western thinkers do not seem to realise that although the Eastern Fathers used the language of philosophy, they imbued it with new meaning. For example, while Hellenic philosophy posited rational being as ultimate reality, the Fathers answered, in effect: yes, truth is being (i.e. ontological reality) but true being is a triune, inter-subjective Godhead, i.e. Persons in communion – in contradiction to ancient Hellenic cosmology, which could not accommodate the experience of three personal and equal divine "Subjectivities".

To the idea that truth can be known rationally, the Fathers answered that the truth can be known, but only experientially in communion – and then only inasmuch as the Divine Persons reveal themselves in their revelatory modes, not in their essence. Thus the words "being" and "knowing" are used entirely differently from how philosophy uses them. And so one could go on. At the same time, the extensive, detailed, nuanced argumentation that was produced by the Eastern Fathers gives the lie to Rahner's claim that the idea of three consciousnesses in God is indicative of pre-reflective tritheism (2.iv. above). It is simply that Eastern theology is not the product of logical deduction, but of experience.

It also seems to be the case that the Eastern reticence to clearly spell out the underlying subtext of their perception of the Trinity in the past has rendered their perception rather inaccessible to the Western mind. While this reticence is understandable in light of the *apophatic* approach to theology and the inexpressible nature of the sublime reality of the Trinity, it has nevertheless constituted a barrier to mutual understanding. However, having taken the trouble to come to grips with and to articulate the Eastern position, the Eastern objections to the *filioque* begin to make a lot of sense.

6.V. COMMENTS: ORTHODOX OBJECTIONS TO THE FILIOQUE

First, if, as the Orthodox assert, the Divine Persons are real, distinct personal Subjects it is quite reasonable to assert that, while one can distinguish the Persons by their relations, one cannot identify the modes of being or relations of origin with the Persons themselves, because to say that the modes/relations cause or *are* the Persons would be to confuse the modes of interpersonal communion with the Persons themselves, which negates the perceived reality that they are real *Hypostases*-Persons *in* relation.

Second, if the Divine Persons are three real *Hypostases*-Persons, the Orthodox rejection of the Western assertion that the economic Trinity *is* the immanent Trinity is also reasonable because this notion implies that the Son and Spirit simply *are* their economic manifestations/acts, which are identical to the relations (of origin), meaning that they are not real Persons who act freely in history; they simply are their acts.

Third, the accusation of Modalism from the East is also understandable in light of the fact that the West seems to confuse the Persons with the modes of being and economic functions, which does not allow for the presence of three "I's" in the Trinity.

Fourth, in this context it seems reasonable to argue that distinguishing the Son from the Spirit by ascribing to Him a dual origin would imply either, as Photius argues, that the Spirit is a composite, which would mean He is not an "I", which is simple, or, as Staniloae argues, that He is an impersonal overflow of the common essence – and that both options thus depersonalise the Spirit.

Fifth, if the Spirit is a distinct "I", then He proceeds from the Father as such; therefore a procession from the Son as a "secondary principle" would not add anything to His existence as a distinct "I" that He does not receive in His procession from the Father, which renders the *filioque* redundant as a way of accounting for the *hypostatic* origin of the Spirit.

Sixth, if the equality of the three Persons is premised on the shared nature, then it is also needless to show the equality of the Father and the Son by means of the *filioque*.

Seventh, the Eastern accusation that the *filioque* subordinates the Spirit seems reasonable in the context of the Eastern understanding of the *hypostatic* (personal) characteristics: if being the cause of other Persons is a *hypostatic* characteristic, then the *filioque* would constitute the only instance in which two Persons share a *hypostatic* characteristic in common; the Spirit would be unequal in dignity as the only Person lacking this characteristic. Conversely, Photius' argument that attributing the same *hypostatic* characteristic to the Father and the Son confuses the two Persons, who are "one in relation to the Spirit", is also reasonable.

Eighth, it follows that the monarchy of the Father, although not philosophically compromised by the *filioque*, is in fact robbed of its intended content. If the Father is "God as such" (to use Rahner's term) due to being the cause of the other two Persons, then the *filioque* introduces the idea of two Gods "as such", because having the *hypostatic* property of causing other Persons is precisely the quality that distinguishes the Father as God proper.

Ninth, the Orthodox are not being unreasonable when they say that the *filioque* goes beyond Scripture, because (a) this notion is not directly specified in any Scripture text[71] and (b) all the biblical texts that are cited by the West to support this doctrine can be shown to have another meaning: those referring to the Spirit of the Son can be shown to allude to the Spirit abiding in the Son, the text "All things whatsoever the Father has are mine" (John 16:15) can be understood as a reference to the common nature and intersubjectivity, while texts that refer to the Spirit of love can be viewed as an allusion to the Spirit, as Person, sharing the divine communion of love with creatures and, as Person, occupying a particular position in the structure of Divine love.

In this context, references to the Son sending the Spirit cannot be seen as a synonym for the eternal procession, but rather as an expression of the common will of the Father and Son in the Spirit with respect to humanity, which is also the will of the Spirit in accordance with their common nature. Moreover, if the Spirit rests eternally in the Son, the implication is that human creatures receive the Spirit by virtue of being united to the Son in whom the

---

[71] We shall deal with the question of whether it is implied when we get to Augustine's thought below.

Spirit abides; thus the sending "from" the Son can be seen as an anthropomorphic expression that cannot be a basis for philosophical definition.

In short, all the objections are premised on the fundamental issue of personhood and if the Persons are in truth three subjective "I's" who subsist in a communion of love, then the Orthodox objections to the *filioque* seem reasonable, not only in terms of the content of the dogma but also in that it threatens the very idea of truth itself as it is understood by the Orthodox, namely that truth is the experientially known reality of Divine Persons in communion.

This seems to support my rather obvious initial observation that, while Scripture is quite properly a normative criterion of truth, the fact that the two traditions arrive at such different interpretations of the Bible means we can only resolve this issue by examining the divergent perspectives that are brought to bear on our readings of both Scripture and tradition.

7 ORIGINS OF THE WESTERN CONCEPTION

We have noted that the West formally received the formula of Constantinople I as ecumenical in only 451 A.D., 70 years after the council. In the meantime, Western thinkers had already developed their own Trinitarian theology and appropriated the formulas of Nicaea I and Constantinople I within their own conceptual system. We have also noted that the ideas that the Divine Persons are relations of origin and that the Spirit proceeds eternally from the Father and Son as from one principle are traceable to St Augustine, who worked out his theology in the period between the Constantinople I and Chalcedon. The following chapters are aimed at grappling with the underlying approach and aspects of Augustine's thought that resulted in a divergent conception to that of the Eastern Fathers. As we have already dealt with the Cappadocians, I shall note relevant differences between their thought and Augustine's as they arise.

7.1. AUGUSTINE'S MYSTICAL EXPERIENCE AND APPROACH

Considering Augustine's immense reputation, one expects him to be a great mystic whose doctrinal authority is premised on this fact. However, a very different picture emerges. As he outlines in books 4–8 of his *Confessions*, Augustine, an accomplished rhetorician and teacher, journeyed through Manichaeism and Neoplatonism before he came to faith in Christ. While the tone of his journey is one of intellectual searching, he reports a "momentary vision"[1] prior to his conversion, in which he describes (in truly Platonic fashion) searching in his mind for "that immutable, true and eternal truth which

---

[1] *Conf* VII.17.23

exists above my changeable mind", with his focus moving from the apprehension of "bodily things" to "the soul and its own understanding and reasoning power", and then above that – in what appears to be a rather *apophatic* transcendence – withdrawing itself from habit and "contradictory phantasms":

> Thus in a flash of trembling sight it [his mind] came to that which is. Then indeed I saw your 'invisible things, understood by the things which are made'. In my frailty I was struck back and I returned to my former ways. I took with me only a memory, loving and longing for what I had [...].[2]

Augustine does not describe exactly what he saw (or "saw"), but it does not seem to be of the same order of mystical encounter as that indicated by the Cappadocians or described by St Symeon the Theologian – apparitions of the manifest Persons and conscious communion with and in the Trinity. I say this, firstly, because Augustine's mystical encounter does not seem to be the sort of "Damascus experience" that results in an immediate acceptance of the Christian faith, which one would expect if it was an actual apparition of the glorified Christ. It rather formed one of a series of events that led to his deeply felt conversion (in 386, five years after Constantinople I), which climaxed in a sense of being touched by the Holy Spirit, who convicted him of sin and brought peace to his heart in his famous garden experience.[3]

The latter account appears to signify a genuine working of the Spirit in his life, leading to a profound conviction of sin and repentance, and moving him to seek an in-depth knowledge of the God in whom he had come to believe.

Here the word "seek" is pivotal. In his introduction to his translation of Augustine's *On the Trinity*, Edmund Hill insists that this work forms a part of his *search* for God: "The overriding concern in *On the Trinity* is to present his quest for God the Trinity as

---

[2] *Ibid* VII.17.23
[3] *Ibid* VIII.12.29

both an all-absorbing personal preoccupation and a kind of plan for the spiritual life of any Christian"[4] – a point that is often lost, from the scholastic period, on academic theologians who mined his work for useful metaphysical material on the Trinity.[5] Augustine himself says: "I have undertaken, not so much as to discuss with authority what I have already learned, as to learn by discussing it with modest piety".[6]

In short, his treatise is a function of a search for the God he had "glimpsed"; it is not an authoritative testimony to the experienced reality of the manifest Trinity. This constitutes an important distinction between the truth claims of East and West: while the Orthodox insist that the Eastern Fathers theologised from the perspective of having entered into a real communion with the Divine Persons, Augustine's exposition is a function of his struggle to understand the Trinity. This is of immense importance to our discussion of the word "Person", because the Orthodox insist that when the Eastern Fathers coined the Person-*Hypostasis* terminology, they simply named a reality they knew mystically,[7] while Augustine was dealing with ideas about the Divine Persons.

This brings us to our second point. Augustine seems to have perceived his own "momentary glimpse" as an illumination of the mind in the Neoplatonic sense of the expression rather than an illumination that occurs in the context of an apparition of God in Christ or an interior communion with the Divine Persons.

This interpretation is supported by his treatment of mystical experience in his writing. He consistently denies the possibility of

---

[4] Edmund Hill, *op.cit*, 21; see also Lewis Ayres, "Sempiterne Spiritus Donum: Augustine's Pneumatology and The Metaphysics of Spirit" in *Orthodox Readings of St Augustine* (Eds Demacopoulos, GE, & Papanikolaou, A) (New York: St Vladimir's Seminary Press, 2008), 143

[5] Edmund Hill, *op.cit*, 19

[6] *Trin.* I.1.8; see also I.1.5; III.*praef*.1; IV.*praef*.1; V.*praef*.2

[7] That is, in (a) apparitions of the Son, in whom the Father's personal presence is discerned and in which the Spirit is discerned as light and/or as the Person who shares His communion with the Father and Son in us. And (b) in the form of interior communion in which three personal presences are discerned – see 4.i.a above.

knowing God "face to face"[8] while still in the body,[9] asserting that the Divine Persons can become visible only by some created effect.[10] His de-legitimisation of mystical experience of God is particularly evident in his treatment of the Old Testament theophanies, which he argues were prophetic visions "seen in spirit by means of psychic images of things",[11] echoing Tertullian.[12] Thus for him apparitions and visions are given the same treatment. For example, in *On the Trinity* II.7.33–34 he places Daniel's visions in the same category as other Old Testament descriptions of apparitions of God. In II.5.17 he argues at length that God made Himself known to Moses through created effects and in II.6.29–31 he interprets the Lord's "back parts" of Moses' encounter allegorically as the flesh of Christ – which he takes to mean the Church. In I.3.16 he says that at the Parousia we will know God and (!) the Father face to face, when the Son reveals the Father and "when there is no more need for the regime of symbols administered by the angelic sovereignties and authorities and powers".[13] In fact, he interprets the text "we see Him in a glass darkly" (1 Cor 13.12) to mean that we see Him in symbols.[14] And in I.3.17: "We shall not seek anything else when we reach that contemplation of him, which is not yet ours as long as we are rejoicing only in hope."

In the meantime, he repeatedly stresses, we know God "by the things that are [made]" (Rom 1:20)[15] and that the Holy Spirit

---

[8] The Orthodox would understand face-to-face encounters with God as apparitions of Christ in His self-manifestation (energies).

[9] See for example *Trin.* II.6.28; *Conf* X.5.7

[10] Edmund Hill, *op.cit*, 45–46; 48; *Trin.* II.2.10–11; 3.12–14; 7.32; by contrast, as we have noted, in Orthodox testimony a face-to-face encounter with God would entail an apparition of the Son in His self-manifestation (energies), in whom the Father is also discerned, while the Spirit is discerned as light and/or the subjective ground of perception.

[11] *Trin.* II.2.11

[12] *Against Praxeas* 14

[13] See also *Trin.* I.3.21 and II.6.28; here of course, Augustine differs from the Eastern Fathers, who say that we see the Father in Christ, and then in His energies (manifestations), not in His essence

[14] *Ibid* I.3.16

[15] For example *ibid* II.5.25; IV.4.21 & 23; VI.2.12

illumines the human mind from sensible things, so enabling one to comprehend divine truth,[16] *contra* the Greek Fathers, who saw knowing God intimately as the very goal of the Christian life.[17] And in *On the Trinity* VII.3.9 he says: "For it [that God is three yet one] is known with complete certainty from the Scriptures [...] and the *mind's eye* can also achieve a faint but undoubted glimpse of the truth [...]" (italics mine). Bradshaw indicates that he does seem to entertain the possibility that biblical "greats" such as Moses and St Paul saw God face to face, as an "intellectual" vision, i.e. "that form by which God is what he is" or "the very substance of God".[18] However, Augustine insists that this was possible only because these saints were taken up out of the body[19] – and what he means by this is indicated in *On the Trinity* IV.5.28: "Of us too it can be said that when we grasp some eternal truth with the mind as far as we are capable of it, we are not in this world."

It is noteworthy that he sees the mind, which he considers "a spiritual substance",[20] as the spiritual component of the human being: "But mind and spirit are not said relatively, but express essence. For mind and spirit do not exist because the mind and spirit of some particular man exists [...] in so far as they are mutually referred to one another they are two; but whereas they are spoken in respect of themselves, each are spirit, and both together also are one spirit; and each are mind".[21] His use of the word "mind" interchangeably with the word "spirit" indicates that he identifies rationality with spirituality.

---

[16] See for example *City of God* 11.2.11; *Trin.* V.*praef*.2; VI.2.12; c.f. Allan & Springsted, *op.cit*, 28

[17] See for example John Meyendorff, *Byzantine Theology* 6–9; 67

[18] David Bradshaw, "Augustine the Metaphysician" in *Orthodox Readings of St Augustine* (Eds Demacopoulos, GE, & Papanikolaou, A) (New York: St Vladimir's Seminary Press, 2008), 248; he cites *De Gen. Ad lit* 12.28.56 & 147.31

[19] David Bradshaw, "Augustine the Metaphysician" in *Orthodox Readings of St Augustine*, 248; he cites *De Gen. Ad lit* 12.27.55, *Ep.* 147.31 & *Ad Simpl.* 2.1.1

[20] *Trin.* XII.2.2

[21] *Ibid* IX.2.2

Bradshaw also cites Augustine as identifying God as "the intelligible Light in, by and through whom all things are illumined"[22] and, like the Good in Plato's *Republic*, "God is the Sun of the intellectual realm".[23] But, unlike the Good (in its Neoplatonic interpretation), "God belongs to the realm of intelligible things"[24] and *reason* lets "you see God with your *mind* as the sun is seen with the eye" (provided the mind is purified).[25] In short, the evidence seems to indicate that Augustine's seeing is a rational "seeing", rather than actual experience of the Trinity in communion.

He consequently equates truth with rational knowing rather than intimately experiencing. Thus Augustine's idea of apprehending divine truth appears to be illumination of the mind in the Neoplatonic sense, which was premised on the idea that divine reality is discursively revealed in temporal reality in varying degrees by a series of emanations from the One.[26] Thus, even Augustine's interpretation of his mystical experience – and perhaps even his naming of his "illumination" as such – was informed by an Hellenic philosophical presupposition that made the rational mind the connecting link between divine and creaturely reality. This appears to be indicative of the fact that, whatever the exact nature of his mystical experience, having been thrown back on his creaturely perspective, Augustine continued to be informed by presuppositions from the Hellenic philosophy in which he was ensconced at the time of his conversion, particularly Neoplatonism.[27] This goes a long way to explaining why – as opposed to the *apophatic* approach of the Eastern monastic movement, which involved emptying the mind of all presuppositions and so creating the space for God to make Himself known personally through the Son and in the Spirit in subjec-

---

[22] *Soliloquiorum* 1.1.3 in David Bradshaw, "Augustine the Metaphysician" in *Orthodox Readings of St Augustine*, 236; see also *Trin.* IV.1.3

[23] *Soliloquiorum* 1.9.16 in *ibid*

[24] *Soliloquiorum* 1.8.15 in *ibid*

[25] *Soliloquiorum* 1.6.12 in *ibid*; see also *Trin.* 1.1.3 & 4, I.4.23

[26] Allen & Springsted, *op.cit*, 9; 24–25; 34; 50–52; *Trin.* IV.4.23–24

[27] John K. Ryan (trans), introduction to *The Confessions of St. Augustine* (New York: Image Books, 1960), 21–23

tive relationship[28] – Augustine's quest was an existential-rational one, as Hill[29] asserts.

7.II. AUGUSTINE AND HELLENIC PHILOSOPHY

Immersed in Neoplatonism just prior to coming to believe in the Christian God, Augustine attributed to Platonism the fact that he was able to overcome his inability to conceive of any reality that was not sensible, thus paving the way for his conversion to Christianity.[30] Thus the discovery that the Christian faith could be shown to be consistent with his philosophical presuppositions was an important factor in his conversion[31] and he retained a great love for philosophical inquiry. Hill comments that Augustine incorporated the metaphysics of the 4th century Arian metaphysicians, notably Eunomius (to whose approach the Cappadocians objected so strongly) into his argumentation "while taking the sting out of their arguments […] He found no difficulty in taking over their metaphysics, as he breathed the same Neoplatonist atmosphere that they did."[32]

He did not make a distinction between philosophy and theology in the vein of the medieval scholastic faith/reason distinction; rather, philosophising about the Christian God and theologising about God meant the same thing to him. He called theology the true philosophy, like his Eastern counterparts, and referred to pagan philosophies such as Platonism "false theologies.[33]

However, he meant something quite different to the Eastern Fathers. Although he says, like them, that "it is necessary for our minds to be purified before that inexpressible reality can be clearly seen by them",[34] what he seems to mean is that the mind is hum-

---

[28] See 3.ii above

[29] *Op.cit*, 20

[30] Allen & Springsted, *op.cit*, 21; 56; Bradshaw, "Augustine the Metaphysician" in *Orthodox Readings of St Augustine*, 234–235

[31] *Conf* 7.20

[32] Edmund Hill, *op.cit*, 49

[33] *Ibid* 22

[34] *Trin*, I.1.3

bled by having to live by faith in the *lesser truth* of historical revelation;[35] thus, for example, he equates Christ Crucified – whom St Paul considered the epitome of the revelation of God (1 Cor 2:2) – with the milk that is fed to babies (I Cor 3:1–2).[36] And in *On the Trinity* I.4.24: "Now just as the rational mind is meant, once purified, to contemplate eternal things, so it is meant while still needing purification to give faith to temporal things." It seems to be with this in mind that, in *On the Trinity* IV.4.20–21, he attacks the pride of the philosophers "who think they can purify themselves for contemplating God and cleaving to him by their own power and strength of character" because "they have been able to direct the keen gaze of their intellects beyond everything created and to attain, in however small a measure, the light of unchanging truth" while ridiculing those who believe in the resurrection.

In the same paragraph he nevertheless gives them their due for being able "to understand the sublime and unchanging substance of God by the things that are made (Rom 1.20)" and being able to "provide convincing proofs that all temporal things happen according to eternal ideas" – an explicit allusion to the Platonic Forms – and for being "superior to others in their understanding of the supreme, eternal ideas".

Augustine's point is not that their ideas are wrong, but that their ideas will not be of any use to them if they do not submit in humility to the Cross. Thus purification of the mind means being purified of pride; it does not seem to include jettisoning the philosophical presuppositions he considered consistent with the Christian faith.

Thus, while for the Eastern Fathers calling theology the "true philosophy" meant "love of God" and true *theo-logia* meant "words about God" uttered when one has achieved *theoria* (the vision of God),[37] for Augustine philosophising *was* theologising, leading to a rational approach to theology and also to the fact that he brought

---

[35] *Ibid* IV.1.2; see also Edmund Hill, *op.cit*, 177, footnote 8, and 182–183, footnote 74

[36] *Ibid* I.4.23

[37] See John of Damascus in Hierotheos, *The Person in the Orthodox Tradition*, 61–63

key Hellenic philosophical presuppositions to bear on the content of his thought.

This is pivotal, because with the reception of Augustine's Trinitarian theology as normative, the presuppositions embedded in his thought have also been received as normative in the West, meaning that the Western interpretation of the theological developments of the 4th century are circumscribed by an approach and presuppositions that owe their normative value to the very developments that are being interpreted.

It seems that one has to be particularly mindful of this when assessing Augustine's thought, both in relation to Eastern assumptions and to his particular polemical situation.

7.III. THE INFLUENCE OF OTHER ECCLESIAL WRITERS

Hill notes the well-known fact that Augustine's Greek was poor[38] and that he was therefore not thoroughly conversant with the writings of the Greek Fathers. He does quote from Latin translations of two of Basil's works and in one case translates a passage from Basil, indicating that his Greek improved later in life. He also quotes from Latin translations of some of Gregory Nazianzen's writings, mainly homilies. But none of these were on the Trinity or the Holy Spirit, and he seems to have mined these works to support his own views on original sin, the fall, grace and predestination, which he was debating with Julian of Eclanum.[39]

Hill notes that he also seems to have read some writings of Didymus the Blind, but cites Tertullian in the early 3rd century, Novatian in the late 3rd century, and Hilary of Poitiers and Marius Victorinus in the 4th as Augustine's primary sources.[40]

However, Augustine's reflection on the Trinity constituted a rather solitary attempt to correct what he perceived to be philosophical deficiencies in the thought of his predecessors and con-

---

[38] Edmund Hill, op. cit, 38; see Conf 1:13, 20; 14:23; Trin. III.praef.1

[39] Joseph T Lienhard, "Augustine of Hippo, Basil of Caesarea and Gregory Nazianzen" in Orthodox Readings of St Augustine, op.cit, 88–99

[40] Edmund Hill, op. cit, 38

temporaries. Hill outlines some of the problems Augustine set his mind to solving, the first being that of subordinationism.

7.iii.a. Subordinationism

Hill notes that a tendency to subordinate the Son was typical of third century Latin thought;[41] for example, Novatian's argument for the divinity of the Son involved vigorously arguing for the inequality of the Son to the Father and even going so far as to assert that the Son was a product of the Father's will. As for Tertullian, while he displays an in-depth knowledge of both Latin and Greek in this work, he misinterprets the monarchy to mean the "sole government" of the Father. He therefore argues that the monarchy (rule) of the Father is not disturbed by the fact that it is administered by the Son and Spirit, "who have the second and third places assigned to them".[42]

In this conception, the Son and Spirit are seen as administrators or executors of the Father's government in the economy [i.e. as in legal *persona*], acting according to the Father's will in what appears to be a rather subordinate way.[43]

This sense of subordination is underscored in Tertullian's use of 1 Corinthians 15:24–28 to demonstrate the Son's subjection to the Father with a view to showing, notably, that the Father and Son are "two separate Persons" without the monarchy of the Father being disturbed.[44] However, he also sees the Son as equal to the Father by virtue of the shared substance, pre-empting the Eastern Fathers by answering the Modalist use of the text "My Father is greater than I" (Jn 14:28) as follows: "The Father is distinct from the Son, being greater than the Son inasmuch as He who begets is one and He who is begotten is another".[45]

---

[41] *Ibid* 42–43
[42] Tertullian, *Against Praxeas* 3
[43] *Ibid* 3–4; 12; 15; 24
[44] *Ibid* 4
[45] *Ibid*

Tertullian also equates the generation of the Son with the economic sending. While he hints that the Son is somehow latently present in God prior to creation, he interprets the "let there be light" of Genesis 1:3 to denote the begetting or nativity of the Son/Word from the Father, which he sees as giving utterance to the Reason that was already present with the Father – in the same way that a thought is given form in a word – "in the beginning"[46] before the creation of heaven and earth and with a view to the Son participating in creation. He pre-empts Arius' "there was a time when the Son was not" by saying that it was only in this begetting as Light that He became Son, because in this begetting He assumed His own distinctive form (i.e. the form of a thought is a word).[47]

This tendency to equate the Trinity with the economy was also present in Novatian's thought, Hill observes.

He notes that in Novatian's case this difficulty was related to how he identified Irenaeus' assertion that the Father is invisible and the Son visible with the Son being the image of the Father, resulting in a failure to distinguish between "what we now call the eternal processions and the temporal missions of the Son and Spirit".[48]

This mindset, which dovetailed into a lingering Arianism in the West after Nicaea I, meant Augustine needed to forcefully distinguish the economic Trinity from the immanent Trinity and affirm the equality and eternity of the Son and the Spirit in line with the faith of the Church.

His opposition to the traditional notion that the Old Testament theophanies were appearances of the Son was largely a reaction to the fact that this idea "had been largely responsible for involving the 'economic' theologians in subordinationism," Hill notes.[49]

In book I of *On the Trinity* Augustine argued for the equality of the Persons from the New Testament, which enabled him to assert – as did Athanasius – that the Son is lesser than the Father in his

---

[46] *Ibid* 19

[47] *Ibid* 5; 7; 19; "form" is probably meant in the Platonic sense; c.f. Edmund Hill, *op.cit*, 42

[48] Edmund Hill, *op.cit*, 43

[49] *Ibid* 45–46; 48

humanity but equal in His divinity. Thus Scripture texts that had been used to support a subordinationist stance could now be shown to apply only to the Son's humanity.[50]

7.iii.b. Confusion of sending and proceeding

To complicate the issue further, Augustine's Western predecessors did not seem to be aware of the precise way in which their Eastern counterparts used specific words. For example, Tertullian used the term "begetting" for the economic Trinity and sometimes "proceeding" as a synonym for both begetting and sending.[51]

St Ambrose, whose preaching contributed to Augustine's conversion,[52] used the word "proceeding" for both the eternal coming forth of the Spirit and the economic sending.[53] Thus Augustine inherited a rather vague use of terminology on the key issue of the Spirit's procession.

Hill adds that the Son's sending was particularly problematic, as the "economic" writers had used this idea to affirm their subordinationist views. They assumed, quite reasonably, that being sent implied the superiority of the sender and the inferiority of the one sent.[54]

Here Augustine could not argue that the Son was lesser only in His humanity, as the sending precedes becoming human, while the Spirit, who is also sent, has no human nature in which to become less than the Father. Augustine argued quite simply that being sent does not imply inequality, but simply that the one sent is *from* the sender. It also implies a manifestation or revelation of the one sent – a similar argument to that used by St Ambrose[55] – who now comes to be among men in a new way.[56]

---

[50] *Ibid* 46; see for example *Trin.* I.3.14 & 4.22
[51] See *Against Praxeas* 5–7; 11; 13; 19; 22
[52] *Conf* 5.13–6.4
[53] See Ambrose, *On the Holy Spirit* 1.1.23 & 25; 1.3.44; 1.11.116–119
[54] Edmund Hill, *op.cit*, 47
[55] *On the Holy Spirit* 1.11.116–125
[56] Edmund Hill, *op.cit*, 47; see also Lewis Ayres, *op.cit*, 130–131; *Trin.* II.1.3 & 2:7–8; III.1.3; IV.5.26–27

He also used this identification of the word "sent" with "revealed" to argue against the idea that it was the Son who appeared to the prophets in the Old Testament theophanies;[57] thus he asks: "If God sends His Son in "the fullness of time" (Gal 4:4) – i.e. in the incarnation, "how could He be seen by the Fathers before He is sent?"[58]

He then distinguished the sending from the processions and explicitly made the eternal "processions" prior to the sending and, in keeping with the idea that the sending is a manifestation or revelation of the one sent, he asserted that the sendings are temporal revelations of the eternal processions.

Thus, Augustine is still arguing from the economy, but while Tertullian argued that the economy *constitutes* the mystery of God, Augustine modified this to say that the economy *reveals* the mystery of God.[59] This aspect of Augustine's thought brings us to the Eastern objection that one cannot deduce the immanent Trinity from the economic Trinity – an idea related to his rational idea of truth as illumination of the mind, along with some others from Hellenic philosophy. In fact, Augustine's notion of truth *is* his justification for arguing that the economic Trinity reveals the immanent Trinity.

7.IV. NOTION OF TRUTH – THE ECONOMIC TRINITY REVEALS THE IMMANENT TRINITY

Augustine's idea that the economic Trinity reveals the immanent Trinity is linked to several Platonic presuppositions, beginning with his understanding of the relationship of time to eternity and his identification of truth with eternity. In book 11 of his *Confessions* he answers a Manichaean attack on Christian doctrine. They had asked: "If God created the world out of nothing, why did He create it at the time He did?" Allen explains that Augustine answered, following Plato,[60] that time began with creation (though Plato did not advocate creation *ex nihilo*, but the ordering of matter). In Him-

---

[57] *Trin.* IV.5.28
[58] *Trin.* IV.5.26
[59] Edmund Hill, *op.cit*, 47–48; see *Trin.* IV.5.29
[60] *Timaeus* 37e–38b in Allen & Springsted, *op.cit*, 6

self, God is eternal and therefore complete, not subject to change. And, as Plotinus had argued, time is a mental phenomenon, not governed by the motions of the heavenly bodies (*contra* Aristotle). The only real time is the present. As He is eternal, for God all time is present. Thus, as God is eternal, we cannot comprehend Him in His essence; we can only make statements about His relation to time.[61]

One would then expect him to sharply distinguish between the economic (revealed) Trinity and immanent Trinity (God as He is in Himself), as the Eastern Fathers did. They used this distinction to say that we cannot know anything about the Trinity beyond what has been revealed to us, as we noted in 1.iv.b above, a conviction consistent with the mystical perception of the impenetrable depths of the Divine Persons as personal Subjects.

However, two fundamental Hellenic philosophical presuppositions that informed both Augustine's idea of truth and his idea of God militate against this view:

First, Augustine identifies absolute truth with eternity and, explicitly agreeing with Plato,[62] eternity with "unchangeableness".[63] Second, he identifies truth, immutability and eternity with the divine substance: "For God's essence, by which he is, has absolutely nothing changeable about its eternity or its truth or its will".[64] His equation of immortality with "unchangingness" led him to conclude that since the simple and unchanging immanent Trinity cannot suffer alteration through an interaction with time, the economic Trinity reveals the immanent Trinity (as in the sendings reveal the immanent processions).[65] As his idea of truth relates to an im-

---

[61] Allen & Springsted, *op.cit*, 7–8; see *Trin.* IV.4.22
[62] *Timaeus* 28
[63] *Trin.* IV.4.24
[64] *Ibid* IV.*praef.*1; see also V.1.3; VI.2.8
[65] *Ibid* I.1.1; I.1.2; here Augustine equates true immortality, as against the relative immortality of the soul, with "unchangingness"; see also *Trin.* I.4.26, II.3.14; IV.4.24; V.1.5; *Conf.* 7.11 and *Civ Dei*, 8.11, quoted in Jean-Luc Marion, "Idipsum: The name of God according to St Augustine" in *Orthodox Readings of St Augustine*, *op.cit*, 171. Here Augustine explicitly credits Plato with this idea.

mutable eternity of substance, Augustine had to legitimise the idea that, albeit a lesser truth, discursive rational truth is the highest form of truth available to us in this world. Thus, he argues, we can only know Truth, which is God, when we come to share in eternity; in the interim, we can know truth only by faith.[66] Thus:

> Our faith will then become truth, when we come to what we are promised as believers; but what we are promised is eternal life, and the truth said – not the truth our faith will become in the future but the truth which is always truth because it is eternity, the truth said – *this is eternal life, that they should know you the one true God, and Jesus Christ whom you have sent* (Jn 17:3); therefore when our faith becomes truth by seeing, our mortality will be transformed into a fixed and firm eternity.[67] (Italics in original)

The implication is that Augustine does not seem to consider it possible to actualise Truth ontologically in this life, even as an interior reality (which again suggests that he himself did not do so). This comment needs to be understood relative to the Eastern idea of actualisation of truth as communion with a triune God who is a threefold communion of Persons, which allows for the interior actualisation of truth as communion while still in the body as a subjective reality (as in "The kingdom of heaven is within you" of Lk 17:21), as opposed to Augustine's idea of truth as immutable eternity of *substance*, which means that in this life truth can be appropriated only in a discursive, temporal and rational form. There is therefore a split in Augustine's thought between the actuality of truth and truth as a set of rational ideas – a split that we shall see echoed in his conception of the Trinity, notably between the historical experience of the Divine Persons and his metaphysics.

Zizioulas and Hierotheos object to both these ideas of truth; firstly, that ultimate truth is linked to the (common) divine substance rather than explicitly to the Persons and, secondly, the

---

[66] *Trin.* IV.4.23–24
[67] *Ibid* IV.4.24

Eunomian idea (that St Basil countered) that a set of ideas about God can be considered truth.[68] Thus, for example, in *On the Trinity* VI.2.10, Augustine equates understanding that God is one yet three with knowing God; i.e. knowing about God is equated with knowing God, in true Eunomian fashion. What is most significant is the different emphases: the Eastern emphasis on the Persons means that truth is actualised in and as relationship with Persons who subsist in an eternal communion; by sharing in this personal communion, we also share in the common life of the Divine Persons, which is a communion of love, by a participation in the *hypostatic* energies (manifestations); thus participation in the divine life is contingent on personal relationship.

By contrast, Augustine's emphasis on truth as unchangeable essence means that he is unable (a) to connect the actualisation of truth to relationship or communion, but only to the consequence of that communion, i.e. the state of being eternal by participation, or (b) to identify the incarnate Son with absolute truth itself; Christ is seen merely as a bridge to truth, as one who leads us from temporality to eternity:

> But eternal life is promised us by the truth, from whose transparent clarity our faith is as far removed as mortality is from eternity. So now we accord faith to the things done in time for our sakes, and are purified by it, in order that when we come to sight and truth succeeds to faith, eternity might likewise succeed to mortality. [...] When the Son of God came in order to become Son of man and to capture our faith and draw it to himself, and by means of it to *lead us on to his truth* [...] Nor [...] could we pass from being among the things that originated to eternal things, unless the eternal allied himself to us in our originated conditions and so provided us with a *bridge* to his eternity.[69] (Italics mine)

---

[68] See 3.ii.a above
[69] *Ibid.* IV.4.24

At the beginning of the next chapter, Augustine states: "There you have what the Son of God has been sent for."[70] The implication is that he has retained the Justinian-Origenistic idea of truth that the Cappadocians steered theology away from in the East, namely that the Christ event does not realise truth, but only reveals a singular and comprehensive pre-existing truth.[71] The idea that the historical Christ *is* truth (Jn 14:6) has effectively been explained away.[72] Augustine has thus justified (a) turning truth about an "intelligible God" into an object of rational speculation, thereby justifying a speculative, phenomenological interpretation of divine revelation and (b) the idea that the economic Trinity discursively reveals the immanent Trinity.

We have also noted that this rational notion of truth goes hand-in-hand with Augustine explaining away the Old Testament theophanies. In the process he ends up undermining the possibility of mystical encounters with God *in principle*. This argument is pivotal because it brings us to the heart of the conflicting truth claims of East and West. The Eastern Fathers subscribed to the notion that it was the Son who appeared to the Old Testament prophets because this interpretation was consistent with mystical experience, in which the Persons are perceived in the form of "uncreated light" (as in uncreated manifestation) and in which the Father is seen visibly only in the Son, never in Himself.[73] This direct experience in turn informed their interpretation of not only the Old Testament theophanies, but also the biblical texts in which the Son is described as the eternal image of God the Father (e.g. Col. 1.15).

---

[70] *Ibid* IV.5.25

[71] John Zizioulas, *Being as Communion*, 78; see 3.i.b above

[72] *Ibid* 75–77

[73] Hierotheos (Vlachos), *The Person in the Orthodox Tradition*, 192; see also 4.i.a above. The experience of uncreated light was central in the *hesychast* debate of the 4th century that resulted in the dogmatisation in the East of the doctrine of uncreated energies, although the distinction was already made by the Cappadocians – see David Bradshaw, *The Concept of the Divine Energies* [online]. http://johnsanidopolous.com./2009/10/-concept-of-divine-energies.html (accessed 16/10/2009), n.pag; see also 4.ii.a above.

Their mystical experience was the hermeneutic key that unlocked the Scriptures for them. By contrast, Augustine, who seems to have had no such experiential reference, had to de-legitimise the veracity and authority of this testimony to support his Hellenic philosophical idea of truth. As Bradshaw indicates, he does this on the basis of his Neoplatonist idea of the divine simplicity and being as undivided wholeness.[74] Thus, over and above the notion, shared with the Eastern Fathers, that God must be identical to His perfections (otherwise He would possess them by participation), he argued in *Civitate Dei* 8.6 and 11.10 that "since God is absolutely and without qualification, for him to live, to understand, to be blessed and to enjoy his own perfections is the same as to be; thus the divine nature 'is the same as itself' and 'is what it has'".

Bradshaw asserts that this leads to the conclusion that "the divine essence is identical with the divine attributes as well as with the divine *esse*, and that all of these are identical with one another".[75] One can see an example of the former in *On the Trinity* VI.1.2–3, in a discussion of the text "Christ is the Power of God and the Wisdom of God" (1 Cor 1:24), in which Augustine collapses the (non-relational) divine names that refer to attributes into each other and into the essence: "The power is of course identical with the wisdom and the wisdom with the power." He adds that this is also true of greatness and "any other things that can be named [...] whatever they [the Father and Son] are called to indicate their substance they are called together." Bradshaw comments:

> Gregory [of Nyssa] is just as emphatic as Augustine in affirming that God is Goodness, Beauty, Wisdom, and the other divine perfections; yet since he also holds that the divine names are names of the divine *energies* rather than the divine essence, he must be understood to be asserting these names on the level of energies. That is, they are names of God *as manifested* in

---

[74] David Bradshaw, "Augustine the Metaphysician" in *Orthodox Readings of St Augustine*, 240–241

[75] *Ibid* 241; see also Edmund Hill, *op.cit*, 92, footnote 18; Hill cites this as a basic axiom of Trinitarian theology; see also *Trin.* V.2.11 & VI.1.3 & 7

his activity. What he clearly does not mean is that God's attributes are identical to his essence, as is held by Augustine.[76] (Italics mine)

As an example of the latter, Augustine argues in *The Trinity* 1.4.26–27 that if the incarnate Son speaks the Father's word, as in Jn 12:49–50, He speaks *Himself* – thus identifying the Son with His acts. He continues that when the Son says, "the Father has given me" (Jn 5:36; 14:31), this is the same as saying the Father has begotten Him, because in the Son that which He is and that which He has (from the Father) are one and the same. Thus the fact that the Father has given the Son life in Himself means the Son *is* eternal life. The context is a discussion in which Augustine attempts to demonstrate that "the words I have spoken, that is what will judge him on the last day (Jn 12:47)" are an allusion to the Son Himself, who *is* the Word of the Father.

What is of interest here is not his final conclusion but the way in which he argues the point; he reasons that inasmuch as the Son's acts are also the Father's acts, the Son's acts are identical not only with the essence and attributes, but also with the begetting. The implications are obvious: (a) without the distinction between energies (manifestations) and essence in Augustine's thought, the revealed Trinity is substantially identical with the immanent Trinity. And (b), because there is no distinction between energies and essence in his mind, there are only two "states" in God – either incorporeal and therefore invisible or incarnate and therefore visible; i.e. there can be no such thing as uncreated light. Because the incarnation had not yet happened, the Old Testament theophanies could not be apparitions of the Son.[77] In short, an affirmation of a Hellenic philosophical presupposition necessitates the negation of

---

[76] *Ibid* 241

[77] He deals with this theme extensively in *Trin.* II.4–7; see for example II.4.18 & 7.32 & IV.*praef.*1; see also II.3.14 and 7.35; this is in all likelihood a counter argument against the Arian doctrine that the Son is a divine energy; Augustine wishes to stress the common essence against this idea, while the stress on incorporeality is an attempt to counter the idea that the Son came into being as light with or just before creation.

the testimony of experienced reality. He even explains away the "Light of Light" of Nicaea I, which, as noted in 4.i.a, was an affirmation of a mystically perceived reality, saying that it denotes the incarnate Christ who illumines us as the revealed wisdom of God the Trinity.[78]

Also, because he understands references to God in the Old Testament as references to the "triad" – i.e. "the supreme and supremely divine and changeless *substance* in which the one and only God is both (sic) the Father and the Son and the Holy Spirit",[79] who act inseparably, he asserts that one cannot argue that one specific divine Person appeared to the Old Testament prophets. And, in any case, the biblical texts do not indicate that a particular Person appeared to the prophets.[80]

This again dovetails into the essence/energies discussion: because he identifies the divine essence with the attributes and acts of God, even if he did distinguish the immanent Persons from the essence as three "I's" (which, as we shall see, he does not), he could not conceive of the Persons manifesting Themselves in their *hypostatic* (personal) energies.

Another important point is that he relates the immutability of God to the divine substance rather than to the incommunicable identities of the three Persons. In his mind, because immutability denotes immortality, if the Persons took different forms it would mean they were mortal.[81] He thus argues repeatedly that if any of the Persons are made visible in the economy, it is not because one of them is eternally visible; the Person becomes visible only through some created effect: "All these visions, however, were produced through the changeable creation subject to the changeless God, and they did not manifest God as He is in Himself, but in a symbolic manner as times and circumstances required".[82]

---

[78] *Trin.* VII.2.4–5
[79] *Ibid* II.7.32 (italics mine)
[80] *Ibid* II.7.32
[81] *Ibid* II.3.14–15; 5.27; III.4.22; here he argues that angels mediated God to the prophets
[82] *Ibid* II.7.32; see also II.2.10–11, 3.12–15; chapters 4 and 5; III.3.19

Ergo, we can only know God from illumination of sensible things (hence the need for the Incarnation, which reveals a pre-existing truth through the "Word being compounded with a man".[83] We see all these presuppositions coming together in *On the Trinity* III.3.21:

I can boldly say with complete confidence that neither God the Father nor his Word nor his Spirit, all of which is one God in *being and identity*, is in any way changeable or variable, let alone visible, like thoughts and memories and wishes, like any incorporeal creature. But nothing that is visible is not also variable. So then the substance, or if you prefer it the being of God, *in which we understand after our limited and partial human manner Father and Son and Holy Spirit*, is in no way changeable or variable, and therefore cannot in itself be visible. (Italics mine)

Augustine has effectively demoted the three Divine Persons to the level of our discursive, partial perception and therefore to the level of a "lesser truth" about the One God. And by explaining away the testimony of the prophets to actual apparitions of any of the Divine Persons he has implicitly undermined the authority of any subsequent testimony to such experiences and thereby (a) justified turning truth, about an "intelligible God", into an object of rational speculation and (b) turned the presuppositions that informed his thinking into criteria of truth, which he reads into Scripture and dogma. In short, he has justified (a) a speculative, phenomenological interpretation of divine revelation and (b) the idea that the economic Trinity reveals the immanent Trinity. On this basis he justifies the idea that the sending of the Spirit reveals the immanent procession of the Spirit and therefore the *filioque*.

This argumentation has a fourfold significance regarding the relationship between Augustine's experience, presuppositions, idea of truth and the content of his explication: First, it underscores the reality that Augustine's approach to truth and his conception of the

---

[83] *Ibid* IV.5.30; IV.3.16

Trinity are informed mainly by Hellenic philosophical presuppositions rather than by experience of God.

Second, by undermining testimony to the reality of experience of God, he has effectively excluded the basis of the Eastern objections to (a) his approach to truth and (b) to his view that the economic Trinity reveals the immanent Trinity, i.e. the argument that one cannot deduce the immanent Trinity from the economic Trinity because the immanent Trinity is beyond our experience.[84]

Third, by identifying truth properly with the substance of God and improperly with rational ideas about the substance, rather than the Persons themselves, he has depersonalised truth: God is no longer the personal Subject of truth known in interpersonal communion, as the Orthodox argue, but rather a rational, immutable, seemingly static and abstract entity.

This depersonalisation is reinforced by the fact that the Platonic equation of immortality with "unchangingness" relates to a changelessness in God that has little resemblance to the personal biblical meaning that, as Wiles[85] indicates, was related to the reliability and consistency of a personal God "[…] in His attitudes of grace and judgment towards men".[86]

Fourth – and here we see how his approach to truth, presuppositions, criteria of truth and content dovetail into each other and are mutually informing – Augustine has made it impossible, on the basis of both his criteria of truth/Hellenic presuppositions and concept of God, to conceptualise the Divine Persons as ontologically distinct personal Subjects because (a) he identifies the *being* with the *identity* of the one "God the Trinity", which militates against the notion of three distinct Persons; (b) his identification of the divine essence with the attributes and acts of God means he could not conceive of the Persons manifesting Themselves in their *hypostatic* (personal) energies; and (c) while, according to Allen,[87] it was axiomatic among Christians of the 4th century that God reveals

---

[84] See 1.i.b above

[85] *Op.cit*, 21

[86] See also David Bradshaw, "Augustine the Metaphysician" in *Orthodox Readings of St Augustine*, 236

[87] In Allen & Springsted, *op.cit*, 58

Himself freely, as an act, rather than by degrees of necessary emanation, as Bradshaw indicates, Augustine infers with his notion of
divine simplicity that God is also identical with His own will –
meaning that God cannot act in any other way to the way He does,
as in Plotinus, who argued that the Good by its nature must produce all that it is capable of producing.[88]

In tandem with the fact that this calls into question the divine
freedom, Augustine's identification of the substance with the acts
and attributes of God, together with his idea that there is only one
identity in God, is prohibitive of the notion that there are three real
Persons in the Trinity who act freely, because they simply are their
acts. Furthermore, in Augustine's thought the Son's acts and the
Father's acts are identical, and the *esse* with the begetting; thus the
Son is merely an act of the Father. This means the Son cannot be a
distinct Person who acts. In short, a rejection of the idea of three
real Persons is built into Augustine's notion of truth, and his notion of truth and content are mutually informing. By contrast, the
Eastern distinction between the divine *ousia* and energies is rooted
in the experiential perception that three distinct personal Subjects
manifest themselves in history in particular ways, which is the reason for which (a) they strongly assert that Father, Son and Spirit are
three distinct, *hypostatic* Persons, (b) that truth is a function of personal communion with the Divine Persons and (c) that the Persons
and their eternal processions are ineffable.

The fact that the divergent conceptions of the Trinity are so
interwoven with differing truth criteria in East and West means we
find ourselves having to decide between two sets of truth claims.
The following is in question: the Eastern truth claim is premised on
the *apophatic* approach to truth, namely, that an essential ingredient
of repentance is that one needs to empty one's mind of all presuppositions regarding God; having undertaken this repentance, the
Fathers experienced the Divine Persons mystically and then attempted to explain and defend what they knew experientially. Their
theology is therefore not a function of philosophy and thus does

---

[88] David Bradshaw, "Augustine the Metaphysician" in *Orthodox Readings of St Augustine*, 241–242

not fit comfortably with key ancient Hellenic philosophical premises, such as those governing categories of unity and personhood.

By contrast, philosophy played an important role in Augustine's conversion to Christianity and his Trinitarian theology does not seem to be the fruit of mystical apparitions of or communion with the Divine Persons – if Hill is correct in saying that his conception is a function of his search for God and if Augustine's Neoplatonic idea of illumination of the mind is indeed indicative of the extent of his inspiration.

But even if this is not accurate, the fact remains that, arguing from Hellenic metaphysical presuppositions, he (a) explained away direct encounters with God and (b) allowed key Hellenic philosophical presuppositions to become his criteria of truth. And because his criteria of truth and the content of his argumentation are mutually informing, his conception of the Trinity and his criteria of truth are self-referential – and actively exclude the objection that his argumentation contradicts experience of God.

7.V. SUMMARY

While Augustine attempted to explicate the orthodox faith as it had been handed down to him, several key ideas in his conception can be attributed to his attempt to fix difficulties posed by the thought of earlier writers, perceived and real – without the benefit of a detailed knowledge of the thought of the Greek Fathers. We have so far touched only on Augustine's conviction that the economic sendings reveal but do not constitute the immanent processions. This constituted his answer to the fact that several of his Western predecessors, such as Tertullian and Novatian, subordinated the Son and the Spirit by positing that the sendings and the processions were identical, and did not distinguish between "sent" and "proceed". Against this backdrop, Augustine needed to assert strongly the equality of the Divine Persons, as the Eastern Fathers did against Arius. However, because he appropriated the Christian faith from the perspective of Hellenic philosophy, he argued his case in a markedly different way from his Eastern counterparts.

It also seems to be the case that, as with the Eastern Fathers, there is a direct link between Augustine's personal journey and the content of his thought; his notion that the economic missions reveal the divine processions, which underpins his justification of the *filioque*, is a function of his approach to truth, which is in turn informed by presuppositions from Hellenic philosophy, which served as a bridge to his own conversion to Christianity, together with an apparent parallel absence of a direct, personal encounter with the Divine Persons. Thus he appropriated the Christian faith via Neoplatonic philosophy, then read philosophical presuppositions into the content of revealed Christian truth, such that his idea of truth and the content of his thought mutually informed each other.

He consequently interpreted Scripture rationally and phenomenologically through the lens of Hellenic presuppositions, which necessitated explaining away the Old Testament theophanies in such a way that he de-legitimised, in principle, the possibility of apparitions of the Son as legitimate criteria of truth. This is in direct opposition to the Eastern approach, in terms of which the truth claim is that the Eastern Fathers' position was a function of their immediate experiences of the self-manifestation of the Divine Persons. The Orthodox consequently argue that one cannot dogmatise as truth an article of faith that is not supported by direct experience of God; thus it is false to read a deduced truth into the biblical revelation.

In short, the truth claims of thinkers of the two traditions that I have sourced indicate that the Eastern perspective is a function of having found God, while Augustine's approach is a function of a seeking God – meaning Augustine's thought is the product of speculation, while the Eastern Fathers' starting point is mystical experience of God and their thought is essentially testimony, albeit couched in language necessitated by polemics. Both the question of whether there are three, real Divine Persons in the Trinity and the question of whether the economic Trinity reveals the immanent Trinity are a direct consequence of these divergent truth claims, which indicates that, ultimately, the East-West impasse over the *filioque* can only be resolved once we have addressed the question: should we limit ourselves to that which can be verified in historical-mystical experience, or is it valid to dogmatise a deduced truth rooted in a phenomenological reading of Scripture that is in turn premised on Hellenic philosophical presuppositions?

8 UNITY TO *FILIOQUE*

Hill attributes the confusion between the economic and immanent Trinities in the writings of Augustine's predecessors to the "want of a sufficiently rigorous and tough metaphysics of the divine nature" to match the Arians, who were "acute practitioners of a metaphysical natural theology".[1] He adds that at least the subordinationist theologians "economic approach" to the Trinity took Scripture and the historical dimension of Christianity seriously, but claims that this approach was "obscured [...] by the 'metaphysical approach' that Nicaea [I] would canonise."

This statement is rather startling in light of Hierotheos' contention that the approach to theology that informed the thought of the Eastern Fathers was mystical and polemical rather than metaphysical – and that they actively resisted the subordination of the Christian faith to Hellenic philosophy that was evident in, for example, the thought of Origen and the Arians.[2] In fact, Anatolios insists that the non-Scriptural term *homoousios* was adopted extremely reluctantly by the council Fathers as a last resort because it was the only way to exclude any suggestion of the Arian idea that the Son was a creature.[3] Hill goes on to applaud Augustine's genius in combining the "economic" and metaphysical dimensions of theologising in his treatment of the Trinity.[4] He continues: "The definition of the Council of Nicaea in 325 did not solve the problem for the orthodox; it only forced them to realise that there was a problem to solve by affirming that the Arian conception was unac-

---

[1] Edmund Hill, *op.cit*, 43
[2] See 3.i.b & c above
[3] Khaled Anatolios, *op.cit*, 11
[4] Edmund Hill, *op.cit*, 43

ceptable."[5] He says Nicaea I left the orthodox with two questions to answer: (a) what does consubstantial mean in this instance? And (b) if it means the Three persons are one numerically identical substance, as opposed to the semi-Arian *homoiousion*, then in what sense are They distinctly three? Wiles pointedly outlines the post-Nicene difficulty in a different way: "The Nicene formula excluded the Arian conception, but only served to restate the problem in a new way: how does one square the divinity of the Son with the monotheistic conception of simplicity and unity that had been imposed by Platonic thought?"[6] This tendency to view the "one substance" terminology of Nicaea I as a function of ancient Hellenic metaphysics is traceable to Augustine. In this chapter I shall attempt to demonstrate that the *filioque* is a function of Augustine's appropriation of the Nicaea I *homoousion* and the person-*hypostasis* terminology of Constantinople I.

8.I. AUGUSTINE'S APPROPRIATION NICAEA I

8.i.a. The divine oneness

Augustine seems to have read the one *ousia* of Nicaea I in the sense in which the unity of the One had been explicated in ancient Greek philosophy – as pure being characterised as a unity without parts, differentiation or difference of any kind.[7] As Bradshaw indicates, this understanding of the divine unity can be ascribed to Augustine's involvement with Neoplatonism at the time of his conversion, influencing how he appropriated the Christian faith.[8]

---

[5] *Ibid*; of course, this was all it set out to do – see Hierotheos (Vlachos), *The Person in the Orthodox Tradition,* 68; 72; 166; 223–224; John Zizioulas, *Being as Communion*, 116ff

[6] Maurice Wiles, *op.cit*, 41–42; see also David Bentley Hart, "The Hidden and the Manifest: Metaphysics after Nicaea" in *Orthodox Readings of St Augustine*, 198–203

[7] Maurice Wiles, *op.cit*, 18–19

[8] David Bradshaw, "Augustine the Metaphysician" in *Orthodox Readings of St Augustine*, 239; see also pp. 234–236 and *Conf.* 7.9 for Plotinus' role in Augustine's conversion

He cites Plotinus' argument in *Enneads* 6.9.1 that anything that "is" is one and that degrees of being vary according to degrees of unity. However, he adds, Augustine differs from Plotinus in that Plotinus does not identify being with the One, which he sees as above being, while Augustine collapsed Plotinus' One and Mind (or intellect) into the One God.[9] Here Bradshaw is referring to Plotinus' reworking of Plato's idea of the One and the Form of the Good to posit three *hypostases* – the One, Mind and the World Soul.[10] In this schema the One is the highest transcendent Good, which is above essence and is characterised by eternal self-contained contemplation. The Mind, which has the potential to know, emanates from the One automatically and its contemplation of the One (which is simple unity) on the level of *neosis* (contemplative knowledge, which sees the whole picture at once) gives rise to the world of Forms, which represent the One on the level of Mind. Below that is the World Soul, which is capable only of discursive thought, but which produces and governs the world from the inside as a succession of discursive thoughts.[11]

Bradshaw posits that the reason for the difference in Augustine's thought seems to be that an important step in his conversion to Christianity was that fact that Platonic thought helped him to recognise God as Truth and also as real (in a schema in which the rational and incorporeal were considered more real than sensible things).[12] Thus, following Plotinus' equation of being and unity, God must consequently also be unity. This Neoplatonic idea of unity as a unity of pure being, which precluded "any distinctions such as those of essence and accident or genus and differentia,"[13] was to profoundly influence Augustine's understanding of the *homoousion* formula of Nicaea I.

---

[9] David Bradshaw, "Augustine the Metaphysician" in *Orthodox Readings of St Augustine*, 238–239

[10] John K. Ryan, *op.cit*, 22

[11] Allen & Springsted, *op.cit*, 50–52

[12] David Bradshaw, "Augustine the Metaphysician" in *Orthodox Readings of St Augustine*, 238–239

[13] *Ibid* 237; in this Augustine agreed with Arius – see Edmund Hill, *op.cit*, 186

8.i.b. Augustine's understanding of substance

Like his Eastern counterparts, Augustine often stresses the insufficiency of human language to express the reality of God.[14] However, while for the Eastern Fathers this expressed the absolute transcendence of three ineffable Persons, for Augustine it seems to be the insufficiency of language to describe the absolute simplicity of God, which in his mind relates to the limitations of rational enquiry to grasp the limitless "indivisible and unchanging [divine] nature".[15] Thus in *On the Trinity* VII.3 he engages in a lengthy discussion about the meaninglessness of the category substance with reference to God. He argues that the word cannot properly be applied to God if it is understood as a generic term or genus or species or common (material) nature or underlying reality, because God is simple and "the total transcendence of the godhead quite surpasses the capacity of ordinary speech".[16] He continues:

> [...] it is improper to call God substance in order to signify Him by a more usual word. He is called being truly and properly in such a way that perhaps only God ought to be called being. He alone truly is, because he is unchanging and he gave this as his name to his servant Moses when he said *I am who I am* [...] whether he is called being, which he is called properly, or substance, which he is called improperly, either word is predicated with reference to **self**, not by way of relationship with reference to something else. So for God to be is the same as to subsist. Therefore if the Trinity is one being, it is also one substance.[17] (Italics in original, bold print mine)

---

[14] See for example *Trin.* V.2.10
[15] *Trin.* V.*praef*.1–2; see also V.1.4
[16] *Ibid* VII.3.7
[17] *Trin.* VII.3.10

Two important points need to be made here. First, Augustine seems to use the word "being" *relatively* to denote that which is in fact above being. This interpretation seems to be supported by Jean-Luc Marion, who posits a compelling argument for the fact that the Thomist identification of God with being was a misreading and distortion of Augustine; a metaphysical interpretation (*ipsum esse* – being itself) was read into an *apophatic* and biblical denomination (*idipsum* – the thing in itself) in key texts, and subsequent translators of Augustine have followed suit.[18] Marion[19] further explains that the context in which Augustine found the expression, Psalm 122 (123), has the connotation of "the thing itself in which we must participate". He also quotes several texts in which Augustine identifies God's essence with his immutability/eternity, such as *On the Trinity* V.2.3, VII.5.10, which, as the above indented quotation indicates, could be interpreted to mean God's personal presence. This brings us to the second point: for Augustine the being of God – or *idipsum* – is the *self* of God.[20] As per the indented text, that which God is in Himself is "I". His being is His "I-ness". Here we arrive at the heart of the matter: while the Cappadocians linked the "I" of God both to being and to *each hypostasis*, because Augustine's conception is premised on the Hellenic idea of oneness and oneness is linked to the essence, or *idipsum* if you prefer, he identifies the "I" with the one essence (commonly translated substance). In linking the being of God to the "I" of God Augustine was not being innovative – this was exactly the point Arius had made, using this observation to assert that there can be only one God – the Father – and that the Son and Spirit are therefore not properly called God. As noted in 3.ii.c, in his fervour to maintain the monotheistic transcendence of the One God, traditionally understood as the Father, Arius had posited that the Son was of a different substance to the Father (as in Origen's distinction between God and "gods") and distinguished between the essence and energies of God to argue that the Son was a product of the uncreated energies of God.

---

[18] Jean-Luc Marion, *op.cit*, 167–189

[19] *Ibid* 182ff

[20] See also *On the Trinity* VII.1.1

A pivotal difference in thought between East and West is the result of the divergent ways in which Augustine and the Eastern Fathers answered Arius.

The Nicene Fathers agreed with Arius – and the tradition of the Church – that the name God applies properly to the Father, enabling them to maintain the emphasis on the monarchy of the Father (the same emphasis Arius wished to uphold); but they also asserted that equal (true) divinity – and therefore also eternity – is predicated of the Son by virtue of the shared substance, i.e. that the Son is *of* the Father and therefore also divine.

This perception is reflected in the symbol of Nicaea I, which states: "I believe in one God, the *Father*", *and* the Son, who is "from the essence of the Father" and is thus "of the same essence [*homoousios*] as the Father" [...] *and* in the Holy Spirit.[21] At Constantinople I additions made to the clause on the Holy Spirit denoted a parallel meaning: "The Lord, the giver of life, who proceeds from the Father",[22] that is, He is also divine because He is *of* the Father. Underpinning this conception was the perception of three personal Subjects in perfect communion – which is how St Ambrose also seems to have understood the dogma.[23] But the ontological reality of the Persons was made dogmatically explicit only at Constantinople I, specifically in opposition to Sabellianism in order to assert that three incorporeal Persons constitute the substance of God, i.e. three "Selves" subsist as One.[24]

Thus, while Arius argued that the "I" in God's "I am" belongs only to the Father, the Eastern Fathers argued, effectively, that the "I" belongs to each Person and that the three Persons tri-mutually constitute the one essence. We therefore have the following schema: God (the Father) is His own substance – as in Athanasius' thought;[25] i.e. in God, personhood is an ontological category. The Father brings forth two Persons, i.e. two ontological "I's" who are

---

[21] See for example Gerald O'Collins, *op.cit*, 115
[22] *Ibid* 15
[23] Ambrose, *On the Holy Spirit* 1.12.26–31
[24] Hierotheos, *The Person in the Orthodox Tradition*, 195–196
[25] See *De Decretis* 22; *Against Arius* 1.14 and 16; *Letter to Serapion* 1.19, 21, 25

of the same substance as Himself and therefore also love, holiness, omnipotence, power, wisdom, eternity, etc. The Father, Son and Spirit indwell one another in a perfect interpersonal communion of love; thus, while each Person has distinct ontological status as a personal Subject, the communion of love is the unity; ergo in the Trinity being is communion and simultaneously the Persons themselves. Thus one is able to assert that the Trinity is indivisibly Persons in communion – each One has distinct Personal being plus common being; He is eternally Himself plus the other two Persons, who indwell Him. This is the doctrine of the unity.

Also, because God the Father is (a) his own essence and (b) the cause of the Son and Spirit, He is also the cause of the common relational being and therefore, as Person, transcends the common being as communion; ergo, the monarchy of the Father is upheld. The Eastern Fathers also reinterpreted Arius' notion of the energies to say that the energies of God refer to the Divine Persons in their economic activity or manifestations. Therefore texts that the Arians used to show that the Son was an energy of the Father such as "Christ is the Power and Wisdom of God" (1 Cor. 1:24), could be shown to relate to the economic activity/manifestation of the Son, i.e. He is the power and wisdom of God (the Father) for us because He is of the substance of the Father and therefore shares all the Father's attributes (including eternity), which He reveals to us in Himself.

Augustine, on the other hand, while agreeing with Arius that the "I-ness" of God should be identified with the being/substance/*idipsum*, argued that the *name* God belongs properly to the *Trinity*, not just the Father – a function of the fact that he identifies the unity with the substance *per se*. He engages in a lengthy discussion of this in *On the Trinity* I.2.8–12[26], in which he bends certain Scripture texts that explicitly refer to the Son (such as 1 Timothy 6:14 and Romans 11:36) quite out of shape to argue that the apostle is in fact not speaking about one Person of the Trinity but all three. Second, both in order to refute the Arians and due to his idea of divine simplicity, he collapses the attributes and *esse* into

---

[26] See especially I.2.10–11; also II.4.18, VI.1.4 & VI.2.9–10; see also David Bentley Hart, *op.cit*, 204

the substance, arguing that "the divine essence is identical with the divine attributes as well as with the divine *esse*, and that all of these are identical with one another".[27]

In his treatment of St Paul's expression "Christ the power of God and the wisdom of God" (1 Cor. 1:24), the structure of which indicates "Son/Word of the Father", Augustine therefore argues that substance words like "God" or "wisdom" or "goodness" are properly predicated of the divine substance, or equally and identically of the Divine Persons without signifying relationship, because the Divine Persons are identical to the substance. Thus one can say of the Father or Son that He is God or good or wisdom, and that the Son is God from God or Light from Light, as in the Nicene Creed. But the Pauline text uses these terms improperly, Augustine argues, albeit legitimately, by predicating Wisdom of the Son and God of the Father, though these terms apply equally to both.[28]

In terms of the name God belonging properly to the Father, he has effectively explained away what appears to be the intended meaning of the text because he reads his notion of simple oneness into Scripture. In terms of the essence/energies issue, he does in fact agree with the Eastern interpretation that the Son is the power and wisdom of God *for us*, but this is limited to the incarnation and, of course, by "God" he means Trinity, not Father. Thus the Son is no longer a revelation of the Father's Person, but of the Trinity.[29]

Thus Augustine's identification of the name God with the Trinity appears to be attributable to his reading of the one *ousia* of Nicaea I in the sense in which the unity and simplicity of the One had been explicated in ancient Greek philosophy. He maintains the personal identity of God by identifying God's being with His "I-ness", but because his idea of unity precluded any distinctions such as those of essence and accident or genus and differentia, he assumed that the doctrines that (a) all three Persons were God and

---

[27] David Bradshaw, "Augustine the Metaphysician" in *Orthodox Readings of St Augustine*, 240–241; he quotes *Civ. Dei* 8.6 and 11.10; see also Edmund Hill, *op.cit*, 92, footnote 18; Hill cites this as a basic axiom of Trinitarian theology; see also *On the Trinity* V.2.11 & VI.1.3 & 7

[28] Edmund Hill, *op.cit*, 187–188; *Trin.* VII.1–2

[29] *Trin.* VII.2.4

(b) that the Persons subsisted as a unity had to mean that all three Persons irreducibly constituted one "I"; thus the three Persons are the one God proper.

This is not the sense in which Scripture posits the oneness of God. As Wiles, indicates the Old Testament simply asserts that there is only one God in contradistinction to the many gods of a polytheistic milieu,[30] as Tertullian and Gregory of Nyssa also point out,[31] and in the New Testament this one God is revealed as *Abba*, Father. The Eastern Fathers and the council of Nicaea I retained the Biblical meaning of the one God, who was identified with the Father, while speaking of the Son and Spirit as God in a derivative sense; i.e. they are of the same substance because they are of the Father. The emphasis, against Arianism, is the equality of the Son by virtue of the shared essence on account of the fact that He is *of* the Father; it is not the ontological oneness of the One. As Athanasius says explicitly: "There is no other God than the Father".[32]

Augustine's idea of unity also sharply contradicts the Eastern Fathers' understanding of oneness as a *comm*unity of interpersonal Subjects,[33] replacing it instead with an abstract idea of unity that cannot be reconciled with the human person's experience of communion with an interpersonal Trinity. Notably, the anti-Nicene party during and after Nicaea I had objected to the term *homoousios* precisely because it was vulnerable to the Sabellian interpretation of "a Modalist reduction of the Trinity to a singular unity"[34] – an idea Gregory of Nazianzus strongly opposed.[35] In answer to such a notion, Athanasius, whose perspective seems to be representative of the intended meaning of the council and who seems to have understood the unity in the personalistic sense of community, contradicts the Sabellian meaning when he asks in 1.20 of his *Letter to Serapion*: "Or how is it really a Trinity if the three are depicted as one?" Au-

---

[30] Maurice Wiles, *op.cit*, 18–19

[31] *Against Praxeas*, 13; 18 and *Letter to Ablabius* respectively

[32] *Letter to Serapion* 1.16 in Khaled Anatolios, *op.cit*, 215

[33] Basil, *De Spiritu Sancto* 45; see 6.iii above

[34] Socrates (Church historian) in Khaled Anatolios, *op.cit*, 7; 11

[35] *Oration at the First Council of Constantinople*, in Colman J. Barry (ed.), *Readings in Church History* (New York: Newman Press, 1960), 87

gustine's philosophical notion of the divine unity was thus a misappropriation of the intended meaning of *homoousios*. His notion of the one substance or "I" of "God the Trinity" in turn constitutes the context for his difficulty with the Person-*Hypostasis* terminology of Constantinople I.

8.II. CONSTANTINOPLE I: PERSON AND *HYPOSTASIS*

It is clear from his argumentation that Augustine was familiar with the Person-*Hypostasis* terminology of Constantinople I but that he did not understand how the Greek Fathers had reinterpreted the terms.[36] His poor Greek, the Eastern Fathers' reluctance to use the word "Person" because of its association with Sabellianism, his lack of familiarity with their writings and his own presuppositions could have all contributed to the confusion. For Augustine the word "person" denoted the human individual, a "rational mortal animal" comprised of body and soul, as the ancient philosophers' described the human being.[37]

To complicate matters, the only Western source at his disposal that asserted that the Father, Son and Spirit were real Persons was Tertullian, whose use of *Persona* was initially rejected by St Basil of Caesarea because it was linked to Sabellianism. Hill[38] also observes this, but without noting the later and more important development in Basil's thought.

Also, Tertullian's notion of the Persons was rooted in a perception of God as a corporeal being and in the idea of human personhood, in which the person shares a portion of nature – which led to an economic, pseudo-tri-theistic view of the Trinity: "The Father is the whole substance, while the Son is derivative and a portion of the whole".[39] He also speaks of the Spirit in the same

---

[36] See *Trin.* V.8.10

[37] See Nancey Murphy, "The Person in Greek Thought" in *Counterbalance*, [online]. http://www.counterbalance.org/neuro/greek-frame.html (accessed24/07/2008), n.d: n.pag; *Trin.* VII.3.7; XV.7.11

[38] *Op.cit*, 44

[39] *Against Praxeas* 9; see also 2; 4; 18; Gerald O'Collins, *op.cit*, 104–105

way.[40] As for *hypostasis*, Augustine understood the word to mean substance (essence) – as it had been used at Nicaea I.[41]

These understandings of person and *hypostasis*, in tandem with his perception of the divine unity, would have rendered the Eastern formula of Constantinople I unintelligible to him, a philosophical anomaly. "Three *hypostases* in one nature" would have meant to him "three substances" or "three (separate) individuals" in one substance.[42] Thus in *On the Trinity* VII.3.8 Augustine asks: "If we call them three persons [using person as a generic name] because what by person is common to them […] why can we not also call them three Gods? […] what we have been saying about person in our way of talking must be understood about substances in the Greek way of talking. They say three substances, one being, just as we say three persons, one being or substance." So, quite rightly rejecting the idea that the Divine Persons are three individuals, he concluded that as a proper term could not be found "to enunciate in words that which they [the Greeks] understood without words",[43] an approximation was used: "[…] by which names it did not intend diversity to be meant, but singleness to be denied".[44] Actually, diversity is exactly what they meant. But what Augustine means is that the Greeks could not have meant three separate individuals (three primary substances in Aristotelian terms.

His confusion over the meanings of the words person and *hypostasis*, together with his understanding of the divine unity and substance, is the pivotal reason for which he perceived a need to distinguish the Persons *ad intra*. This seems to be true of a pool of Western Christian philosophers. Hill states that the formula "God is one *ousia*, three *hypostases*" was not helpful; it did not answer the

---

[40] *Ibid* 26

[41] *Trin.* VII.4.7; 6.11; see also Gerald O'Collins, *op.cit*, 117–118

[42] *Trin.* VII.3.8; V.2.10; c.f. Gerald O'Collins, *op.cit*, 118; Ayres, *op.cit*, 133; this seems to be true of Western academics to this day, judging by the comments of Western thinkers I have sourced, such as Rahner, O'Collins, Cross, Hill and Meredith, who consider Eastern thought flawed because they read it as if it were metaphysical speculation argued according to the criteria of ancient Hellenic philosophy.

[43] *Trin.*V.9.10

[44] *Ibid* VII.3.8

question "three what?" Victorinus coined the expression one substance, three *subsistentiae*, but this did not explain how "the three
persons, or subsistences, or *hypostases*, or substances, were really
distinguished from each other while remaining numerically one and
identically the same God, one divine substance".[45]

Thus Hill asks: "What were their distinguishing marks or
properties?"[46] He comments that Hilary of Poitiers, whom Augustine quotes in *On the Trinity* VI.2.11, suggested distinguishing properties in terms of certain attributes – eternity, form and gift, seemingly an allusion to the Father's transcendence and the Son's and
Spirit's roles in the economy. Victorinus, arguing philosophically,
does the same, calling the Father the being of God, the Son the life
and Spirit the knowledge of God, and elsewhere distinguishes the
Persons by their economic activities.[47]

None of this was particularly helpful, Hill argues, because, as
the Arians pointed out, both the attributes and activities of the Father belong properly to Him. Thus if the Son and Spirit are truly
God, these acts and attributes must be common to them too; they
cannot be distinguished by attributes or acts.[48]

O'Collins[49] raises another set of issues in his summary of Ath-
anasius' theology. While categorising the different activities of the
Son and the Spirit, Athanasius simultaneously asserted that all three
Divine Persons were present in every activity of the economy:
"The Father does all things through the Word in the Holy Spirit".[50]
O'Collins protests that this conception of the Persons' *ad extra* ac-
tivities makes it difficult to distinguish the relations *ad intra*.[51]

Also, with respect to St Paul's description of the Spirit dis-
pensing the divine gifts, the saint writes: "The Apostle does not
mean that the things which are given are given differently and sepa-

---

[45] Edmund Hill, *op.cit*, 45; see also pp. 51–52
[46] *Ibid* 44
[47] *Ibid*
[48] *Ibid* 44–45
[49] *Op.cit*, 128
[50] *Letter to Serapion* 1.27
[51] Gerald O'Collins, *op.cit*, 130

rately by each Person, but what is given is given in the Triad, and that all are from the One Triad".[52]

O'Collins questions whether he means "given *by* the Triad" rather than "*in* the Triad",[53] but I think the point Athanasius is trying to make is that the gifts are the fruit of being in communion with and therefore "in" the Trinity by virtue of being in the Spirit; the gifts are not external to God Himself. In fact, he prefaces the above statement with a lengthy description of the divine communion in which we are invited to participate.[54] If the Eastern paradigm of communion were an important emphasis in Western theological consciousness, such questions would not arise.

Also, in this same letter, Athanasius affirmed the divinity of the Spirit who "proceeds" from the Father and is given by His Son. That is, He receives his whole divine nature and existence from the Father and is sent on His mission by the Son.[55] O'Collins notes the criticism this notion elicited: if both the Son and Spirit are of the Father, this would imply that there are two Sons. How then could the Son be the only begotten?[56]

Of course, the first difficulty is a function of reading the formula of Constantinople through the lens of Augustine's notion of unity. If one understands the Divine Persons to be real, incorporeal "I's" in *comm*unity, *contra* Hellenic metaphysical conceptual categories, they are distinguished by the very fact of being Persons, i.e. relational "I's". Their unique identities are distinguished by their names, which also denote their unique relationships within the intra-Trinitarian communion, as Gregory of Nazianzus and Didymus the Blind proposed.[57] That takes care of distinguishing the Persons *ad intra*, while the distinction between begetting and proceeding is suggestive of a distinction of origin, accounting for the fact that the Son comes forth specifically as Son while the Spirit does not (see 1.iv.b above). This takes care of the "two Sons" accusation. (Of

[52] *Letter to Serapion* 1.31
[53] Gerald O'Collins, *op.cit*, 130
[54] *Letter to Serapion* 1.30
[55] *Ibid* 1.20
[56] Gerald O'Collins, *op.cit*, 130128–129
[57] Edmund Hill, *op.cit*, 45

course, the Eastern Fathers consign the mechanics of the generation of the Son and Spirit to the realm of mystery, which Hill finds
rather irritating.[58]

Thus, from an Eastern perspective, Augustine's real problem
was that he read the formula of Constantinople I as abstract metaphysics rather than as an affirmation of three real, incorporeal Persons and thus found himself having to answer irrelevant questions:
What are the three *hypostases* and how do we distinguish them *ad
intra?* That is, how do we to square the formula of Constantinople I
with the Hellenic idea of unity?

8.III. AUGUSTINE'S SOLUTION

Augustine, Hill asserts, with reference to the use of the word "person", "will cut the Gordian knot by saying that it does not matter
what word you choose, it is purely a matter of convention and
convenience. And surely he is right; finding a word in this instance
does not really tell us anything or solve anything".[59] Here Hill
stumbles on the tragedy of the East-West schism: for the Eastern
Fathers, the word "Person", joined to *Hypostasis*, meant everything;
it constituted the most accurate language conceivable to articulate
the sublime, experientially perceived reality of the Trinity as a
communion of incorporeal personal Subjects and to convey, in
opposition to the Hellenic vision of rational being, a new way of
perceiving divine reality: that the cause of life and being itself was a
Person (the Father), that the Trinity was three personal Subjects in
perfect communion and that our redemption lay precisely in participating in this communion. But, not understanding the subtext of
the formula, Augustine set his mind to solving the perceived puzzle
using Gregory Nazianzus' and Didymus' notion of interpersonal
relations,[60] which he interpreted using Aristotle's categories. This is
pivotal because Arius had also argued within Aristotelian categories

---

[58] *Ibid*
[59] *Ibid*
[60] *Ibid*

and there is a huge difference in the way Augustine and the Cappadocians answered him.

Aristotle had argued that things exist in themselves, not in some universal concept (as in Platonic thought). Thus substance, according to Aristotle, is the seat of existence as opposed to form and is that which is perceived by the senses. Thus things exist in substance.[61] In his *Categories*, Aristotle posited that individuals – persons, horses, cabbages – were primary substances, while the genera (genus/species) to which individuals belonged were secondary substances. Notably, the word genus comes from the Greek word genesis, meaning "birth".[62]

General qualities that are "present in" a primary substance that can also be present in other individuals – such as green in a cabbage – he called predicates or "accidents". Thus green can be predicated of a cabbage or a dress. But the most important thing we predicate of individuals is the genus or species. The genus tells us the essence of a thing, that is, what it is or what kind of thing it is. Thus an individual is defined in terms of species but distinguished or identified by attributes (quantity, quality, relation, place, time, posture, having, action, and being acted upon). Thus in a primary sense only the individual substance has being (*ousia*).[63]

Now, according to Hill, the Arians, using these categories, had pointed out that one couldn't speak of accidents with reference to God (the Father), because God is wholly simple. He just is, as He states in Exodus 3:14: "I am who I am." Thus, for example, God does not have wisdom; God is His wisdom.[64] Therefore there cannot be a distinction in the divine substance as between distinct (human) persons (individuals) and the distinction used by the Fathers between unbegotten and begotten cannot be used in terms of these categories because there cannot be two contradictory qualities

---

[61] J. Justus, *Aristotle's Antithesis*, 2003 [online]. http://www.cleff-publishing.com/articles/a20040303jj.htm (accessed 19/12/2008), n.pag

[62] Allen & Springsted, *op.cit*, 65–67

[63] *Ibid*; see also Edmund Hill, *op.cit*, 49–50; Augustine argues this rule in *Trin.* V

[64] Edmund Hill, *op.cit*, 50; Augustine echoes this argument in *Trin.* VII.3.10 with respect to God's goodness

in the same substance. If God is called unbegotten then He is un-begotteness; if He is called begotten He is His begotteness. He cannot be both.[65]

Notably, the Cappadocians transcended these categories in order to explain the distinction of personal Subjects in the God-head, because they could not accommodate the experienced reality of three divine personal Subjects. As Allen explains, Gregory of Nyssa, for example, used the example of three individual men (primary substances) distinguished by their peculiar properties but who share a common *genus* (secondary substance) to demonstrate analogously the difference between *hypostasis* and *ousia*. However, he qualified this by saying that the Divine Persons do not share one nature in the same way that human beings share a common *genus* (or species); rather, they are the nature – a notion that implied and was later developed more explicitly into the doctrine of *perichoresis*. And nor, with respect to Platonic thought, do the Persons share one nature as particulars participate in the Forms (which are more real than the particulars); the Persons personally constitute the na-ture.[66] The Persons are therefore not functions of nature but trans-cend it. Thus when Gregory of Nyssa says analogously: "Suppose we say 'Paul'. We set forth, by what is indicated by the *name*, the nature subsisting",[67] his central point is that in the Trinity three "who's" (Persons) are the essence of being, not the "what" (sub-stance), or rather the "who's" *are* the "what".

By contrast, Augustine argued within Aristotelian categories of thought. He agreed with Arius about the simplicity of God and that in God there can therefore be no accidents,[68] but, premising his argumentation on his identification of the one substance (one God/Self) with the Trinity, he reinterpreted Aristotle's categories, as Hill[69] indicates, by finding a loophole: one of the attributes, that of relationship, implies change or becoming when applied to creat-

---

[65] *Ibid*
[66] Allen & Springsted, *op.cit*, 67–71
[67] *Letter 38* in *ibid* 69
[68] *Trin.* V.1.3; VI.1.6; VI.2.8
[69] *Op.cit*, 50; 186

ed substances, but when applied to God, relations are not accidental but subsistent:

> Wherefore, although to be the Father and to be the Son is different, yet their substance is not different, because they are so called, not according to substance, but according to relation, which relation, however, is not accident, because it is not changeable.[70]

Thus, as Hill indicates, Augustine introduced a new distinction with reference to God: we no longer speak just about substance and accidents; we distinguish between words that say something about the subject in itself, or absolutely, without reference to another, and words that say something with reference to, or relatively, to another.[71]

This is another pivotal difference in thought between Augustine and the Cappadocians: Augustine argued, against Arius, that the names Father and Son, "unbegotten" and "begotten", are said only in reference to one another; they are not said in reference to themselves "substance-wise".[72] The Cappadocians argued, effectively, that the names Father and Son are also said "self-referentially" because the Person is an ontological reality in relation. Thus being a Person is the fundamental ontological reality, while relation denotes a subsistent identity.[73]

These divergent premises underpin the *filioque* on the one hand and the Eastern objections to it on the other.

---

[70] *Trin.* V.5.6; c.f. V.1.6

[71] Edmund Hill, *op.cit*, 50

[72] *Trin.* V.1.6

[73] Here they echo St Athanasius' argument that the Son cannot be another Father because "it belongs properly to the Godhead alone, that the Father is properly Father, and the Son properly Son, and in Them, and Them only, does it hold that the Father is ever Father and the Son ever Son" – see *Against the Arians* 1.21; *Letter to Serapion* 1:16

8.IV. THE *FILIOQUE*

8.iv.a. *Filioque* mooted

We have noted that Origen and Tertullian in the 3rd century both posited that the Spirit came into being through the Word[74]as a function of the Neoplatonic schema of three descending *hypostases*. Hilary of Poitiers in the 4th century also wondered aloud whether "to receive from the Son is the same thing as to proceed from the Father".[75] The NAOCTC further cites Ambrose of Milan, who "writing in the 380s, openly asserts that the Spirit "proceeds from (*procedit a*) the Father and the Son", without ever being separated from either[76] – although, as noted above, Ambrose used the word "proceed" both for the economy and eternal processions; it is therefore debatable whether he denoted the eternal procession.

Also, as O'Collins indicates, Marius Victorinus, whose conversion story played a role in Augustine's conversion,[77] drew on John 16:14 ("He [the Spirit of Truth] will take what is mine and declare it to you") to argue that the Son, together with the Father, "produced" the Spirit.[78]

I do not have the space here to investigate the nuances of thought of these writers. Suffice it to say that the notion had been posited in the general pool of Western thought since the 3rd century, although in the context of differing conceptions, and it seems likely that the *filioque* was a presupposition that became fixed in Augustine's mind during his formative period, although he was to give it the distinctive meaning that came to be accepted in the Western Church.

---

[74] See 3.i.b above
[75] *De Trinitate* 8.20 in NAOCTC, *op.cit*, n.pag
[76] *On the Holy Spirit* 1.11.20
[77] *Conf.* 8.2; 8.4
[78] Gerald O'Collins, *op.cit*, 138–139

8.iv.b. The Spirit as Gift

Hill[79] comments that with Augustine's metaphysical distinction concerning relations in God, which is developed in book V of *On the Trinity*, he has established a metaphysical "rule" for himself that provides the contours of thought for the *filioque*. In this regard, Augustine has a further difficulty to solve – that the name Holy Spirit is not a relational name in either of its parts; to be holy and to be spirit are attributes of all three Persons.[80] Thus, Hill argues, this name does not seem to tell us anything about the constituent relationship of the Spirit to the other two persons. Therefore Augustine opted for the name "Gift", which implies a relationship with the giver.[81]

Hill notes that the trouble with this is that the name also implies a relationship with the receiver and therefore takes us into the sphere of the relationship of God with creatures, who receive the Spirit from God. Thus "Gift" is really a functional or economic name. Thus, despite his best attempts, Augustine ends up reading an economic function back into the relations of origin.[82]

In actual fact, Augustine begins to call the Spirit "Gift" before he has established his rule regarding the relations of origin.[83] In the earlier context his use of this name for the Spirit appears to be (a) a function of his idea that the economy reveals the immanent Trinity and (b) his identification of the divine essence with the *esse*, which is the pivotal rationale for the *filioque*. In *On the Trinity* II.1.4 – before he has arrived at his metaphysical rule regarding relations of origin – Augustine therefore argues that the Son simply *is* His life, as we have noted; thus the text "'He (the Father) gave the Son life' (Jn 5:26) means nothing else than 'He begot the Son who is life'" and "He begot the Son who is His teaching".[84]

---

[79] *Op cit*, 51

[80] *Trin.* V.3.12; VI.1.7; in the latter he includes charity as that which the three have in common; love is therefore the substance of God, along with the other attributes held in common

[81] Edmund Hill, *op.cit*, 51; Lewis Ayres, *op.cit*, 141–142; *Trin.* V.3.12.

[82] *Ibid* 51

[83] See for example *Trin.* IV.5.29

[84] See also *Trin.* IV.5.29

Noting parallel biblical texts in relation to the Spirit, Augustine then introduces the question of why the Spirit is not also a Son.[85] In V.3.15 he answers his own question by asserting: "He comes forth, you see, not as being born, but as being given, and so He is not called Son, because He was not born like the Only Begotten" – the same distinction as that made by the Eastern Fathers, except that Augustine uses "given" as a synonym for "proceed". As noted in 6.iii above, Gregory of Palamas later argued that, in a certain sense, the Spirit is "given to" the Son in His procession and abides or comes to rest eternally in the Son and thus radiates from Him. Augustine could be understood to be making a similar connection, although his perception is differently framed.

This is Catholic apologist Lewis Ayres'[86] line of argument in his attempt to demonstrate the harmony of the Eastern and Augustinian conceptions in his treatment of Augustine's notion of the Spirit as love, which forms part of his attempt to show that Augustine preserves the monarchy of the Father.[87] But Augustine does not stop there. True to his notion that the sendings reveal the processions and that the essence is identical with the *esse*, he identifies "proceed" with "sent", stating that just as the Son's being sent indicates that He is of the Father, so "for the Holy Spirit His being gift of God means his proceeding from the Father, so His being sent means his being known to proceed from Him".[88]

Augustine continues, arguing from the economy, that the Spirit being sent from the Son means He also proceeds eternally from the Son. Ayres argues that he qualifies this assertion with the statement: "The source of all Godhead, or if you like deity, is the Father. So the Spirit, who proceeds from the Father and the Son, is traced back, on both counts, to the Father".[89] Ayres argues that the

---

[85] *Trin.* II.1.5

[86] *Op.cit*, 129

[87] Edmund Hill (*op.cit*, 203, footnote 24) warns against this reading.

[88] *Trin.* IV.20.29 in Ayres, *op.cit*, 130; (IV.5.29 in Hill's translation)

[89] *Trin.* IV.5.29; Augustine cites Jn 15:26: "whom I will send from the Father" as the premise of his argument. It is noteworthy that in book IV Augustine has not yet set up his metaphysical rule of the relations of origin; his use of the *filioque* at this early stage therefore seems to support

missions of the Son and Spirit therefore reveal their interconnection with the Father as their source.[90] As we have seen, some Western thinkers use this distinction to expound the *filioque* in terms of *per filium,* as the Clarification does. Ayres[91] also tends towards this option. But Augustine's later argumentation contradicts this position. He continues that the Spirit is also given to creatures, who therefore call Him "our Spirit", but as those who have received it from the Son. Thus the Father and Son are both the origin of the Spirit relative to creatures:

> If therefore what is given [the Spirit] also has Him it is given by as its origin, because it does not receive its proceeding from Him from anywhere else, we must confess that the Father and the Son are the origin of the Holy Spirit; not two origins, but just as the Father and Son are one God, and with reference to creation of creator and one Lord, so with reference to the Holy Spirit they are one origin; but with reference to creation Father, Son and Holy Spirit are one origin, just as they are one creator and one Lord.[92]

Augustine continues that the Son receives not only his identity but also his being in being born and asks whether the Spirit receives His being only in being given – or if he proceeds/is given without there being anyone to give Him to? Or does He simply proceed in time in such a way as to be always giveable?[93] He reasons, in V.4.17, that "we should not be disturbed at the Holy Spirit, although he is coeternal with the Father and the Son, being said to be something from the point of view of time". He goes on to rea-

---

the idea that it was a presupposition for him, although he has not yet thought it through to its logical conclusion.

[90] Lewis Ayres, *op.cit,* 131

[91] *Ibid* 149

[92] *Trin.* V.3.15

[93] Here we see that Augustine is not thinking in terms of the Spirit being given to the Son, as in Palamas' thought.

son that since God is unchangeable, what is true of Him in time must be true of him outside time as well; thus the relationships in God are not changed by His interaction with creatures in time.

He picks up this theme again in book XV. In XV.6.47 he follows this time-eternity logic to its final conclusion and says definitively: "Therefore anyone who can understand the generation of the Son from the Father as timeless should also understand the procession of the Holy Spirit from them both as timeless." And, arguing from Jn 5:25 ("Just as the Father has life in Himself, so He has given the Son to have life in Himself"), he asserts:

> And anyone can understand that when He said this [Jn 5:25] He did not mean that the Father gave life to the Son already existing without life, but that He begot Him timelessly in such a way that the life which the Father gave the Son by begetting Him is co-eternal with the life of the Father who gave it, should also understand that just as the Father has it in Himself that the Holy Spirit should proceed from Him, so he gave to the Son that the Holy Spirit should proceed from Him too, and in both cases timelessly; and thus that to say that the Holy Spirit proceeding from the Son is something which the Son has from the Father [...] the Spirit proceeds principally from the Father, and by the Father's wholly timeless gift from both of them jointly."[94]

Addressing the question of whether the Spirit is not then a Son of the Father and Son (which would make the Son also the Father of the Spirit), he uses the same distinction between proceeding and begetting that he used to argue that the Spirit is not a Son of the Father, but now to support the *filioque*:

> Clearly, then, it would be the height of absurdity to call the Holy Spirit the Son of them both, since just as generation from the Father *bestows being* on the Son without any beginning in

---

[94] *Trin.* XV.6.47

time [...], so does procession from them both *bestow being* on the Holy Spirit without any beginning in time.[95] (Italics mine)

Thus, while Augustine's thought – as a function of the fact that his writing constitutes a process of working out his thought – is not particularly systematic, he does arrive at the conclusion that the Father and Son are together the eternal ontological cause of the Spirit, a logical outcome of his identification of "proceed" with "sent" and the essence with the *esse*, which are in turn a function of the fundamental philosophical presuppositions regarding the divine simplicity, unity and immutability that appear to inform his thought from the beginning to the end of his *On the Trinity*.

8.V. SUMMARY

The primary perceived difficulty Augustine attempted to solve with the *filioque* seems to be how to metaphysically define and distinguish the three *hypostases* in the Trinity while maintaining the unity of God. From an Eastern perspective, this problem was already solved with the assertion of three, subsistent incorporeal Persons-*Hypostases*, while the *monotheistic* oneness was upheld by the monarchy of the Father and the threefold unity by the tri-mutual indwelling; i.e. the oneness and unity are not necessarily identical.[96] Augustine's difficulty with this solution seems to be a function of two parallel problems:

First, he misappropriated the Nicaea I *homoousion* terminology in light of the Platonic notion of the simple unity of the One, which he identified with the divine substance. It followed, in Augustine's mind, that the one God proper is the Trinity, rather than the Father, an idea he read back into Scripture and dogma.

Second, there was a parallel misappropriation of the formula of Constantinople I; Augustine did not realise that the Cappadoci-

---

[95] *Ibid* XV.6.47

[96] In a footnote, Ayres (*op.cit*, 134) rightly question assertions that the Cappadocians' emphasis was on the Father as God proper to the exclusion of the first emphasis – see footnote 16

ans had imbued the words "person" and *hypostasis* with new meaning in order to assert the experientially known truth that the Trinity was constituted by three subsistent incorporeal real personal Subjects who subsisted in a communion of love. The underlying difficulty appears to be that he appropriated the formulas as if they were functions of philosophy rather than of experience of God. Premising his conception on his notion of divine simplicity, and consequently that the one God is the essence, which he identified as the "I" of "God the Trinity", he solved the philosophical conundrum of how to distinguish the divine *Hypostases ad intra* with his notion of subsistent relations. However, (a) because of his identification of the "I" of God with the being of the One God and (b) because Augustine argued within Aristotelian categories, which allow for only one primary substance and are therefore prohibitive of the notion of three "I's", in contrast to the traditional view that "God proper" is the Father and the Trinity is a communion of three interpersonal Subjects, Augustine arrived at a conception of "God the Trinity" that is a single Self in whom there are three self-referential relations.

Within this context, Augustine's demonstration of the *filioque*, which appears to have been a presupposition for him, is a pivotal aspect of his attempt to answer the question "how do we distinguish the Persons *ad intra*" – which he answers with his notion of diverse relations of origin, as well as the question "why is the Spirit not a Son of the Father and Son?" – using the same distinction between begetting and proceeding that the Eastern Fathers used to argue that the Spirit is not another Son of the Father. We have also established that Augustine meant that the Spirit takes his *being* from the Father and the Son, as opposed to the *per filium* interpretation the PCPCU's Clarification emphasises and that this notion is justified on the basis of his identification of "proceed" with "sent" and the essence with the *esse*, which are in turn contingent on his philosophical presuppositions regarding the divine simplicity, unity and immutability.

9 AUGUSTINE'S PSYCHOLOGICAL ANALOGIES

In this chapter I shall outline Augustine's famous analogies, indicate how they relate to his metaphysics and Neoplatonic cosmology and then assess the Orthodox objections to the *filioque* in relation to his conception of the Trinity as a whole.

9.1. AUGUSTINE'S ANALOGIES

As Hill indicates, believing (notably) that we have no direct access to the inwardness of God in Himself, Augustine sets out from Book VIII of *On the Trinity* to search inwardly for a reflection of God in His image, which he identifies as the human self.

He first identifies truth and goodness – knowing and loving in psychological terms – as that which the human mind and God have in common. That is, God is absolute truth and absolute goodness, which is reflected in our "better part" (the higher mind).[1] "Truth is that in terms of which we know and understand whatever we know and understand, while goodness is that in terms of which we desire, approve and love whatever we desire, approve and love".[2]

This gives him his first psychological Trinity, which he uses as an analogy to explain how an individual triune God can subsist as three yet one:[3] the mind, the mind's knowledge of itself and love of itself, which he posits as a faint vestige of the Trinity in the human mind.[4] This analogy is echoed in *City of God* 11:26 as the soul's sense of self in knowing that one is and in loving this knowledge.

---

[1] Edmund Hill, *op.cit*, 52
[2] *Ibid* 24
[3] *Trin.* IX.3ff; 15.6.10
[4] Alasdair Heron, *op.cit*, 90

These images are useful, he argues, because mind, its self-knowledge and self-love are co-extensive, co-equal and consubstantial. Also, as we conceive (beget) ideas, thought language seems appropriate for the Son.[5] As we have noted, there was a precedent for this argument in the *Logos* language of earlier Christian thinkers. As for the Spirit, Augustine follows the logic that we cannot love what we do not know; thus the love proceeds from the mind and its self-knowledge.[6] Ergo, we have the psychological demonstration of the *filioque* to which Zizioulas objects so strongly.[7]

This also enables Augustine to illustrate that the Spirit is not a Son, because we do not speak of conceiving love; "it is not a generation or conception," as Hill indicates, "it is rather an issue which joins together, as Augustine quaintly puts it, quasi-parent (mind) and quasi-offspring (mind's self-knowledge)".[8] One cannot fail to notice that this analogy is an image of one mind that has two attributes, faculties, powers or acts, depending on the lens through which one views it. Mirroring his metaphysical explanation of the Trinity as a single "I", Augustine has an image of an individual God (self/mind) in whom there are three overlapping and interlocking substantives, in contradistinction the Eastern perception of three personal Subjects subsisting in communion. Hill frames the difficulty in linguistic-metaphysical terms:

> There are [...] some obvious defects in this mental trinity as so far established. Knowledge and love signify acts, and acts that refer to an object; they are conjugated with the relative proposition "of", they are used *relatively*. But mind signifies just a thing, substance. It is said *absolutely*, without reference. We lack a relative term. This trinity of *mens, notitia sui and amor sui* corresponds to God, Son and Holy Spirit, not to Father, Son and Holy Spirit.[9] (Italics in original)

---

[5] Edmund Hill, *op.cit*, 52
[6] *Ibid* 53
[7] See 5.iv above
[8] Edmund Hill, *op.cit*, 53
[9] *Ibid* 52

Augustine seems to have realised this problem, because he developed his thought further, adjusting the image, from Book X of *On the Trinity*, to self-memory, knowledge and love, because memory is a relative term.[10] This idea is echoed in his *Confessions*, in which he deals extensively with memory: "There [in memory] too I encounter myself and recall myself, what and when and where I did some deed, and how I was affected when I did it."[11] Augustine's argument is that you can remember yourself in the same way that you can forget yourself by a kind of absence of mind and remember yourself by becoming present to yourself again. In this context, memory is the mind's presence to itself, or mindedness, which, Hill argues, "is basically given in the very fact of its being mind; rather as you might say the Father is the basically divine person, since he is just God, whereas the Son is God from God."[12] He continues:

As soon as the mind activates its self-presence by remembering itself, this act of self-minding breeds the second act of understanding itself, thinking itself with the mental word of self-understanding, saying explicitly "Me"; and from these two conjoint, co-extensive, conmental acts of me minding me, and me saying me to myself, there issues the third co-extensive, conmental act, as it were joining together quasi-parent and quasi-offspring, of me liking me, me willing me, self-willing.[13]

Thus we have a trio of mental acts, Hill remarks, not powers or faculties – self-remembering, self-understanding and self-willing.[14] We also have two versions of the Trinity in Augustine's writing, both of which are used by Western thinkers to demonstrate the Trinity: (a) mind, knowledge and love, which translates into God/Father, Son and Spirit; and (b) mind equals memory,

---

[10] *Ibid*
[11] *Conf.* 10.8.14
[12] Edmund Hill, *op.cit*, 53
[13] *Ibid* 53–54
[14] *Ibid* 53

knowledge and love, which translates into God equals Father, Son and Spirit. Against this backdrop I think we can safely argue that Augustine's analogous illustration of the Trinity is an image of a single Self in whom there are three acts or powers; i.e. an image of God in the image of the individual human mind.

However, this conception is not informed by psychology alone. It also seems to be informed by Hellenic metaphysics and cosmology, which in turn provided the impetus for his exploration of the mind, indicating that Augustine's psychological exploration and philosophy were mutually informing.

9.i.a. Augustine's analogies and Neoplatonic thought

Augustine's use of the human mind as an image of God derives from the Middle Platonists of the 1st century B.C., who identified Plato's Forms with the divine Mind.[15] As noted in 3.i.b above, Neoplatonic philosopher Plotinus had reworked this schema to posit three *hypostases* – the One, Mind and the World Soul, from which the world emanates, and argued that we could be united with the Good because our higher intellect perfectly conforms to it on the level of Mind and is therefore made like it,[16] giving Augustine his methodological foundation for this model. We have touched on the fact that identifying the Son with the knowledge (or *Logos*/Reason) of the One had a long history in Christian thought and went hand-in-hand with a rational approach to truth.[17]

We have also noted that Augustine rejected Origen and Tertullian's use of the Neoplatonic descending degrees of divinity, strongly asserting the equality of the three "Persons".[18] However, as in Origen's schema, he collapsed Plotinus' first *hypostasis*, the One, into the second *hypostasis*, the Mind (reverting to the middle Platonic Mind) to arrive at his idea of a simple "God the Trinity",

---

[15] Allen & Springsted, *op.cit*, 5–6; 9–10; 47
[16] *Ibid* 53–55; John K. Ryan, *op.cit*, 22
[17] See 3.i. above; Allen & Springsted, *op.cit*, 10; 29–32; 51
[18] 3.i.b and 7.iii.a above

while retaining the earlier Platonic *Logos* emphasis with respect to the Son as the knowledge of God.

Augustine then reworked Plotinus' third *hypostasis*, the World Soul, which is capable only of discursive thought, but which produces and governs the world from the inside as a succession of discursive thoughts.[19] O'Collins claims that the concept of the Holy Spirit as the love of God was a novelty, derived from Christian experience,[20] though one cannot fail to notice the connection between the Christian experience of God in the Spirit and the Neoplatonic treatment of love, as well as the idea that the Holy Spirit constitutes the Trinitarian communion.

As Allen explains, in Plotinus' thought love is the power that enables Mind to think, producing the Forms as the content of its thought and making the union between Mind and the One possible. But this love is distinct from the state of knowing – it facilitates a self-transcendent ecstasy alongside and independent of the knowing, raising the mind above itself[21] – the same language Augustine used to describe his mystical vision.[22]

Thus, one can see a clear correlation between Augustine's analogies and the later Platonic *hypostases*, along with Neoplatonic epistemology, although he reinterpreted the Neoplatonic schema to fit in with his idea of the Christian God. He also amalgamated these notions with the Aristotelian categories he used to arrive at his notion of three internal relations in God the Trinity.

9.i.b. Substantive relations and Augustine's analogies

Allen outlines how Augustine develops his metaphysics using his analogies: In order to maintain the Oneness of God (one *ousia* or primary substance) while avoiding tritheism (i.e. three primary substances), he posits one primary substance – the mind of the human being – as an analogy or image of the Father, which, as a subjective

---

[19] Allen & Springsted, *op.cit*, 50–52
[20] Gerald O'Collins, *op.cit*, 136
[21] Allen & Springsted, *op.cit*, 53–55
[22] See 7.i. above

cognitive entity, is personal.[23] The mind's knowledge (Son) and love (Spirit) of itself are powers (as opposed to Hill's acts) that are distinct from the mind without being properties (as are colour and shape) or attributes; therefore they are substantive and not reducible to one another. In terms of this analogy, the subject and object are one; that is, the subject's object of loving and knowing is itself. As Allen explains: "(1) Knower and lover, (2) object of knowledge and love, and (3) knowing and loving are relations that do not exist without one another. If there is a knower and a lover, there is knowing and loving, and there is also an object known and loved."[24] As such:

> Although distinct, the relations of subject, object and knowing and loving are inseparable and wholly involved in one another. They are thus a substance. Its oneness is not the *subject* to the exclusion of being the object or to the exclusion of being its powers; nor is the oneness the object to the exclusion of being the subject and powers; nor powers to the exclusion of being subject and object. What is the substance? It is subject, object and powers. [...] It is not that one is subject, another object and the third powers that relate subject to object; each is a power (act); each is an object (of the other's acts); each is a subject (with the others as the objects of its acts). They are thus one *God* who is Father, Son and Holy Spirit. [25] (Italics in original)

This is a brilliant piece of philosophical argumentation. Augustine has collapsed Aristotle's substantives into Plato's forms by positing that that which exists in the mind is substantive. Then, arguing within the confines of Aristotelian logic, his analogies demonstrate – quite brilliantly – how God can be one yet three. Philosophically, he has avoided tritheism by showing that each

---

[23] Allen & Springsted, *op.cit*, 72

[24] *Ibid* 73

[25] *Ibid*; see also Edmund Hill, *op.cit*, 50–51

"Person" is not an individual (primary) substance and taken the sting out of Modalism by showing that the "Persons" are not accidents because the relations (one of Aristotle's attributes) are substantive.[26] And, polemically, he has answered the Arians on their own terms. It all seems so logical. So what's the problem?

9.II. ANALYSIS

9.ii.a. Starting with the Substance

It does seem to be true that Augustine starts with the substance, as the Orthodox claim, although it would be more accurate to say that he starts with the ancient Hellenic metaphysical idea of the divine oneness, which he links to being/substance/*idipsum*.

This appears to be a deviation from tradition, understood as the faith of the worshipping community. It was not the idea of oneness posited at Nicaea; while the Nicene Father's posited the *homoousios* formula to mean that the Son is of the same substance as the Father in a derivative sense and is therefore both divine and eternal, Augustine appropriated *homoousios* to denote the unity of the Trinity, which is a separate doctrine and was understood as community in the East. This is also true of the Western worshipping community, if Ambrose's thought is indicative of 4th century Western piety.[27] Crucially, this perception implies that Father, Son and Spirit are three personal Subjects.

This appears to be the pivotal cause of the divergence in thought between the two traditions and is a function of Augustine arguing within ancient Hellenic conceptual paradigms rather than from an experiential perspective. The first conceptual difficulty with Augustine's idea of unity is its implication for the monarchy of the Father. The Cappadocians, in accord with the faith of the worshipping community and the Nicene faith, identified the name God with the Father, while Augustine, consequent on identifying the common divine essence with the "one God the Trinity", identified the name God with the Trinity, marking a significant deviation

---

[26] See *Trin.* V.5.6
[27] See, for example, Ambrose's *On the Holy Spirit*, 1.11–12

from the faith of the Church. He even speaks in a derogatory way
of those who hold this view.[28] With this pivotal premise, on which
his whole conception turns, Augustine destroyed the biblical premise of the monarchy on which the Orthodox insist, namely that
God proper is the Father.[29]

9.ii.b. Mere relations?

This also appears to be true with respect to the perception that
Father, Son and Spirit are three personal Subjects, which brings us
to the pivotal Eastern objection that the Augustinian conception of
the Trinity reduces the Divine Persons to mere relations – an issue
that arises due to the differing ways of understanding Person in
relation to substance. *Substantia*, a popular Latin translation of *ousia*
(being), was the word Nicaea I had used to assert the common essence. Thus, because Augustine identified being (properly) or substance (improperly) with the Divine "I" and the "I" with the Trinity, the impression is created that the Trinity is a single Self (or personal Subject). Lewis Ayres refutes this idea. Quoting from book
VI of *On the Trinity* he argues that Augustine in fact saw the divine
essence in the same way as the Eastern Fathers – constituted by the
three Persons themselves:[30]

> Nor since he is Trinity [*trinitas*] is he, therefore, tripartite [tri-
> plex]; otherwise the Father alone or the Son alone would be
> less than the Father and the Son together. [...] since the Father

---

[28] *Trin.* II.3.14–15; 5.27; his subordinationist opponents seem to have
argued for the mortality of the Son and Spirit on the grounds that change-
ability implied mortality and they were changeable because they took different forms. The Eastern Fathers, by contrast, claim the Son is the image
of the Father on the basis that, mystically, the Father is perceived in the
Son and because the Son is described as the eternal image of God *the Father* in Scripture (e.g. Col. 1.15). See also *Trin.* III.3.21

[29] John Behr (*op.cit*, 161–165) comes to the same conclusion

[30] Richard Cross (*op.cit*, 474-476) posits the same argument with respect to Aquinas' thought – the divine substance is nothing other than the
Persons themselves

is with the Son and the Son with the Father always and insepa-
rably [...] *because they are always mutually in one another.* In God
Himself, therefore, when the equal Son adheres to the equal
Father, or the equal Holy Spirit to the Father and the Son,
God does not thereby become greater than each one separate-
ly, for there is nothing whereby that perfection can increase.
But he is perfect whether the Father or the Son or the Holy
Spirit.[31] (Italics mine)

Ayres interprets this to mean that "the Father generates the
Son as one who is irreducibly all that it is to be God, and thus is
necessarily perfect God in himself and necessarily a 'person' or
'agent'".[32] He quotes Augustine's *Ep.* 120.12: "[...] the Father, the
Son and the Holy Spirit are a Trinity and that there is, nonetheless,
one God, not that the divinity is common to these as if it were a
fourth, but that it is itself the inseparable Trinity".[33] And *Ep.*
120.3.17: "[...] we should believe the Trinity is of one substance in
the sense that the essence is nothing other than the Trinity itself."[34]

His main point is that, for Augustine, God's being is none
other than three Divine Agents who, by virtue of their irreducible
unity, can be spoken of as a single I. Thus Augustine does not see
the Trinity as an intelligible simple reality who must somehow be
divided, he argues, nor as a simple reality with internal divisions
constituted by relations, but rather that each Divine Person is the
irreducible fullness of God.[35] Ayres adds that Augustine himself
clearly argues that the divine names are spoken relative to one another and that "every essence which is spoken of in relation is certainly something besides that relation".[36] Ayres' argument, which I
am unable to do full justice to here, is extremely compelling. However, the difficulty remains that Augustine was unable to pinpoint
what that "something besides" was. Thus, although he found a

---

[31] *Trin.* VI.7.9 & 8.9 in Lewis Ayres, *op.cit*, 133
[32] Lewis Ayres, *op.cit*, 134
[33] In *ibid* 136
[34] In *ibid*
[35] *Ibid* 135; see also *Cat.* 253, 255 (quoting the Council of Florence)
[36] *Trin.* 7.1.2 in *ibid*; see also *Cat.* 252; David Bentley Hart, *op.cit*, 204

metaphysical rule that enabled him to distinguish the Persons *ad intra*, by his own admission he did not really answer the question "three whats?"[37] And the reason for this is that, even if his subtext was personalistic, the categories of thought in which he worked out his distinction-by-relation rule could not accommodate the subjective perception of three personal Subjects in the Trinity. Two primary points are at issue:

First, the fact that he approaches the question of the Trinity from the impossible perspective of identifying the Substance with the "I" of God and identifies God *the Trinity* as one "I" or "Self" in whom there are three persons, militates against Ayres' personalistic interpretation. An "I", or a distinct identity, is incommunicable; if an "I" is an ontological category, the very essence of what God is (which is the basis of Augustine's identification of the being of God with the "I" of God), one "I" cannot be predicated of three subsistents simultaneously. Thus it is incoherent to suggest that one "I" can *be* three "I's". It is both conceivable and consistent with (mystically) experienced reality that three "I's" (subsistents) can subsist as one in perfect inter-subjective communion, but Augustine explicitly rejects this idea because he cannot accept the idea that being could be relationship.

He asserts that if in God it is the same thing to be as to subsist, "then it ought not to be said that there are three substances [which is how he understood *hypostases*] because then substance will no longer be substance because it will be relationship; every single thing that is, after all, subsists with reference to itself. How much more God [...]?"[38]

This constitutes an explicit rejection of the Cappadocian position – that in God, *contra* Hellenic philosophical conceptual categories, the common substance *is* relationship, in a sense; this was possible because they had redefined the meaning of *hypostasis* to say that God is substantially three Persons (subsistents) in communion (being) – i.e. Zizioulas' "being as communion" (see 3.ii.c above). The communion is a function of the fact that the Persons are love;

---

37 *Trin.* V.2.10
38 *Trin.* VII.1.2; see also VII.3.9

because the Father is love and because the Son and Spirit are of the Father, they are also love. While this conveys an indivisible reality, the Persons-*Hypostases* are distinguished from the *ousia* (being as communion) to draw out two conceptual aspects of the one reality, while monotheism is upheld by the fact that the One God is the Father. Thus there are two completely different paradigms: in the Eastern paradigm, three Persons subsist as one in community; in Augustine, one Person *is* three Persons, which is an anomaly if you understand a person to be an incommunicable "I".[39] Thus Augustine saying, "they are always mutually in one another", as quoted above, cannot be interpreted in a personalistic sense. In a nutshell, Rahner's explication (1.iv.a above) appears to be more representative of Augustinian-Western Trinitarian thought than Ayres' personalistic reading.

Second, the Aristotelian categories he used to argue his case do not allow for three real Persons, because in terms of these categories a person is an individual substance – which for Augustine is the Trinity as a whole. Thus he argues in *On the Trinity* V.1.3: "There is at least no doubt that God is substance, or perhaps a better word would be being [*ousia*]" and goes on to identify the substance with the "I am" of God (the Trinity) in Exodus 3:14 (i.e. God = substance = "I"). Earlier, in III.3.21, he similarly refers to God the Father, His Word and Spirit as being "one God in *being* and *identity*" (italics mine). Thus he asserts against the Arians: "If everything that is said about God is said substance-wise, then 'I and the Father are one' (Jn 10:30) is said substance-wise. So the substance of the Father and the Son is one" (i.e. they are one "I").

He continues in V.1.6: "If [...] what is called Father were called so with reference to itself and not to the Son, and if what is called Son were called so with reference to itself and not to the Father, the one would be called Father and the other would be called Son substance-wise"[40] (i.e. each Person does not have distinct ontological status). In V.1.7 he applies the same principle to the Spirit.

---

[39] The idea that many persons can be one person is echoed in Augustine's suggestion that the Church and Christ can be said to be one person, because the head and the body make up "one person" – see *Trin.* IV.2.12

[40] See also *Trin.* VI.1.3

He continues by arguing, against the Arian notion that the distinction between unbegotten and begotten denotes different substances, that what makes the Son equal to the Father "cannot be what he is called with reference to the Father" (V.1.7) because these titles are reference terms (i.e. Father is not essentially Father and Son is not essentially Son) – in contradiction to the Athanasian and Cappadocian understanding of Nicaea I, which affirmed the equality of the Son precisely on the grounds that He is equal to the Father because He is *of* the Father and therefore of one and the same *ousia* with the Father.

This then enables one to argue, with the relevant qualifications, the Father and Son are of the same substance yet ontologically distinct, i.e. Divine Person of Divine Person. But Augustine explains away this interpretation in *On the Trinity* VI.1.3, where he interprets "God from God and Light from Light" – to mean "this which the Son is not without the Father from this which the Father is not without the Son".[41] Thus, to return to V.1.7, in contrast to the Cappadocian interpretation, Augustine goes on to affirm that what makes them equal is that they simply *are* one substance: "So it follows that he is equal substance-wise. Therefore the substance of each is the same." Apart from the fact that it is a circular argument, the implication is that the Son is equal to the Father because He is also the whole Trinitarian substance, as is the Father:

> The chief point that we must maintain is that whatever that supreme and divine majesty is called with reference to itself is said substance-wise; whatever it is called with reference to another is said not substance- but relationship-wise; and that is the force of the expression "of the same substance" in Father and Son and Holy Spirit, that whatever is said with reference to self about each of them is to be taken as adding up in all three

---

[41] In *Trin.* VI.1.6 Augustine toys with the Cappadocian understanding, but ultimately rejects it; see also Edmund Hill, *op.cit*, 214, footnote 6

to a singular and not to a plural ... the supreme triad is not three Gods but one God.[42]

But considering the one substance is identified with the "I" of God, the implication is that Father and Son are one "I": "But as for the things each of the three in this triad is called that are proper or peculiar to himself, such things are *never said in reference to self* but only with reference to each other or with creation"[43] (Italics mine). In other words, Aristotelian categories do not allow for each divine Person to have ontological status.

As a consequence of "starting with the substance" and identifying the substance with the "I" of God, Augustine's inability to accord the Father, Son and Spirit distinct ontological status as Persons (or "I's") while arguing that they are only distinct "relationship-wise" seems to validate the Eastern objection that he reduces the divine Persons to "mere relations". Furthermore, Augustine has inverted the intended meaning of the formula of Constantinople I, namely that three Persons = substance and communion (in three modes) = relations. In Augustine's thought substance = Self and relations (modes) = Persons. Consequently, while Western apologists such as Cross[44] and Ayres' insist that the Augustinian-Thomist and Eastern "models" of the Trinity are metaphysically the same, because in both conceptions the divine essence is nothing other than the three Persons,[45] the subtext is entirely different – and all the Orthodox objections to the *filioque* are a function of this irreconcilable divergence.

9.ii.c. Contingent objections

If there is only one "I" in "God the Trinity", i.e. Father, Son and Spirit are jointly the one God and therefore one "I", then the Father, as the principle cause of the other two Persons, is the only

---

[42] *Trin.*V.2.9
[43] *Ibid* V.3.12
[44] Richard Cross, *op.cit*, 474–475
[45] David Bentley Hart (*op.cit*, 214) makes the same point.

Person in the Trinity who has ontological status with reference to Himself alone. As Augustine argues, the Father is His own substance, i.e. the "I" or Self or personal Subject or Person (whichever word has the least baggage for you):

> [...] the substance of the Father is just the Father, not insofar as he is Father, but insofar as He just is; so too the person of the Father is just the Father. He is called person with reference to himself, not with reference to the Son or the Holy Spirit, just as he is called God with reference to himself.[46]

Thus when the Father begets the Son by communicating His essence, i.e. Himself, to the Son, this has to mean that Father communicates his own "I-ness" to the Son in such a way that the two are one "I" or Self. Because there is only one Self in God, the Father and Son constitute one "I", who spirate the Spirit as one by communicating the common essence, i.e. the Father and Son as one "I", to Him.

Thus we have the following schema: the Father is His own substance and also the substance of the Son. Both the Father and the Son are the substance of the Spirit. Therefore the Father and Son are both causes of the Spirit's *identity* as Spirit; however, although the Spirit takes His being from the Son, the Son is not a cause of the substance of the Spirit, because the ontologically prior substance is the Father.[47] Thus the Father is the principle cause of the Spirit, meaning the monarchy is not compromised in terms of metaphysical criteria. Also, the consubstantial oneness of God is upheld, the Persons are clearly distinguished in terms of relations of origin and the Spirit is shown to be not another Son. Again, it all sounds perfectly logical.

The difficulty is that because the Father is the only Person who is His own substance, he does not generate a second "I" in

---

[46] *Trin.* VII.10.11
[47] C.f. Lewis Ayres, *op.cit*, 146–149

begetting the Son, but *Himself* in an internal relationship to Himself, which in turn generates a third internal relation. Consequently:

First, with respect to the Son, when discussing the Word as the Wisdom of God, Augustine explicitly speaks "of the Word equal to Himself [the Father] with which he always and changelessly utters *himself* [...] he is not to be understood singly, but together with that Word without which he would not be uttering"[48] (italics mine).

As Photius deduced, this implies that the Father and Son, being one in relation to the Spirit, have a shared *hypostasis*,[49] meaning a shared "I" or personal subjectivity.

Second, and likewise, Augustine's model enables him to distinguish the Spirit as a relational identity, but it does not allow for the Spirit to be an ontologically real Person, an "I" in Himself; the Spirit is not Himself plus the Father and the Son (i.e. an "I" indwelt by another two "I's"), He is simply the sum of the Father and Son, i.e. the Father and Son as mutual essence. Thus Photius would seem to be correct in saying that the *filioque* implies that the Spirit, as the sum of the Father and the Son, is a composite:[50] the Son simply *is* the Father's self-expression and the Spirit simply *is* the Father and the Son; He is not a distinct *Hypostasis*-Person in Himself, i.e. distinct from the common essence as a Person whose distinctive subsistence is Himself. The Orthodox are therefore right in saying that the *filioque* depersonalises the Spirit.

Third, on the other hand, if the Spirit *is* a distinct "I", then proceeding from the Son as a secondary cause would not add anything to the ontological reality that He is a Person. Thus it is anomalous to say that the relationship of the Father and Son to the Spirit is that of a common nature that *causes* the Spirit to be a Person or anything at all other than the sum of the Father and Son; the Son's relation to the Spirit can only be an interpersonal relationship, or mode of being, as the Cappadocians defined it.

Therefore it is incoherent, from an Eastern perspective, to posit the relation, i.e. the fact that the Father and Son indwell the

---

[48] *Trin.* VII.1.1
[49] See 2.i above
[50] See 2.i above, fourth point

Spirit, as a cause of the personhood of the Spirit. This is to transpose arguments for the mutual indwelling into arguments for the origin of the Son and Spirit. Fourth, from an Eastern perspective, this means Augustine confuses the economic Trinity (the modes of being, which are revealed in time) with the immanent Trinity (relations of origin, which are beyond conception).

Fifth, we get back to the question of the monarchy. The fact that, in the Augustinian conception, the Son and Spirit are not ontologically distinct Persons (i.e. being their own "I-ness) means that the Father does not (a) bring forth two distinct personal Subjects and therefore (b) He cannot be viewed as causing the Trinitarian being as communion. Thus, while the monarchy of the Father is upheld in a metaphysical sense, it is nevertheless undermined in the sense that, as the Eastern Fathers argued polemically, the Father is God proper and the cause of the Trinitarian being (as communion) because He is the sole cause of the other two *Hypostases*-Persons who, together with the Father, constitute the Trinity.

If one were to give Western thinkers such as Ayres the benefit of the doubt and argue that Augustine understands each Person to be a distinct divine Agent or personal Subject, one can only do this by abstracting the essence from the Persons: i.e. the Father begets the Son by imparting the essence – a constituent element of Himself – to the Son, meaning that the Father is not wholly an "I" and therefore not simple; the Son and Spirit then impart this same constituent element of themselves to the Spirit in bringing Him forth.

This would mean that the Son is a function of the Father's essence and the essence of the Father and Son are the substance of the Spirit in the way that human creatures are persons, who in being conceived come to *have* a biological substance that we receive from our parents; that is to say, the Father and Son's essence is the substance of the Spirit in a parallel way to the way that creatures have a common substance, in which the substance is an underlying reality that is shared by three "I's".

But, apart from the fact that Augustine himself rejects this notion because this would mean God was not simple,[51] this still does

---

[51] *Trin*.VII.3.10–11

not explain how the Spirit comes to be a *Hypostasis*-Person as a consequence of receiving the common essence from the Father and Son together; we are back to the idea that He is a composite, but this time of the underlying nature of the Father and the Son and therefore simply the common nature.

Alternately, one can argue that a divine "Person" is something other than an "I" – which is, of course, precisely what Augustine does. Thus, in terms of Augustine's schema, the *filioque* could simply be taken to mean that in spirating the Spirit, the Father and Son impart their common "I-ness", which is fundamentally the Father's "I-ness", to the "Person" of the Spirit, or that the common "I-ness" is in itself a third expression of the "I-ness" of the One God. But then this would mean that the Son and Spirit are simply distinct "forms" or modes of being a single "I".

This brings us to a sixth difficulty, namely that Augustine's conception would then be Modalistic, only instead of the idea of one God, i.e. one Divine "I", with three modes of being in relation to the world, one now has one "I" that has three relations to itself that are constituted by three internal acts that are simultaneously a single act. This becomes particularly clear when we consider Augustine's use of his analogies to demonstrate the divine processions. He appropriates mindedness (consciousness) to the Father, knowledge to the Son and love to the Spirit, which are all in reality common attributes of the nature but used to denote internal acts.

Both Hill and Ayres insist that Augustine intended to show, with his analogies, how the Trinity was constituted by the Persons' internal acts towards one another[52]– implying that each Person is a real Person.

However, this is impossible, once again, against the backdrop of (a) Augustine's identification of the common being with the "I" of God; (b) with the fact that he ultimately calls the Persons "memory" (self-presence), "self-knowledge" and "self-love" – an image of one Self being aware of, knowing and loving Himself; and (c) in light of the fact that Augustine has appropriated different common attributes to each person, that he collapses the attributes

---

[52] Edmund Hill, *op.cit*, 53; Lewis Ayres, *op.cit*, 43

and *esse* into each other and into the one substance, such that God's power is His wisdom, is His goodness, is His love, etc.

So what he has done is to appropriate to particular "Persons" the attributes that seem to best describe their acts in the *economy*, in which the simple One is discursively revealed. Thus the three "Persons" are in fact not really distinct in *reality*, but only distinct in our minds as a discursive revelation of the one God, the single "I", and simply *are* their acts in the economy, meaning that the Trinity is an immanent-economic self-referential manifestation of the transcendent, simple, unchanging and inconceivable One.

The Trinity turns out to be a lesser reality in Augustine's thought; the only true reality is the transcendent, simple, unchanging and inconceivable One, while the Persons are simply His acts; they are not distinct, ontological Persons *ad intra* – echoing the ancient Roman view of personhood,[53] defined according to their role in society, but ultimately only an expression of the monistic One.[54]

The difference is that in ancient Rome the human person has several different relations to society, while in Augustine's Trinitarian thought the Persons simply *are* the self-referential acts/relations of the One. They are not distinct "I's". This is acutely clear when we assess Augustine's analogies in relation to Neoplatonic thought.

9.III. THE HEART OF THE MATTER – THE PARADIGM OF LOVE

9.iii.a. The attributes appropriated as internal relations

It appears that the use of analogies drawn from human psychology is not necessarily an issue in itself; it is rather the context in which an analogy is used (i.e. the supporting argumentation) and what one uses the analogy to demonstrate that matters. For example, because St Gregory Palamas used the analogy of the Spirit as love in the context of a different conception of the Trinity to Augustine, the analogy took on a different meaning. Also, such analogies are use-

---

[53] See 4.ii.a above
[54] See Allen & Springsted, *op.cit*, 26–27

ful for demonstrating the incorporeality and consubstantiality of the Persons, as Augustine rightly observes.

St Symeon the Theologian also used the analogy of a man's *nous* and his word to explain the inseparability of the Father and Son, but consciously as a limited, inadequate example to emphasise the difference between uncreated and created reality.[55] But Augustine, arguing from created reality, appropriates common attributes to particular persons to demonstrate both the oneness of God and the distinctions between the Persons *ad intra*, as well as the divine processions, eliciting the objection that Augustine confuses the common attributes with the Persons and the Persons with the nature, and consequently divides the nature.

By positing only one "I" in God and appropriating common attributes to particular Persons to distinguish the Persons *ad intra*, in particular to distinguish the Spirit as the love that *constitutes* the Trinitarian communion of love,[56] Augustine also creates the impression that love is distinct from the Father (Mind). This (a) creates an impression that God the Father's love is an act of the will and the Spirit is consequently a product of the Father's will, (b) undermines the idea that the Father is the source of the unity, or intra-Trinitarian communion and (c) contradicts the experientially known central revelation of Christ, namely that God *the Father* is love.[57] This is the epiphany of the Father imparted to us by, in and through the Incarnate Son and in the Holy Spirit and, in my view, was the whole point of the Incarnation; on the level of revelation, to reveal that God is Father or *Abba*, the name with which the Son addressed Him (Jn 17:6) so that we might know, love and trust Him; ontologically, it was to reconcile the world to God the Father (Eph 2:16; Col 1:20–22), i.e. to bring us into real communion with the Father, who *is* paternal love (Jn 17:3). The fact that the Son and Spirit reveal this to us as Persons – i.e. as distinct personal "Others" is pivotal: the Son reveals the Father's love to us in the Incarnation in Person as the image of the Father's love for us by virtue

---

[55] Hierotheos (Vlachos), *The Person in the Orthodox Tradition*, 186–187
[56] See Lewis Ayres, *op.cit*, 144
[57] Of course, Augustine makes this point elsewhere; see e.g. *Trin.* 1.3.21; nevertheless, the point holds that his analogies obscure this reality.

of the common nature and by virtue of His relationship to the Father – as the Son who wholly loves and trusts the Father in a filial way, living His life in loving and trusting dependence on the Father as the One who is the cause of His being (e.g. Jn 5:19, 6:57; 8:28) – and submitting to the helplessness of death on the Cross, trusting the Father to raise Him up again.

The Spirit, on the other hand, manifests the Son's communion in us by revealing the Father's love in us *personally* by engaging our subjectivity, so enabling us to share His love for the Son *in us* in the same way that the Father loves the Son and by loving the Father *in us* in the likeness of the Son's love for the Father.

This brings us to a further set of difficulties with using the analogies to distinguish the Persons *ad intra*: to distinguish the Spirit as love, as if love within the Trinity were a distinct entity rather than a common attribute of all the Persons *because of the Father* (i.e. because the Son and Spirit are love by virtue of being *of* the Father) and to demonstrate the Son's identity in terms of knowledge, de-emphasises both the personal love of the Son who died for us on Calvary and the Son as the personal revelation of the *Father's* love. Conversely, identifying the Spirit solely with love (distinct from knowledge) undermines the biblical conception of the Spirit as the *Spirit of Truth* who illumines us inwardly by revealing the divinity of Christ (the image of God the Father) to us as communion.

If we examine the analogies in relation to Neoplatonic cosmology, we arrive at another set of difficulties.

9.iii.b. The analogies and Neoplatonism

We have noted how Augustine collapsed Plotinus' One into the Mind to arrive at the idea of the One God, in which the Father (mind/memory/self-presence) is the only real "Self" in the Trinity, the only one who is self-referential, as Augustine puts it, and therefore the substance of God, while the Son and Spirit are loosely identified with the Forms of the Good (self-knowledge immanently and revealed knowledge economically) and the Spirit as love replaces the World Soul (who constitutes the inter-Trinitarian love immanently and draws creatures into this love economically), and how he then collapsed the knowledge (the Forms) and love (the World Soul) into the Mind/One. Augustine thus ends up with an image of the Father (Mind/Memory/Self-presence) bringing forth two self-referential subsistent relations or acts within Himself.

This leads to a complicated set of theological difficulties. *Economically*, Augustine is able to show that the Father (Mind) is no longer the passionless, transcendent One who does not interact with the world;[58] but this is at the expense of the real, ontological status of the Son and Spirit as Persons because they are merely the Father's acts/self-expressions in the economy.

In Augustine's thought God's acts are identical with Himself, so this in turn implies that somehow the Father became incarnate in Christ in his Self-expression as knowledge – which implies Patripassionism. The idea that the Son is not a real Person in eternity also makes nonsense of biblical texts that, at face value, refer to the Son (a) seeking the Father's glory, not His own, such as Jn 8:18 & 17:4–5 – a reference to a distinct "Other", (b) revealing God *the Father* in Himself, particularly from the gospel of John (the most mystical Gospel), such as Jn 14:1 & 6–9, and (c) the Son reconciling the world to God *the Father* – i.e. a distinct personal Other – through Himself, such as Jn 17:1–3, 2 Cor, 5.18–19; Col 1:19–20.

The only way to get around this is to argue that the Son became a distinct Person only in the incarnation. Augustine himself seems to imply this when he says: "So a man was coupled with and even in a sense compounded with the Word of God as one Person".[59] This non-personal conception of the eternal Son preemptively contradicts the formula of the Council of Chalcedon (451), which dogmatised the truth that the incarnate Son is one divine Person in two natures, as Hill also notes.[60] The Spirit, as an act of the Father, is personal only in the sense that He is the Father's love, but in Himself this means He is an impersonal power.

On the other hand, when one uses the analogies to demonstrate the *immanent* relations, Augustine's reinterpreted notion of the Platonic One, in which the One/Mind knows and loves *Himself* in such a way that His knowing and loving is subsistent, translates into an image of a narcissistic Father – the only ontologically "self-

---

[58] See Allen & Springsted, *op.cit*, 26; Gerald O'Collins *op.cit*, 92
[59] *Trin.* IV.5.30; see also IV.3.16
[60] Edmund Hill, *op.cit*, 181, footnote 54

referential" and therefore real "I" – eternally involved in Self-contemplation and self-love – i.e. we end up back at the idea of the transcendent passionless One who is above being and therefore unknowable as a tangibly real Presence.

This brings us back to the argument that self-love is not love – at least if the love of the crucified Son is our norm, because true love as revealed by Christ Crucified is a *self*-sacrificial love of others (as Christ Himself indicates – see Jn 15:13). If the self-sacrificial love of Christ is a definitive image of the love of God, we have to conclude that the Father's love is also "self-sacrificial" love (in a superlative, transcendent sense) for "others".

This means in turn that it is necessary to show (a) that the Father's immanent love is a self-sacrificial love of distinct "others" and consequently (b) that the Divine Persons are three *real* personal Subjects in relation, or communion, not one "I" in relation to Himself, because otherwise it would not be love in the distinctly Christian sense of the word, but only self-love in the sense of the Platonic One. Because Augustine's image of the Trinity presents the latter image, this implies that "God the Trinity" is love *only* in relation to the world, meaning that in God love for other personal Subjects is contingent on creation.

This is one of the logical reasons (experiential ones remain primary), I believe, for which it was so important to the Eastern Fathers to assert, in *contradistinction* to the rational, narcissistic and transcendent One of Hellenic philosophy and in continuity with tradition, that the Person of the Father is the "One" who is above being and the loving cause of the Son and the Spirit as distinct, ontological Persons and simultaneously the immanent One who governs the world from the inside (*contra* Plotinus' World Soul) *as love*. And this in turn is why it is so important to insist (a) that the name God belongs properly to the Father (b) on the monarchy of the Father as the originator of the Son and Spirit as personal Subjects, and (c) that the Person is a unique ontological reality that cannot be determined by nature.

This is also why the Orthodox will insist that one cannot distinguish love from the Father and ascribe to it a separate identity of its own – as if this were the Spirit's unique, immanent identity and as if love within the Trinity were a distinct entity rather than the primary ontological attribute of all the Persons *because of* the Father.

This not only undermines the central revelation of Christ – that the Father, the source of being, is wholly paternal love and that He loves us with an infinite compassion and solicitude – but also the monarchy of the Father as the source of the inter-Trinitarian communion of love of inter-subjective "others". Augustine rejects this schema because (a) he does not understand how the Eastern Fathers reinterpreted the word Person, (b) it contradicts his idea of unity, derived from Hellenic cosmology and (c) because if in God love is relationship, this in turn implies that substance is relationship – because Hellenic metaphysics do not allow for it.

Thus, in the final analysis, the issue is centred on what our criteria of truth are: the historically-mystically known reality of the Divine Person or Hellenic cosmology and metaphysics.

9.IV. SUMMARY

If one evaluates Augustine's conception of the Trinity and the *filioque* in particular on its own terms, i.e. as a function of Hellenic metaphysics, which allows for only one "I" in the Godhead, it makes a great deal of logical sense. However, when evaluated against the historical-mystical perception of the Eastern Fathers, it becomes extremely problematic every which way one looks at it.

The fundamental point of departure is that the pivotal premise of the Augustinian conception is the Hellenic oneness and simplicity of God the Trinity, allowing for only one "I" in God, while the pivotal premise of the Eastern conception is that the Father is God proper and each Person-*Hypostasis* is a distinct subsistent in the sense that being is identical with interpersonal Subjectivity, and the unity is a community of Persons. The relations of origin – begetting and proceeding – tell us that the Son and Spirit come forth from the Father as distinct Persons with separate identities, but not the mechanics of their origination.

From this perspective, the Orthodox objections to the *filioque* seem to be valid: the *filioque* undermines the monarchy of the Father, causes the Father and Son to be one *hypostasis* in relation to the Spirit, unambiguously depersonalises the Spirit by turning Him into a composite and can be shown to be unnecessary because (a) Augustine could just as well apply the begetting/proceeding distinction to the Spirit's procession from the Father, as he does with respect to the Spirit's "procession" from the Father and the Son

and (b) because if the Spirit proceeds from the Father as an ontologically distinct Person, His proceeding from the Son would add
nothing to his status as Person. Furthermore, it is underpinned by a
conception in which the modes of being (economic Trinity) are
confused with the divine processions (immanent Trinity).

Also, Augustine's conception of a single "I" in three relations
appears to be distinctly Modalistic. In the Augustinian-Western
conception, the Son and Spirit are no more than the economic acts
of the one God that are individuated by relation only. Thus, to the
Eastern mind, while there is agreement that the relations of origin
are intrinsic to the identities of the Persons, the Western model
confuses relation with existence, or subsistence, and thus the
modes of being with the divine processions, and fails to show how
the Spirit as a Person is ontologically distinct from the common,
tri-personal nature; He simply *is* the Father and the Son or, from
another angle, a substance common to the Father and the Son.
This is markedly different from saying that the Spirit, a distinct
"Other", shares all things in common with the Father and Son and
is, for this reason, rightly called Spirit – a statement of identity rather than ontology – as St Basil argues.[61]

If one perceives the Persons to be wholly subjective "Others",
one can argue that the Spirit is the sum of the Father and Son only
by separating philosophical logic from subjectively perceived reality, and thus abstract the Trinity.

With respect to Augustine's analogies, by using the common
attributes – which should be used to argue the *oneness* of a Trinity
of real Persons in community – to demonstrate the *distinctions* in
"One God the Trinity" and by positing that the Spirit as love *constitutes* the Trinitarian communion, Augustine's analogies seem to
confuse the attributes with the Persons and the Persons with the
common nature and thus divide up the nature.

His conception thus reduces the Persons to mere relations
and/or their economic acts, destroys the simplicity of God, depersonalises the Spirit and invalidates the monarchy of the Father as
the cause of the Trinitarian communion.

---

[61] *De Spiritu Sancto* 18–22; 36

Moreover, distinguishing the Spirit from the Father as the love that constitutes the Trinitarian communion, thereby implying that the Spirit is a necessary bond between the Father and Son, undermines the very heart of the Christian gospel; i.e. Augustine is unable to make explicit *what* Son and the Spirit reveal – namely that everything that is, including being itself, is because *Papa* loves wholly and infinitely with a paternal love.

Nor does he adequately link this to the ontological premise of the revelation, namely that the reason we know God the Father as *Papa* is (a) because the eternal Son revealed this by incarnating His eternal interpersonal relationship with the Father historically and because He shares one nature with the Father (and therefore attributes) and calls us to share in the same relationship; and (b) because the Spirit, who personally shares the life/communion of the Father and Son wholly in eternity and thus also the one nature (and attributes), shares this relationship with us inwardly.

He consequently also undermines the truth that the Son is also love and the Spirit is also the Spirit of Truth.

These difficulties appear to be a function of the fact that Augustine (a) did not grasp the intended meaning of the formula of Constantinople I, (b) worked out his exposition within Hellenic conceptual categories and therefore had no way of explicitly articulating the fact that the Father, Son and Spirit are three real Persons, (c) identified the one substance with the one God and the One God with the Trinity – which was consequent on collapsing the Neoplatonic One, Mind and World Soul into each other, (d) sought the image of God in the mind of the human individual – consequent on the converse Platonic notion that the human soul is a copy of and akin to the world of Forms, and (e) presupposed that divine reality is discursively reflected in creaturely reality.

Augustine's conception is thus premised on a complex set of mutually informing ideas in which he both reinterprets Neoplatonic thought and Aristotelian categories in light of the Christian faith and conversely reinterprets the Christian faith in light of Neoplatonic cosmology and Aristotelian categories, using his psychological analogies to demonstrate his conception. Thus, in contrast to the Eastern conception, he arrived at a conception of the Trinity that is not rooted in historical-mystical perception of the Persons, but rather reflects Neoplatonic cosmology.

When one compares Eastern historically-mystically known truth to the analogies in relation to ancient Hellenic cosmology, another set of difficulties emerges. Again the pivotal point of departure is Augustine's idea of unity. His identification of divine Being with Mind/Self/the One, *contra* Neoplatonic thought, appears to have been an attempt to show – over against the Neoplatonic passionless and transcendent One, which is above being – that the Creator is in fact a personal Subject whose "I-ness" is pure being. That is, that the true God is an "I" who created the world *ex nihilo* and who interacts with creatures in an interpersonal way, that the world is not a necessary emanation from the One but an act of His will/love, while knowing Him is not a consequence of actualising a necessary link between God and man, but a consequence of His personal self-revelation.

However, because Augustine identifies the one "God the Trinity" with the Mind and the Mind with the Self and the Father, who brings forth two "subsistent relations" (or powers, act or attributes, depending who you read), which he has appropriated to the Persons in light of their economic functions – the Son (knowledge) and Spirit (love) – within Himself, the image is of one Self, the Father, in whom there are two relations *to Himself.*

Thus, while this schema enables Augustine to demonstrate "God the Trinity's" love for the world, with respect to the immanent Trinity we arrive at a reinterpreted image of the Neoplatonic One who is eternally involved in self-contemplation – and we end up back at the idea of the transcendent passionless One who is above being and therefore unknowable as a tangibly real Presence, a notion that the Orthodox consider an image of a narcissistic God, in contradistinction to the Eastern perception of three ineffable Persons who eternally and wholly indwell the other two in an ecstasy of divine love.

Augustine's conception thus contradicts the revealed truth of God's self-sacrificial love, which implies a self-giving to *others* – and therefore that love is relationship with "others".

Notably, one reason for Augustine's rejection of this schema is that he rejects the notion of being as relationship, which brings us back to the point that he inverts the intended meaning of the formula of Constantinople I, namely that three Persons = substance and communion (*perichoresis*) = relations, while in Augustine's thought substance = Self and relations = Persons.

The fundamental reason for this divergence in thought seems to be that Eastern Fathers premised their conception on experientially (historically-mystically) known truth, while Augustine argued philosophically, phenomenologically and existentially, and read presuppositions from ancient Hellenic philosophy into Christian revelation. The result, from an Eastern perspective, is that Augustine's conception is an abstract conception of the Trinity that has lost touch with experientially known truth and therefore with reality.

10 CONCLUSION

I believe I have adequately demonstrated that the East-West impasse over the *filioque* is not simply a misunderstanding, as some Roman Catholic polemicists attempt to show; the clause represents a significant divergence in thought between the two traditions, underpinned by irreconcilable understandings of the Trinity, and that there has been a great deal of talking at cross-purposes between the two traditions, with the same language often used to denote different meanings. The result is that on the surface, the two traditions often seem to be saying the same things – and some Western polemicists go to great lengths to demonstrate the harmony of the two conceptions on this basis – but in fact the "common ground" has a fundamentally different subtext.

This is an important reason, I believe, for which the East-West impasse on the issue of the *filioque* has been so difficult to resolve; the Orthodox objections seem absurd when viewed through the lens of Western assumptions, while Western attempts to demonstrate a harmony between the two conceptions seem conversely absurd to the Eastern mind. In my view this reality needs to be faced head on if we are to move forward.

I have demonstrated that the fundamental point of departure between the Eastern and Western traditions is different understandings of the word "person" in relation to the Divine Persons and parallel divergent notions of the divine unity. I have also argued that while the Western conception makes perfect sense in terms of Western criteria of truth, if we take seriously the experientially known truth that the Father, Son and Spirit are real personal Subjects, the Eastern objections to the *filioque* seem reasonable because the *filioque* is a function of categories of thought that do not allow for the affirmation of three real personal Subjects in the Trinity to be made conceptually explicit.

I have also found that these differences are in turn consequent on differing experiences, approaches and consequently criteria of truth; the Cappadocians made a case for the *subjectively* and *mystically* perceived reality of God in relation to the biblical witness and the faith of the worshipping community, and in opposition to heretics (who subverted the experienced faith of the Church with their philosophical argumentation), while Augustine argued *philosophically* and *objectively* (phenomenologically) from the biblical revelation and *existentially* in his attempt find a reflection of God in himself. As the thought of these Fathers is regarded as normative in their respective traditions, we have a situation in which, in Eastern thought, mystical perception takes priority over philosophical logic and the resultant conception is regarded as authoritative, provided it is consistent with revelation and in continuity with the experiences of the Apostles and the saints, and the *lex orandi lex credendi* rule of faith.

The Western conception, conversely, is rooted in presuppositions informed by ancient Hellenic philosophy. Thus, the Eastern Fathers asked: How can the revelation of three divine Subjects be reconciled to the Judeo-Christian belief in one God? Augustine, on the other hand, asked: How can the Christian revelation of three divine Subjects be reconciled to the Hellenic philosophical notion of immutable, simple unity?

This appears to be the reason for his identification of the one God with "God the Trinity" as opposed to what seems to be the traditional perception that God proper is the Father, while the Son and Spirit are God in a derivative sense, allowing for the articulation of the experienced reality that all three Persons are real Personal Subjects in communion. Augustine's conception of unity, which allows for only one real "I" in the Trinity, in turn necessitates the formulation of his metaphysical rule of distinctive relations, which underpins his argument for the *filioque*.

His idea that the sendings reveal the immanent processions is premised on the related Hellenic notion of the immutability of the simple One, which is transcendent, impersonal Being, rather than the personal God (the Father) of Scripture who is unchanging because He is incommunicably who He is, namely a personal Subject who is paternal love. As the *filioque* is a function of these differences, the disagreement over the clause will have to be battled out in the arena of criteria of truth in the two traditions.

In short, we need to choose between experiential perception of God and a phenomenological reading of Scripture interpreted through the lens of Hellenic philosophy. In relation to content, the questions are: (a) is our criterion of truth the experiential, subjective perception of three ontologically distinct Persons or the ancient Hellenic idea of divine unity and simplicity? And (b) can one deduce the relations of origin phenomenologically from the historical revelation (economic Trinity), or should we confine ourselves to that which we know experientially? And consequent on the latter: (c) is it legitimate to interpret the unchangingness of God in terms of the ancient Hellenic philosophical notion of immutable substance, which underpins Augustine's view that the immanent Trinity can be deduced from the economic Trinity, or should one rather prioritise the biblical, personalistic meaning of the unchanging nature God? Due to space constraints, I am not able to argue the merits of the two approaches here in any detail, but I would like to make a few observations.

The question of whether it is legitimate in the first place to dogmatise a logically deduced idea requires more extensive discussion than I am able to enter into here. Suffice it to say that in my view the uniqueness and power of the Judeo-Christian proclamation is precisely that we testify to Who we know experientially, not what we have deduced logically (see e.g. Jn 3:11; Gal 1:11–12; 1 Jn 1–3). Our faith rests entirely on our acceptance of such truth claims and it is precisely such truth claims that ground our faith in experientially known reality and separates Christianity from the general pool of "belief systems". Thus by dogmatising rationally deduced ideas as truth we weaken the force of our testimony.

In the Christian witness, both what and how we know is pivotal: (a) we know the Son historically because of the Incarnation. His disciples and followers testify to their experiences of Him and the biblical account of the Incarnation thus gives us an objective criterion of truth. But (b) the Apostles and biblical writers bear witness to the communally experienced reality that it is in the Spirit – who leads us into all truth, showing us things we "cannot bear now" (Jn 16:12), i.e. which cannot be comprehended "in the flesh" (i.e. phenomenologically), by making Himself tangibly present in our subjectivity – that we are able to recognise the Son's divinity and that in the Spirit and through the Son we know God the Father as He truly is, as loving *Papa*. As the Apostolic witness is premised on these truth claims, if mystical experience of God that is in accord with that of the Apostles is regarded as less authoritative than speculative reason about God, you have effectively destroyed the basis of the Christian faith; to reject affirmations of truths that arise from direct encounters with God on the basis that they do not conform to speculative logic that in any case is premised on presuppositions that go hand-in-hand with an incompatible cosmology is equivalent to rejecting the truth claims of the Apostles, because it places hypothesis above the experience of God, implying a rejection of the notion of first-hand testimony to real experience of God. In my view, this amounts to unbelief.

Moreover, it is not adequate, in my view, to draw solely on the testimony of the prophets and Apostles, as recorded in Scripture, and to argue phenomenologically from their testimony, because the questions that need to be answered differ in every era. Therefore those who have mystical experience of God will frame their description of their experience in relation to the questions of their era while not necessarily describing features of their experience that are relevant to questions that have not arisen. In the context of the 4th century, different questions were at issue to those that faced the Apostles – such as those posed by Sabellianism and Arianism, the latter particularly in its Eunomian form.

The Eastern Fathers answered both heresies from the perspective of their mystical experience; i.e. they were illumined by direct encounters with the manifestation of the Son in the Spirit and therefore knew, by recognition, that the Father, Son and Spirit were distinct divine personal Subjects who indwelt one another, the latter because they found themselves indwelt by the Three. They therefore asserted a particular aspect of experiential knowledge of God because that was what was required in their context, while the Apostles had no need to assert this point because the question was not at issue in their time.

By contrast, the evidence I have gathered so far appears to support the Orthodox view that ancient Hellenic cosmology and its imbedded presuppositions are unable to accommodate the experienced reality of three divine personal Subjects because ancient Hellenic conceptual categories were a function of a cosmology that was very different to that espoused by Scripture and the Apostles. This means Augustine's use of presuppositions from ancient Hellenic philosophy was an attempt to reconcile the truth claims of two fundamentally incompatible cosmologies. In my view, the fact that the Eastern Fathers simply named an experienced reality, while

Augustine's conception is the product of logical deduction premised on presuppositions that are not intrinsic to experiential revelation, tips the scale in favour of the Eastern conception.

Another consideration is the relationship between dogma and Christian *praxis*. It seems to me that, in every manner of self-manifestation, the aim of the Trinitarian God was to facilitate a subjective relationship of love between the Father and humanity, from Abram's call to faith (as trust) to the lawgiving, the Incarnation, Crucifixion and Resurrection and the sending of the Spirit, the ultimate aim being the inclusion of humanity in the interpersonal Trinitarian communion of love. This suggests that our theology and dogma should be at the service of this subjective end and provide the conceptual co-ordinates that orient us towards this goal.

There are several implications: as God the Father has revealed Himself as essentially personal, through the Son and in the Spirit – as a Subject to be loved (in fact, this is the first commandment), a subjective approach to truth conforms to both the subjective reality of a personal God and the end to which we are called. Ironically, this is also a more scientific approach, because it limits what we know about God to that which is experienced – and the only way Christian truth can be verified, albeit not proved, is experientially. Therefore, in my view, it makes sense that, in the formulation of our faith, experiential perception of the Trinity in the context of a communion of love should be the fundamental source of the raw data of our faith and our criterion of truth – and our conceptual systems should be subordinated to this perception, not vice versa.

This is exactly what the Eastern understanding of knowledge of God is: knowing the Trinity as three interpersonal "Subjectivities" in a communion of love and confining what we can positively say about the Divine Persons to what is known from this experience. As Orthodox dogma simply asserts this experientially known reality over and against heresies (innovations), there is no separation between theory and practice.

In Western thought, by contrast, (a) knowledge of God is understood as ideas about God. In my view this turns God into an object to be analysed rather than a Subject to be loved, which creates an existential barrier between the human person and God; one cannot truly surrender oneself in love to an object that one is analysing, because this requires the objectification of one's Subject.

Furthermore, (b) because the Western conception does not allow for the reality of three ontological divine Persons in communion, it de-emphasises the experientially known truth that eternal life is communion with and in God. In this regard it is noteworthy that, while Western academics such as O'Collins, Ayres and Coffey subscribe to the Augustinian conception of the Trinity, they also speak of "the *self*-giving of the Father being a condition for the *self*-giving of the Son" (italics mine) and a "supremely intense and blissful mutual presence",[1] while Coffey protests that the subjective nature of the Persons is described "elsewhere".[2] Thus, while Augustine's philosophical explication of the Trinity – on which Western Trinitarian dogma is premised – does not allow for the Divine Persons to be real "Subjectivities", they are spoken of as if they were. This is an anomaly in Western thought.

Thus, while in Eastern thought there is a demonstrable harmony between dogma and experience of God, this does not seem to be the case in Western Trinitarian doctrine. O'Collins implicitly concedes this point when, speaking of Rahner's explication of the Trinity, he says: "Who can adore Rahner's 'three distinct manners of subsisting' […]? The somewhat Modalistic language of Rahner […] is not well adapted for private prayer or public worship."[3] As Rahner's exposition seems to be true to Augustine's conception, this indicates a split between Augustine's philosophical rationale, in which the Western conception is rooted, and the common experiential sense of the Divine Persons among Western Christians – that happens to be in harmony with the East on an intuitive level. Thus there is a contradiction between perception and conception in the Western explanation of the Trinity.

As Augustine's abstract conception of the Trinity does not adequately convey the experienced, living reality of God, it has no relevance for Christian *praxis* because it does not orient the believer towards the divine inter-subjective communion. This means that it is not simply the case that the Eastern and Western traditions be-

---

[1] Gerald O' Collins, *op.cit*, 178
[2] See 3.iii above
[3] Gerald O' Collins, *op.cit*, 175–176

lieve the same things while expressing these truths in different conceptual systems; it is rather that the conceptual system used by Augustine constitutes a barrier to articulating experienced truth.

Also, if the object of God's economic activity is to enable human creatures to enter into a subjective relationship with the Father (e.g. Jn 17:3), then we need to ask ourselves what is truly necessary to know about God in order to facilitate this. St Basil thus makes a valid point when he asserts that knowing *that* God is (along with what He is like, e.g. a loving *Papa*) is adequate to facilitate worship (i.e. appropriate relationship); we do not need to know how He subsists. Consequently, it is not necessary to explain anything about God that lies beyond the scope of that which can be known in relationship – such as the exact nature of the origins of the Son and the Spirit. It therefore seems legitimate (and more intellectually honest) to affirm that which we know experientially, while also admitting that we don't know certain things (e.g. how the Son is begotten or the Spirit proceeds) because our experience does not stretch that far.

In short, it makes sense to dogmatise only those truths that are verifiable in both the historical and Pentecostal experience if our proclamation is to be grounded in living reality – which enables us to assert the real immediacy of God in our lives – rather than hypothesis. This means that (a) it makes more sense to say that we know that there are three divine personal Subjects because this is what experience tells us, than to collapse the three Persons into one "I" because ancient Hellenic hypotheses dictate that that is how we should perceive God. And (b), while it might be terribly interesting to know exactly how the Son and the Spirit originate, it might be safer to say that we don't know than deduce an answer based on presuppositions that are not intrinsic to the Christian revelation, which we cannot verify and which in any case militate against the experientially known truth that Father, Son and Spirit are ontologically distinct personal Subjects.

In my view these considerations constitute at least a few compelling reasons to jettison the pagan criteria of truth that have dominated this pivotal aspect of dogma in the Western Church in favour of the *lex orandi lex credendi* rule of the "primitive" Church in tandem with the mystical-historical approach of the Eastern monastics, which appears to be realistic and in accord with the experience and approach of the Apostles. In terms of this approach, there is only one way in which we can know God – not in the sense of mind being illumined by the rational One, but as personal subject/s knowing personal Subject/s in a communion of love.

The primary strengths of this approach are that (a) it in continuity with the Apostolic witness and (b) there is a correlation between the subjective form of knowing, the Subject/s known and the goal of the Christian life; i.e. while as creatures we cannot fully accommodate the reality of the Trinity conceptually, we can know the Divine Persons subjectively – and, according to the testimony of the Eastern saints, when we enter into communion with them or perceive them in mystical apparitions, we discover the Father, Son and Spirit interiorly as three tri-mutual Presences – which the Eastern Fathers named *Hypostases*-Persons.

This fundamental, historically and mystically known truth, which is supported by the biblical witness, is the reason for which the Orthodox are so insistent that the experientially known reality that the Trinity is a communion of three interpersonal "Subjectivities" should be fundamental to any logical, polemical argumentation regarding the Trinity and must be objectively reflected in dogma. And it is precisely this that the Augustinian metaphysical-existential conception fails to do. If we concede this point then all the Orthodox objections to the Western conception as a whole and the *filioque* in particular become extremely compelling.

Moreover, if we concede that an experiential approach to truth should take priority over rational, phenomenological deduction, then we must also concede that it is illegitimate to dogmatise a rationally deduced and hypothetical article of faith as saving truth, as is the case with the *filioque*.

Moreover, the evidence gathered so far also seems to indicate that Augustine's conception of the one "God the Trinity", which underpins his inability to show that the divine Persons are real, ontological "I's", constitutes a deviation from the Apostolic faith and that of the worshipping community, as expressed in the formulas of Nicaea I and Constantinople I.

It seems that Augustine's identification of the name God with the Trinity rather than God the Father – the pivot on which his conception turns – was an innovation, perhaps not unique to Augustine, but nevertheless in sharp contradiction to the original faith of the worshipping community. As I have indicated, the New Testament Scriptures appear to denote the Father when referring to God. This also appears to be true of Athanasius, Origen, Tertullian, the Cappadocian Fathers, Ambrose and even the Arians; it was the very reason for which Arius and his followers questioned the Son's equality with the Father. The Fathers of Nicaea I answered with the assertion: "We believe in one God, *the Father* [...] *and* in one Lord, Jesus Christ, begotten of the Father [...] *of* the essence of the Father, God of God, Light of Light, true God of true God [...] *and* the Holy Spirit"[4] (italics mine).

This wording seems to indicate that the Nicene Fathers thought of the Father as "God proper", in continuity with the apostolic faith, and the Son and Spirit as distinct personal Subjects of whom "Godness" is derivatively predicated by virtue of their origin in the Father.

I have noted that the need for further clarification of this perceived truth arose because difficulties persisted, as St Gregory Nazianzus stated in his opening oration at Constantinople I, with the "Sabellians, assaulting the Trinity in the interest of the Unity, and so destroying the distinctions by a wicked confusion; not, like the Arians, assailing the Unity in the interest of the Trinity and by an impious distinction overthrowing the Oneness".[5] Augustine seems to have fallen into the same error as the Sabellians. Thus while the Cappadocians retained the Apostolic emphasis on the Father as God proper and therefore the "source of unity" in the Trinity,[6] and the Father Son and Spirit as three distinct Subjects, Augustine, reading the Hellenic philosophical idea of unity into the formula of Nicaea I, interpreted the *name* God and therefore the "I (am)" of God to denote the Trinity. He consequently inverted the intended meaning of Constantinople I.

Thus, although the clause "and the Son" was used by some thinkers in the West prior to Augustine and although it seems to have been a presupposition for him, the way in which he appropriated the clause and the meaning with which he imbued it seems to be premised on a conception of the Trinity that constitutes a devia-

---

[4] Colman J. Barry (ed.), *op.cit*, 85

[5] In *ibid* 87

[6] Gregory Nazianzen, *Oration at the First Council of Constantinople*, in *ibid*

tion from the Apostolic faith and that of the worshipping community up to the 4th century. Furthermore, it undermines insights gained through mystical experience of the Divine Persons by subordinating the Christian faith to Hellenic philosophy. The Eastern charge that it is heretical therefore seems reasonable.

This conclusion is premised on the understanding that the *filioque* means that the Father and Son are together the cause of the Spirit's subsistence – a point some Western thinkers downplay, but which nevertheless seems to be both Augustine's and the official Roman Catholic view. We have noted that some Western sources argue that the clause should be understood in the sense of "through the Son" and this is sometimes posited as a way forward. This certainly seems a possibility, although it should be clear that this would be acceptable to the Orthodox only if it was understood as pertaining to the economic Trinity. However, the difficulty then arises that the *filioque* is placed in the Creed in a parallel clause to the Son's eternal begetting, implying that it is a statement about the Spirit's eternal origin – which is the meaning on which the interpolation is premised. With these considerations in mind, I cannot see the Orthodox embracing the clause.

This means that, in the event of union, we would still have a situation in which East and West are using differing Symbols of faith, which would constitute a problem in a united Church. I therefore cannot envisage how the *filioque* could be maintained in the Symbol of Faith in a united Church, even in the modified form of "through the Son", in the event of the re-establishment of communion between the Roman Catholics and the Orthodox.

BIBLIOGRAPHY

BOOKS

Allen, D. & Springsted, E. *Philosophy for Understanding Theology* (Atlanta: John Knox Press, 1985/2007)

Alfeyev, H. *The Mystery of Faith* (London: Darton, Longman & Todd, 2002)

Anatolios, K. *Athanasius* (London & New York: Routledge, 2004)

Ayres, L. "Sempiterne Spiritus Donum: Augustine's Pneumatology and The Metaphysics of Spirit" in *Orthodox Readings of St Augustine* (Eds Demacopoulos, G. E., & Papanikolaou, A.) (New York: St Vladimir's Seminary Press, 2008), pp. 127–152

St Athanasius "Letter 1 to Serapion" in Anatolios, K. *Athanasius* (London & New York: Routledge, 2004), pp. 214–233

St Augustine *The Trinity* (Trans. Hill, E.) (New York: New York City Press, 1991/2007)

_____. *The Confessions of St Augustine* (trans. Ryan, J. K.) (New York: Image Books, 1960)

Barrois, G. (trans./ed.), *The Fathers Speak: St Basil the Great, St Gregory of Nazianzus & St Gregory of Nyssa* (New York: St Vladimir's Seminary Press, 1986)

Barry, CJ (ed.), *Readings in Church History* (New York: Newman Press, 1960)

Behr, J. "Calling Upon God as Father, Augustine and the Legacy of Nicaea" in *Orthodox Readings of St Augustine* (Eds Demacopoulos, GE, & Papanikolaou, A) (New York: St Vladimir's Seminary Press, 2008) pp. 153–165

Bloom, A. *God and Man* (London: Darton, Longman & Todd, 1971/2004

Bradshaw, D. "Augustine the Metaphysician" in *Orthodox Readings of St Augustine* (Eds Demacopoulos, GE, & Papanikolaou, A) (New York: St Vladimir's Seminary Press, 2008), pp. 227–251

Cooper, D. E. *World Philosophies, An Historical Introduction* (Oxford & Cambridge: Blackwell, 2003)

O' Collins, G. *The Tripersonal God* (London: Geoffrey Chapman, 1999)

Daniélou, J. *From Glory to Glory: Texts from Gregory of Nyssa's Mystical Writings* (New York, St Vladimir's Seminary Press, 1961/1995)

Demacopoulos, G. E. & Papanikolaou, A. "Augustine and the Orthodox" in *Orthodox Readings of St Augustine* (Eds Demacopoulos, G. E. & Papanikolaou, A.) (New York: St Vladimir's Seminary Press, 2008) pp. 11–40

Frank, G. L. C. "The Church in Society" in *Church History: Only Study Guide for KEA302-H* (Pretoria: Unisa, 1992), pp. 1–18

_____. *Christian Foundations 1: Community Life, KEA301-G/ KGE511-M (Tutorial letter 105)*, Pretoria: Unisa, 1997)

Gonzalez, J. L. *A History of Christian Thought* (Nashville: Abingdon Press, 1971/1987)

John-Paul II *Orientale Lumen* [photocopy] (1995)

Livingstone, E. *A Concise Dictionary of the Christian Church* (London: Omega Books Ltd., 1977/1988)

St Gregory of Nazianzus "Oration at the First Council of Constantinople" in *Readings in Church History*, (Ed. Barry, C.J.) (New York: Newman Press, 1960), pp. 86–88

Hart, D. B. "The Hidden and the Manifest: Metaphysics after Nicaea" in *Orthodox Readings of St Augustine* (eds Demacopoulos, G. E., & Papanikolaou, A.) (New York: St Vladimir's Seminary Press, 2008), pp. 191–226

Heron, A. I. C. *The Holy Spirit* (Philadelphia: Westminster Press, 1983)

Hierotheos (Vlachos) of Nafpaktos *The Person in the Orthodox Tradition* (Levadia-Hellis: Birth of the Theotokos Monastery, 1999/2002)

_____. *A Night in the Desert of the Holy Mountain* (Levadia-Hellis: Birth of the Theotokos Monastery, 1991/1998)

Hill, E. (trans) *Introduction to St Augustine's The Trinity* (New York: New York City Press, 1991/2007) pp. 18–56

Hussey, J. M. *The Orthodox Church in the Byzantine Empire* (Oxford: Clarendon Press, 1986/1990)

Latourette, K. S. *A History of Christianity, Volume 1: Beginning to 1500* (San Francisco: HarperSanFrancisco, 1953/1975)

Lienhard, J. T. "Augustine of Hippo, Basil of Caesarea and Gregory Nazianzen" in *Orthodox Readings of St Augustine* (eds Demacopoulos, G. E., & Papanikolaou, A.) (New York: St Vladimir's Seminary Press, 2008), pp. 81–99

Livingstone, E. A. *A Concise Dictionary of the Christian Church* (London: Omega Books Ltd, 1977/1988)

L'Huillier, P. *The Church of the ancient councils* (New York: St Vladimir's Seminary Press, 1996)

Lossky, V. *Orthodox Theology: An Introduction* (New York: St Vladimir's Seminary Press, 1978)

Louth, A. *Maximus the Confessor* (London & New York: Routledge, 1996)

Marion, J. L. "Idipsum: The name of God according to St Augustine" in *Orthodox Readings of St Augustine* ((eds Demacopoulos, G. E., & Papanikolaou, A.) (New York: St Vladimir's Seminary Press, 2008), pp. 167–189

Meredith, A. *The Cappadocians* (London: Geoffrey Chapman, 1995)

Meyendorff, J. *Byzantine Theology* (New York: Fordham University Press, 1974/1979)

Neuner, J. & Dupuis, J. *The Christian Faith* (Dublin & Cork: The Mercier Press, 1973,)

O'Collins, G. *The Tripersonal God* (New York: Paulist Press, 1999)

Pomazansky, M. *Orthodox Dogmatic Theology* (New York: Holy Trinity Monastery, 1963/1994)

Rahner, K. *The Content of Faith* (New York: Crossroad, 2000)

Ryan J. K. (trans) *The Confessions of St. Augustine* (New York: Image Books), 1960)

Schatz, K. *Papal Primacy – from its origins to the present* (Minnesota: The Liturgical Press, 1996)

Schmemann, A. *The Historical Road of Eastern Orthodoxy* (New York: St Vladimir's Seminary Press, 1963/1977)

Staniloae, D. *Theology and the Church* (Crestwood: St Vladimir's Seminary Press, 1980)

Vatican *Catechism of the Catholic Church* (London: Geoffrey Chapman, 1994)

Ware, K. *The Orthodox Way* (New York: St Vladimir's Seminary Press, 1979/1993)

Wiles, M. *The Christian Fathers* (London: SCM Press)

Zizioulas, J. D. *Being as Communion* (New York: St Vladimir's Seminary Press, 1985/1993)

_____. *Lectures in Christian Dogmatics* (London: T&T Clark, 2008)

JOURNAL ARTICLES

Barnes, M. R. "Augustine in Contemporary Trinitarian Theology" in *Theological Studies* (Vol. 56 Issue 2, 1995), pp. 237ff

Coffey, D. "The Roman 'Clarification' of the Doctrine of the Filioque" in *International Journal of Systematic Theology* (Vol 5, 2003), pp. 4–21 (Oxford: Blackwell Publishing)

Cross, R. "On generic and derivation views of God's Trinitarian substance" in *Scottish Journal of Theology* (UK: SJT, 56(4), 2003), pp. 464–480

Dragas, G. D. "The Eighth Ecumenical Council: Constantinople IV (879/880) and the Condemnation of the Filioque Addition and Doctrine" in *The Greek Orthodox Theological Review* (44/1–4, 1999), pp. 357–369

McCarthy, J. F. "On the Procession of the Holy Spirit" in *Living Tradition* (no. 66, September, 1996)

Pugliese, M. A. "How Important is the Filioque for Reformed Orthodoxy?" in *Westminster Theological Journal* (66, 2004), pp. 164ff

Tavard, G. H. "A Clarification on the Filioque?" in *Anglican Theological Review* (Evanston: Summer, Vol. 83, Iss. 3, 2001), pp. 507ff

Turcescu, L. "'Person' versus 'individual', and other modern misreadings of Gregory of Nyssa" in *Modern Theology*, (Oxford: Blackwell Publishing, October, 2002)

INTERNET SOURCES

St Alexander (Bp), *Deposition of Arius* [online].
newadvent.org/fathers (accessed: 30/04/2010)

St Ambrose, *On the Holy Spirit*, [online].
http://www.newadvent.org/fathers (accessed: 12/10/2010)

Anonymous, (n.d.) *Concerning the Neoplatonist Heresy against Orthodox Christian Anthropology* [online] www.new-ostrog.org/tollhouse2.html (accessed: 15/01/2010)
(Posted on the website of the Canadian Orthodox Monastery of All Saints of North America)

St Aquinas, T. *Summa Theologica* [online]. http://www.newadvent.-org/summa (accessed: 16/10/2008, 11/08/2008)

St Athanasius *Against the Arians* [online].
http://www.newadvent.org/fathers (accessed 23/12/2007)

St Augustine *On the Trinity*, [online].
http://www.newadvent.org/fathers//130101.htm
(accessed: 25/01/2008)

_____. *City of God* [online]. http://www.newadvent.org.fathers (accessed 30/01/2008)

St Basil of Caesarea *De Spiritu Sancto*, [online]. http://wwwnewadvent.org/fathers (accessed 02/05/2008)

Bebis, G. S. (PhD *Orthodox Church Beliefs*, 2007 [online]. http://www.mbsoft.com/believe/txw/orthobel.htm (accessed: 18/01/2008)

Bickmore, B. *Tertullian on the Trinity*, 1997. [online] http://www.geocities.com/Athens/Parthenon/2671/ECTert.html? 20094 (accessed: 04/09/2009)

Bradshaw, D. *The Concept of the Divine Energies* [online]. http://johnsanidopolous.com./2009/10/concept -of-divine-energies.html (accessed 16/10/2009)

Bromily, G. W. *Elwell Evangelical Dictionary in Filioque Controversy: Advanced Information*, n.d. [online]. http://mb-soft.com/believe/txn/filioque.htm (accessed: 07/08/2008)

Geddes L, "Person" in *New Advent Catholic Encyclopedia*, Vol 11, New York: Robert Appleton Company, 1911 [online] http//www.newadvent.org/cathen/11726a.htm (accessed 24/07/2008)

Gilbert, P. *The Filioque, a very basic introduction*, n.d. [online]. http://bekkos.wordpress.com/filioque-introduction/ (accessed: 28/01/2010)

St Gregory of Nazianzen, *Theological Orations* [online]. http://wwwnewadvent.org/fathers/ and http://www.ccel.org/print/schaff/ (accessed: 22-02-2008)

St Gregory of Nyssa, *On 'Not Three Gods, to Ablabius* [online] http://wwwnewadvent.org/fathers/ (accessed: 20-05-2009)

St John in the Wilderness Adult Education and Formation, Survey of Theology 2: *The Doctrine of the Trinity* [online]. http/www.stjohnadult.org (accessed: 09/04/2008)

Joint International Commission for the Theological Dialogue between the Roman Catholic Church and the Orthodox Church, *Ecclesiological and Canonical Consequences of the Sacramental Nature of the Church: Ecclesial Communion, Conciliarity and Authority*, 2007, [online]. http://www.prounione.urbe.it/dia-int/o-rc/doc/e_o-rc_ravenna.html (accessed: 02/10/2008)

Justus, J. *Aristotle's Antithesis*, 2003 [online]. http://www.cleffpublishing.com/articles/a20040303jj.htm (accessed 19/12/2008)

Loughlin, J. "St Ambrose in *The Catholic Encyclopedia* (New York: Robert Appleton Company. Ed. K Knight, 1907) [online]. http://www.newadvent.org/cathen/01383c.htm (accessed: 12/10/2009)

Maas, A. *Filioque in New Advent Catholic Encyclopedia*, 1909. [online]. www.newadvent.catholic.org (accessed: 24/6/2008)

Meyendorff, J. "On the Question of the Filioque" from *The Orthodox Church*, 1981, NY: Crestwood [online extract]. www.ocf.org/OrthodoxPage/reading/filioque.html (accessed: 16/08/2008)

Moore, E. "Origen of Alexandria" in *Internet Encyclopedia of Philosophy*, 2005 (online). http://iep.utm.edu/origen-of-alexandria/ (accessed: 9/11/2008), n.pag

Murphy, N. "The Person in Greek Thought" in *Counterbalance*, [online]. http://www.counterbalance.org/neuro/greek-frame.html (accessed 24/07/2008)

Origen, *On First Principles*, http://www.newadvent.org/fathers/0412.htm (accessed: 9/11/2008)

The North American Orthodox-Catholic Consultation, *The Filioque: A Church Dividing Issue?* 2003 [online]. http://www.usccb.org/seia/filioque.html (accessed: 13/09/2008)

Pearse, R. *Tertullian's Theology,* n.d. [online]. http://www.tertullian.org/theology.htm (accessed: 10/08/2009)

Percival, H. (trans), "Synod of Constantinople (A.D. 381): The Synodical Letter", from *Nicene and Post-Nicene Fathers, Second Series, Vol. 14*, edited by Philip Schaff (Buffalo, NY: Christian Literature Publishing Co., 1900.) Revised and edited for New Advent by Kevin Knight. [online] http://www.newadvent.org.fathers/3809.htm (accessed: 12/03/2009)

St Photius, *Mystagogy of the Holy Spirit*, c.886 [online] http://geocities.com/trvalentine/orthodox/mystagogy/html (accessed 03/09/2008)

Pontifical Council for Promoting Christian Unity, 1995, *The Greek and Latin Traditions about the Procession of the Holy Spirit*, [online]. http:www.agrino.org/cyberdesert/statement.htm (accessed 11/09/2008); or http://www.ewtn.com/library/CURIA/PCCUFILQ.HTM (accessed 15/09/2008)

Roberson, R. G. (C. S. P) "Balamand and Beyond: The State of Catholic-Orthodox Relations" in *CNEWA Magazine* (vol. 21:2, July 1995,) [online]. http://www.cnewa.org/mag-article-bodypg-us.aspx?articleID=670 (accessed 03/10/208)

———. Appendix III to *The Eastern Christian Churches – A Brief Survey*, 2008 (7th edition) [online]. http://www.cnewa.org/ecc-bodypg-us.aspx?eccpageID=3&IndexView=toc (accessed 02/10/2008)

Schaff, P. *Historical Excursus on the Introduction into the Creed of the Words 'and the Son' from Nicene and Post-Nicene Fathers: Series II/Volume XIV in Filioque Controversy*, 2007 [online]. http://www.mbsoft.com/believe/txn/filioque.htm (accessed 07/08/2008)

Steenberg, M. C. *Gregory of Nyssa: Luminous Darkness*, 2002–2009 [online]. www.monachos.net (accessed 20/05/2009)

Tertullian (c. 160 – c. 225) *Adversus Praxean* [online] http://www.newadvent.org.fathers (accessed 24/04/2008

Vatican, *The Vatican Clarification on the Filioque*, 1995, [online] http://www.geocities.com/trvalentine.orthodox

———. *The Spirit and the Filioque Debate, General Audience of November 7*, 1990 [online]. www.vatican.va/holy_father/john_paul_ii/audiences/alpha/data/aud19901107en.html (accessed 11/09/2008)

Zizioulas, J. D., *One Single Source: An Orthodox response to the Clarification of the Filioque*, 2007 [online]. http://www.orthodoxresearch-institute.org/articles/dogmatic/john_zizioulas_single… (accessed 06/06/2008); see also http://geocities.com/trvalentine/-orthodox/zizioulas_onesource.html (accessed 20/12/7007)

INDEX